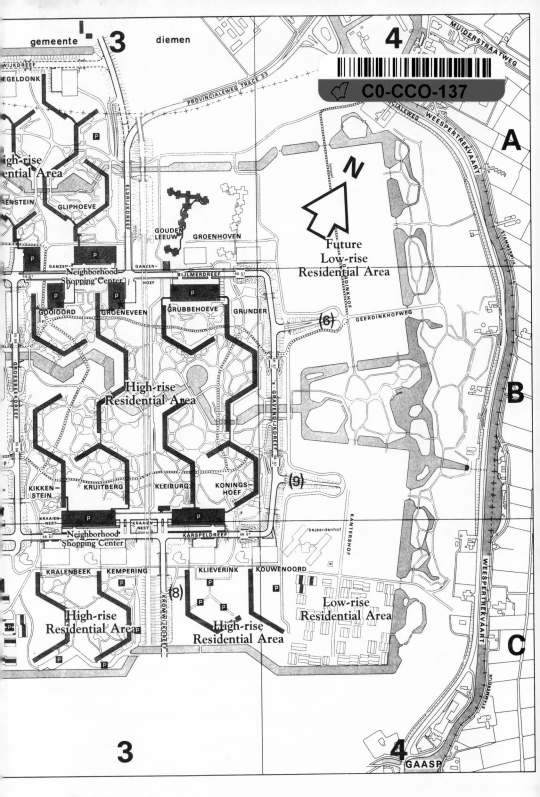

C0-CCO-137

Footpaths/Service roads
Parking garages

The
Urban
Habitat

The Urban Habitat:

Past, Present, and Future

Mary Jo Huth

Nelson-Hall, Chicago

41569

Our thanks for permission granted to reprint a passage from
Daniel P. Moynihan, ed., *Toward a National Urban Policy*,
copyright © 1970 by Basic Books, Inc.

LIBRARY OF CONGRESS CATALOG IN PUBLICATION DATA

Huth, Mary Jo.
　　The urban habitat.

　　Bibliography: P.
　　Includes index.
　　1. Urbanization—United States.　　2. Urbanization—Europe.　　3. Sociology, Urban.　　4. City
planning.　　I. Title.
HT123.H88　　　　301.36′1　　　　77-7273
ISBN 0-88229-333-8

Copyright © 1978 by Mary Jo Huth

All rights reserved. No part of this book may be reproduced in any form
without permission in writing from the publisher, except by a
reviewer who wishes to quote brief passages in connection with a review
written for broadcast or for inclusion in a magazine or newspaper.
For information address Nelson-Hall Inc., Publishers,
325 West Jackson Boulevard, Chicago, Illinois 60606.

Manufactured in the United States of America.
10　9　8　7　6　5　4　3　2　1

To my father and mother
for their lifelong encouragement
of my scholarly endeavors.

Contents

41569

41569

Preface

This book on the urban habitat constitutes a systematic approach to the study of man's relationship to the urban environment, tracing, first, the evolution of the urbanization process from preindustrial to industrial societies, continuing with an analysis of the major sociological perspectives on the urban community; proceeding to an examination of various concepts of the ideal city from ancient times to the present, as well as of American and European urban planning policies and programs which have implemented some of these ideals; and ending with the prescription of a national urban policy and new towns as the formula for a more humane urban America. Chapters 1 through 3 (Part I), which constitute the theoretical portion of the book, consume only one-third of its total content. Two-thirds of its content, Chapters 4 through 6 (Part II), deal with practical and workable solutions to the problems associated with urban growth in Europe and the United States.

The urban problems of the industrialized nations have already reached crisis proportions—in congestion, decay, sprawl, and inhuman living conditions. Inasmuch as an estimated 80 percent of the world's population will be living in urban communities by the year 2000 (in comparison with approximately 40 percent in 1970), solutions must be found and implemented quickly, not only for the industrialized countries but for the developing nations currently undergoing industrialization and urbanization.

The city, then, is where the action will be in the final quarter of the twentieth century. The study of urban sociology should be required for every college student today. In countries like the United States, such learning is especially crucial because, unlike the situation which prevails under democratic socialism (e.g., Sweden and Britain) and scientific socialism (e.g., communistic regimes of Eastern Europe) where the government can impose urban programs on the populace, here the impetus must come from the populace. Citizens must be strongly committed to rebuilding and revitalizing our sick cities and to constructing new towns which are compatible with human needs and the natural environment before Congress will enact the legislation and appropriate the funds necessary to achieve such results. If a large proportion of our citizens were exposed to the concerns of urban sociology, they might, it is hoped, develop a commitment to an ideal living environment which by the end of the twentieth century might be translated into political action at all levels of government. Indeed, my prime motivation for writing this book was that it might make some contribution toward the realization of humane urban living.

It is significant that the predominant theoretical perspective among contemporary urban sociologists is an ecological rather than a demographic or juridical one, demonstrating that even on the conceptual level there is greater concern today for the city as a living organism than as a mere aggregation of people with certain measurable characteristics or as a power center. The viability of the ecological approach to the urban environment became strikingly apparent to me when I visited and studied the new towns and satellite communities of Great Britain, the Netherlands, and Scandinavia, as well as Columbia, Maryland, and Reston, Virginia, during the summers of 1970, 1971, and 1972.

I wish to thank the University of Dayton's Research Council for a grant during the summer of 1970 that made possible my first contact with Europe's new towns; Hani Fakhouri, currently teaching at the University of Michigan and formerly my esteemed colleague in the Department of Sociology, Anthropology, and Social Work at the University of Dayton, who inspired me to undertake this project; the National Association of Schools of Public Affairs and Administration for appointing me a 1972–1973 Public Administration Fellow at the Department of Housing and Urban Development (HUD) in Washington, D.C., which facilitated my research for this book; Joseph Sherman, former director of the Building Technology and Site Operations Division at HUD and my fellowship mentor, for his cooperation and understanding during my preparation of the final draft of the manuscript; and Nancy Schiml, without whose conscientious and efficient secretarial services this book could not have been completed.

Part I

The Urban Habitat: Theoretical Perspectives

While the primary emphasis of this book is on the enhancement of man's relationship to the urban environment through planning, for the benefit of the interested reader or student with a minimal background in sociology and the history of social thought, Part I of this book will summarize the history of the worldwide urbanization process, the major sociological perspectives on the urban community which have emerged in response to this process, and a history of ideas regarding the nature of the "good" city.

THE WORLDWIDE URBANIZATION PROCESS

Although mankind has inhabited the earth for an estimated two million years, it was not until relatively recently—during the Neolithic age some 10,000 years ago—that the foundations of urban life were established in the form of relatively permanent agricultural villages representing primarily the achievement of more effective means of collective adaptation to the physical environment. On the other hand, the culmination of this "primordial urbanization" in the "definitive city" (achieved successively but inde-

1

pendently in the Tigris-Euphrates Valley, in the Indus Valley, in the Huangho Basin, in Mesoamerica, in the Central Andes, in northern Europe, and in sub-Saharan Africa, between 4000 B.C. and A.D. 1000) was primarily an expression of the greater size and complexity of the social unit rather than a reflection of any major changes in subsistence technology. A very strong case can be made, however, for the crucial role of the social component in the development of *both* primordial and definitive urbanization, for without social organization technology is often not applied to improve subsistence, and once the specialized functions characteristic of the definitive city emerge they seem to "expect" social control, directly or indirectly, to assure their continued and effective performance. Nevertheless, the fact that definitive urbanization was not a uniform process in the several areas of the world where it developed between 4000 B.C. and A.D. 1000 attests to the adaptive character of population concentrations in their continuing accommodation to particular sets of demographic and environmental exigencies.

The progression from primordial to definitive urbanization will be discussed in Chapter 1, followed by a description of definitive urbanization before and after the eighteenth century—the "classic" versus the "industrial." While the classic was characterized by a coherent and ascending order of socially static settlements—from hamlets, to villages, to towns, and, finally, to capital cities—and by largely local and unspecialized productive activity, the industrial, completely lacking in pattern, has been characterized as an incessant process resulting in increasingly differentiated structures and functions. Among the more significant of the great changes which have characterized the modern era are the increases in the size and concentration of world population. Cities of a million or more population are largely the product of nineteenth- and twentieth-century social and technological forces. Moreover, while only 1.7 percent of the world's people lived in cities of 100,000 or more population in 1800, by 1970 over 13 percent of the world's people resided in such large urban centers, and by the year 2000, urban places of various sizes are expected to engulf approximately 80 percent of the world's population.[1]

Whereas Eric Lampard has delineated two categories of definitive urbanization, Gideon Sjoberg has posited three: the preindustrial, the transitional or modernizing, and the industrial. The major features of preindustrial cities, which have functioned primarily as political and religious centers, are the following: (1) a wide gap separates the small elite who reside in or near the inner city from the masses of lower-class people who reside at the periphery; (2) the kinship group is not only the primary socializing agent, but the determiner of one's occupation and the focus of leisure-time activity; (3) economic development is retarded not only by the low esteem with which the elite regard manual labor and commercial activity, but by the relative lack of standardization in the production process and by the meager facilities for credit and capital formation; and (4) the bureaucratic structure of the political and religious institutions is a potent integrating and stabilizing force.

The social structure of a transitional or modernizing city undergoes the following processes almost simultaneously: (1) the persistence of traditional forms; (2) the revision or modification of traditional forms; (3) the disappearance of traditional forms; and (4) the emergence of new structures. A major dilemma facing transitional cities is the resistance of the elite to the dissemination of scientific and technological knowledge through the formal education system which they control and, indeed, their reluctance to assimilate such knowledge themselves. At the same time, the ruling elite realize that unless their societies industrialize and urbanize, they may become subject to some national power, a possibility which they find even more repugnant. The adaptation of the lower social strata to an emerging industrial-urban milieu is an even more complex problem, for just when their life condition begins to improve with industrial progress, they develop a desire to acquire the traditional ideals which previously only the elite enjoyed. The mass media and informal subsystems, however, are rapidly contravening this tendency, socializing the common man in transitional cities to an industrial-urban way of life. In the Soviet Union, China, and India, formal organizations such as political parties and labor unions perform the function of the mass media. Finally, in most transitional societies, nationalism, by glorifying history and traditional culture, provides the lower social strata with a sense of identity and continuity which facilitates their adoption of new structural forms.

In contrast to preindustrial cities, industrial ones revolve about a commercial and/or industrial focus rather than a religious-governmental complex; the privileged classes live beyond the city's core, leaving the central area largely to groups of low status; a large category of middle-class functionaries mediates between the upper and lower classes and distinctions between socioeconomic, racial, and ethnic groups are less clearly drawn; there are more opportunities for social mobility; the conjugal family associated with the heightened status of women and children predominates; both in and outside the home there is no well-defined male-female division of labor; extended leisure becomes increasingly the prerogative of the laboring classes, while many high-status persons work long hours; bureaucratic organization characteristic of only the political and religious institutions in preindustrial cities permeates nearly every area of activity; political leaders feel compelled to at least give lip service to the "consent of the governed" as the justification for their rule; the legal system, rather than relying on magic-religious rituals to determine innocence or guilt, depends upon standardized rules and rational processes; formal education for the elite only is replaced by mass formal and informal education; daily life becomes secularized (relatively free of religious influence), and what religious norms do exist are permissive rather than prescriptive. Scientism, nationalism, and hedonism have been substituted for religion by many industrial urbanites in their quest for "meaning" or "purpose" in life.

Once nineteenth-century industrialization had laid the foundation for the modern city, a variety of twentieth-century factors transformed it into a metropolis—a multinucleated territorial system characterized by the decentralization of many activities, the separation of residential and work areas, and extensive spatial mobility. Primary among these factors have been: (1) the worldwide population explosion; (2) migration from rural areas precipitated by technological progress in agriculture; (3) the "revolution of rising expectations"—that is, the desire for a higher standard of living; (4) racial prejudice, notably in the United States; and (5) improvements in transportation and communication facilities. Urban growth in the underdeveloped countries, which is proceeding twice as fast as in the advanced nations of the world, is due mainly to the first factor—overpopulation. Consequently, if migration from rural areas were encouraged in the underdeveloped countries, their urban populations would grow at a disastrous rate. Even without encouragement, thousands of squatters from the rural areas have settled at the fringes of all their major cities. With this combination of circumstances, the underdeveloped nations find it virtually impossible to expand facilities and services fast enough to accommodate their constantly swelling urban masses. Urbanization has not been a problem-free process even in the advanced nations of the world, as evidenced by the race riots of the 1960s and the continued concern about urban crime, racial and class polarization and conflict, and urban decay. It seems obvious, therefore, that the future welfare of the world's cities depends upon mankind's implementing effective population controls and engaging in creative physical and social planning on a metropolitan and regional basis. The importance of urban sociology in delineating alternative theoretical orientations to the urban community must be taken into consideration by any agency which hopes to successfully direct or undertake such creative planning.

Major Sociological Perspectives on the Urban Community

Urban sociology, which had its "birth" at the University of Chicago during World War I under the guidance of Robert Park and Ernest Burgess, has since undergone several major changes. First, there has been a shift of emphasis from the study of the social problems of central cities to an analysis of the relationships between communities within metropolitan areas and regions in recognition of the twentieth-century trend from city to metropolis and from metropolis to megalopolis. Second, three distinct theoretical perspectives have emerged—the juridical, the demographic, and the ecological—reflecting the growing complexity of urban communities throughout the world under the pressure of increasing population growth. Third, considerable interest has developed in comparative urban research, which is really an extension of the first trend, namely, the expansion of the geographical perspective of the urban sociologist in an age of unprecedented international travel and communication.

The ecological and demographic approaches rank first and second in popularity amon the three contemporary theoretical perspectives in urban sociology. The ecologists, who are concerned with the factors determining urban spatial patterns as well as with the social impact of these patterns, may be classified into four categories: (1) traditional materialists; (2) socioculturists; (3) neoclassical materialists; and (4) social-area analysts. Traditional ecologists, following Park and Burgess, reflect the heavy influence of classical economics and Social Darwinism, attributing the spatial arrangement of urban populations and activities to the operation of competitive economic and social forces. Moreover, traditional ecologists have contended that certain social variables—social status, family types and age groups, as well as deviant behavior (anomie, alienation, mental illness, delinquency, crime, divorce, illegitimacy, drug addiction, alcoholism, suicide)—have distinct spatial configurations within urban communities. In general, all traditional ecologists, but especially Louis Wirth, Robert Redfield, and Lewis Mumford, have evaluated the city negatively, characterizing the "urban way of life" as secular, impersonal, and segmental, and the urban setting as unconducive to personal and social integration.

Not only do traditional ecologists underestimate the strength of social organization in the slums and the grip of bureaucracy on most American city dwellers, but their theory that urbanization leads inevitably to social disorganization has not been substantiated by comparative urban research. Oscar Lewis's data from Mexico City, for example, testify to the fact that urbanization is not necessarily accompanied by destruction of the traditional social and moral order. Indeed, it is upon comparing cities in highly divergent cultures that we perceive the enormous value of the socioculturists' perspective on urban sociology—namely, that values are the key determinant of a city's ecology. And in the United States, William H. Whyte, Jr., and Paul Meadows have demonstrated the relationship between city planners' ideology and their proposals for revitalizing our central cities, which is a very significant finding in terms of the increasingly important role of purposive city planning in the shaping of urban life in our country as well as in Europe.

Unlike the socioculturists, neoclassical materialists such as Otis Duncan, Leo Schnore, Jack Gibbs, and Walter Martin ignore the importance of values in shaping the urban milieu, and unlike the traditional materialists who credit competitive economic and social forces, they stress the importance of technology in determining urban spatial and social patterns. But just as comparative urban research has invalidated the traditional materialists' theory and confirmed that of the socioculturists, it has refuted the technological bias of the neoclassical materialists; the Berlin Wall is a prime example of how political ideology can override technological factors in determining urban migration and residential patterns.

Of the social-area analysts who, in the tradition of Burgess with his "concentric zones," have contributed the terms "sectors" and "nuclei" to the urban sociologist's ecological vocabulary, only Scott Greer has explained how a city can achieve and maintain social order in the presence of so many different enclaves of homogeneous population. He simply states that the continued functioning of the highly differentiated set of activities characterizing city life makes the operation of effective integrating mechanisms imperative. Thus, Greer maintains that the city as an organizational unit displays massive uniformities, orderly change, and remarkable stability in spite of its widely divergent and spatially segregated population groups. Consistent with this observation is Greer's conclusion that urbanization involves *organizational transformation* rather than *organizational disruption or dislocation*, as the traditional materialists contend.

The second most popular theoretical perspective in urban sociology, the demographic, analyzes the relationship between population balance in an urbanizing nation and four interdependent variables: the amount of land available, the level of knowledge concerning land use, the state of the technical arts, and the prevailing system of allocation. Thus, Kingsley Davis differentiates between the over-urbanized underdeveloped nations of the world, where city growth is largely a product of population explosion, and highly urbanized advanced nations whose cities grow primarily as the result of migration from rural areas.

Finally, the juridical approach, credited initially to Max Weber, regards political power at all levels as the critical independent variable explaining urban growth and land use patterns. At the same time, the city, as the headquarters for the political, educational, religious, and other "controlling" institutions of a society, can generate sweeping changes in life patterns by giving birth to new ideologies and social movements. As Oswald Spengler so aptly stated, " ... after folk societies evolve into urban concentrations, further urbanization ensues during which diverse sociocultural trends are unleashed with fateful consequences for all."[2] Fortunately, however, most social historians and philosophers have been less fatalistic than Spengler about the potential for realizing "the good life" in an urban community.

VARIOUS CONCEPTS OF THE IDEAL CITY

Throughout history, men have envisioned ideal communities and, interestingly enough, from Plato in the fourth century B.C. to Ebenezer Howard in the late nineteenth century, they have been defined largely in terms of the city. But while the correspondence between ideal and real communities extends from antiquity to the present, prior to the nineteenth century the real usually preceded the ideal, as illustrated by the best-known utopian works—Plato's *Republic,* inspired by a Spartan community, and More's *Utopia,* based on the Incan empire of Peru. During the nineteenth century, however, over two hundred assorted religious zealots, intellectuals, and opportunists established with their followers various types of unprecedented utopian communities in the United States, the most prominent being George Rapp—Harmony, Pennsylvania (1803) and New Harmony, Indiana (1815); Robert Owen—New Harmony, Indiana (1824), after purchasing the community from the Rappites; Charles Fourier—Red Bank, New Jersey, and Brook Farm, Massachusetts (during the 1840s); Etienne Cabet—Nauvoo, Illinois (1847); and John Humphrey Noyes—Oneida, New York (1848). Some of these communities failed because their leaders died, left, or lost their charisma; others, because their leaders were too idealistic to cope effectively with internal and external opposition or with exploitative businessmen; and, still others, because their members lacked organized and disciplined action.

During the twentieth century, two prominent nineteenth-century utopian ideals have been successfully implemented: Arturo Soria y Mata's "linear city" (1882) concept, by the world-renowned Greek architect, Constantinos Doxiades, at Islamabad, the new capital of Pakistan; and Ebenezer Howard's "garden city" concept, first in over thirty British new towns and, successively, in hundreds of other new towns and satellite communities from Canada to Brazil and from the United States to the Soviet Union. Ideal communities are not only examples of how broadly an unfettered mind can think and dream, but as models for real communities they have called public attention to alternative living patterns with their social benefits, and have inspired a spirit of healthy criticism toward the prevailing urban environment, two extreme evaluations of which are discernible within the past two hundred years.

Intellectuals imbued with the philosophy of the eighteenth-century Enlightenment—Voltaire, Adam Smith, and Fichte—elaborated upon the city as virtue, the source of every society's progress in wealth and civilization. Dramatic increases in the rate of urbanization and the establishment of industrial towns during the nineteenth century, however, resulted in the city's becoming stigmatized as the symbol of social vice. Negative responses to the urban-industrial environment have been of three types: (1) archaists like Coleridge, Ruskin, Freytag, Dostoevsky, and Tolstoy, who totally rejected it and sought a return to agrarian or small-town society; (2) futurists like Engels and Marx, who wanted to reform it; and (3) twentieth-century fatalists epitomized by Spengler, who consider the modern urban condition unalterable and who simply make it endurable through a stance compounded of stoicism, hedonism, and despair. America's foremost urban critic during the twentieth century, who might best be classified as a futurist, is Lewis Mumford, whose principal suggestions for urban reform are based upon Piotr Kropotkin's advocacy of deconcentration, Patrick Geddes's concern for regional planning, and Howard's garden city concept. All of these ideas Mumford and two associates in the Regional Planning Association of America, Henry Wright and Clarence Stein, incorporated into America's first new town, Radburn, New Jersey, constructed between 1928 and 1929. Underlying Mumford's rejection of such urban "solutions" as slum clearance and urban renewal and his repudiation of concentrated power, materialism, and economic competition in the metropolis is his concern for the dignity of the human person within the urban environment.

The principal ideas which the twentieth-century urban planning profession has borrowed from the aforementioned urban critics are that it is not only desirable but possible to manipulate the human environment, that the "good man" is a product of a healthy community, and that the ideal urban setting is a balanced one, providing occupational, recreational, and cultural opportunities as well as housing. Such borrowing is significant, because an important indicator of the maturity of any profession is the degree to which succeeding generations of practitioners have built upon earlier ideas and experiences.

Chapter 1

The Phenomenon
of Urbanization

Among the most significant of the great trends which have characterized the modern era is the tremendous increase in the size and concentration of world population. It has been estimated that for some 600,000 years of the Paleolithic period, world population growth approximated only 0.02 per thousand per year.[1] By the end of the Neolithic period (some 10,000 years ago), world population had reached an estimated 10 million, and by the beginning of the Christian era it probably reached between 200 and 300 million.[2] The rate of world population growth increased to about 0.4 percent per year by the start of the modern era (1650) when world population numbered about 500 million.[3] To produce a world population of about one billion persons took only two hundred more years (1850), but another billion were added by 1925 and a billion more by 1962, when world population reached the three-billion mark.[4] At the present rate of world population growth, 2 percent per year, a fourth billion will be attained around 1977 and a fifth billion by about 1985.[5] Thus, it may be stated that in the course of man's development since the Paleolithic period, his rate of population growth has risen from about 2 percent per millennium to 2 percent per year—a thousandfold increase.[6]

Similarly, although man has inhabited the earth for an estimated two million years, permanent human settlement was not achieved until the Neolithic period about 10,000 years ago. The first villages, however, were restricted by their limited technology to a small population of a few hundred persons each, and it took at least 1,500 years, from 5000 B.C. to 3500 B.C., for them to evolve into cities. Moreover, it is unlikely that cities as large as 100,000 existed prior to the Greek or Roman period, and cities of a million or more did not appear until the nineteenth century. Hence, in 1800 when reasonably accurate data on the urban population of the world began to become available, about 1.7 percent of the world's estimated population of approximately 900 million persons lived in cities of 100,000 and over; 2.4 percent in cities of 20,000 and over; and 3.0 percent in urban places of 5,000 or more inhabitants.[7] Since that time, however, accelerating world population has been accompanied by an even more rapid increase in urban population, a trend which is expected to continue for some time. Between 1920 and 1980, for example, while world population is expected to have increased 132 percent (from 1,860 to 4,318 million), population in places of 20,000 or more will have increased an estimated 407 percent (from 267 to 1,354 million) ; in places of 500,000 or more, 522 percent (from 107 to 665 million) ; and in places of 2.5 million or more, 875 percent (from 36 to 351 million).[8] As a consequence, between 1920 and 1980 the proportion of the world's population residing in cities of 20,000 or more people will have increased from 14.4 percent to 31.4 percent; in cities of 500,000 or more people, from 5.8 percent to 15.4 percent; and in cities of 2.5 million or more people, from 1.94 percent to 8.13 percent.[9]

Even more startling is the realization of the fact that the world urbanization process will not even then (1980) have come to a halt, for by the year 2000 urban residence is expected to claim approximately 80 percent of the world's population, the most dramatic increase occurring in the developing nations. Although these countries already have many large cities due to their booming populations, they are still characterized by a low level of urbanization (the percentage of their total populations residing in urban areas). Thus, while urbanization and the growth of cities have been companion processes historically in many instances, the two trends are not parallel. For example, the cities of today's most advanced countries are still growing at the expense of the rural areas, but they are doing so at a decreasing rate. In other words, the rate of urbanization in these countries has decelerated. In the underdeveloped countries, however, cities are growing rapidly due mainly to natural increase and without appreciably reducing the rural proportion of the population. Consequently, their levels and rates of urbanization remain low. Summarizing, the process of urbanization—the transition from a spread-out pattern of human settlement to one of concentration in urban centers—has a beginning and an end, but the growth of cities has no inherent limit, because even with little or no rural-urban migration, cities can grow through sheer excess of births over deaths.

THE HISTORY OF WORLD URBANIZATION

The history of world urbanization may be divided into two stages: (1) *primordial urbanization*: the initial achievement of urban organization as a more productive mode of collective adaptation to the physical and social environment, and (2) *definitive urbanization*: the culmination of primordial urbanization in the definitive city.[10]

PRIMORDIAL URBANIZATION

The comparative study of primordial urbanization in eleven Old World and seven New World areas reveals what Robert J. Braidwood and Gordon R. Willey have termed "the varieties of ecological conditions and cultural buildups leading to the thresholds of urban civilization." [11] Granted that marked contrasts existed among the areas in regard to climate, topography, natural vegetation, cultivated crops and domesticated animals, in the extent of dependence upon irrigation, in the time required for the emergence of cult and ceremonial centers, and in the size, density, and social differentiation of their populations—the process beginning with the cultivation of wild cereals and the herding of wild animals and culminating in year-round sedentary agricultural villages, such as Jarmo (c. 6750 B.C.) in Iraqi Kurdistan and Mesa de Guaje in Mexican Tamaulipas (c. 1500 B.C.), was a painful and protracted one in every instance.

Both the technological (cultural) achievement of food production and the social organization of village agriculture were necessary conditions for the appearance of primordial urbanization.

However, although these developments were prerequisites to the attainment of primordial urbanization, they did not *inevitably* guarantee it or even facilitate changes in that direction. Progress toward primordial urbanization, therefore, seems to have been contingent mainly upon interaction between, and the symbiotic exploitation of, closely associated but diverse cultures. Eventually, with increasing contact and exchange, a more formalized interdependence developed, demanding more complicated social organization and culminating in a cultural product which was sufficiently large to enable village settlements to assume the characteristics of definitive cities.

DEFINITIVE URBANIZATION

Definitive urbanization was finally achieved in the Fertile Crescent of the Middle East by the fourth millennium B.C., in the Indus Valley and Huangho Basin from the third to the second millennia B.C., in Mesoamerica very late in the first millennium B.C., and in the Central Andes, northern Europe, and possibly in sub-Saharan Africa during the first millennium A.D.[12] The contention that the transition from primordial to definitive urbanization was primarily a social rather than a technological process has been most succinctly stated by Robert M. Adams in his discussion of the immediate origin of cities during the fourth millennium B.C. in Mesopotamia: "The rise of [definitive] cities . . . was pre-eminently a social process, an expression more of changes in man's interaction with his fellows than in his interaction with his environment. The novelty of the city consisted in a whole series of new institutions and in the vastly greater size and complexity of the social unit, rather than in basic subsistence innovations [technology]."[13] V. Gordon Childe, however, attributes the advent of definitive urbanization to *both* social and technological factors, as illustrated by his facous criteria: (1) a compact settlement with at least 4,000 to 5,000 inhabitants; (2) full-time craftsmen and artists; (3) an effective capital surplus based on agriculture; (4) "foreign" trade; (5) monumental public architecture; (6) writing or other script system; (7) calendrical or mathematical sciences; (8) social stratification; and (9) political hierarchy.[14] Thus, a combination of the Adams and Childe analyses results in a comprehensive concept of definitive urbanization as the response of a given population to its environment via the mechanisms of technology and social organization.

Nevertheless, it is the author's position that organization is *the* crucial ecological variable because without it the frequency and level of social interaction declines, technology lies dormant, and population cohesion tends to diminish or even completely disappear. When such conditions prevail, definitive urbanization, with its many specialized functions demanding governance to assure their continued and efficient performance, cannot take place. The two stages in the transition from primordial to definitive urbanization in Mesopotamia, for example, were both primarily contributions of social organization, for the demographic, economic, and technological aspects of the change were determined largely by the structure of the religio-political and military-political institutions. During the first stage of the transition, which occurred in the Ubaidian period (c. 4000 B.C.), several interconnected temples were constructed at Eridu which were markedly different from the more independent shrines characterizing village settlements to the north. The hub of this new social order was the "temple city" whose social and political life were both dominated and sanctioned by "sacred officials," resulting in a rather exclusive definition of urban communities. During the ensuing Early Dynastic period (after 3000 B.C.), the second stage of the transition was characterized by the appearance of momumental royal palaces and a clearly defined political tradition which was apparently precipitated by a rising feeling of insecurity in the community generated by outside threats and by the concomitant escalation of organization for war. While the resulting gradual reduction of the political influence of the temple hierarchy did not weaken its priestly functions, some reorganization of authority and a greater reliance upon secular power occurred. The development of monarchical institutions altered the social stratification of urban populations, for the construction of defensive installations and the organization of professional military forces necessitated a different apportionment of surplus capital than had prevailed during the earlier stage in the evolution of definitive urbanization. That class differences were accentuated was exemplified by the contrast between the simple graves of the Ubaidian period and the ornate tombs of the royalty and the elite at Ur in the latter part of the Early Dynastic period.

While definitive urbanization was first achieved in the Fertile Crescent, the process did not occur evenly there. Rates and levels of urbanization in Egypt, for example, were considerably lower than in Mesopotamia because the former's physical and social settings were both less susceptible to city building. John A. Wilson has dramatically described the situation as follows: "For 3,000 years, until the founding of Alexandria, ancient Egypt was a major civilization without a single major city."[15] The continuity brought by the Nile River's passage over a distance of 5,000 to 6,000 miles that simplified the problem of water management and facilitated navigation and communication, together with the country's relative isolation from other city-states and predatory nomadic peoples, were major explanations. Moreover, Egypt attained an unprecedented degree of political unity at a very early period in its history, passing over a city-state phase comparable to that experienced by protoliterate and Early Dynastic Mesopotamia. This accounts for the absence of massive fortifications around early Egyptian cities of the kind commonly found in Mesopotamia. The fact that major differences between Egyptian and Mesopotamian urbanization persisted, despite frequent interaction by land and sea (c. 3000 B.C.), clearly demonstrates that contact alone is an insufficient condition for the displacement of a native "lower" cultural form by an external "higher" form. In one important respect, however, Egypt's and Mesopotamia's experience with definitive urbanization has coincided; in both areas, the vast majority of the people have continued to live in agricultural villages.

In other areas where definitive urbanization was achieved between 4000 B.C. and A.D. 1000—in the Central Andes, in Mesoamerica, in the Indus Valley, and in the Huangho Basin—it did not follow the sequence, let alone the pattern, which characterized the process in the Middle East. Not only has definitive urbanization proceeded differently in each of its geographical contexts, but, as an increasing amount of archaeological evidence accumulates, it becomes more and more difficult to establish any particular trait or combination of attributes as uniquely associated with definitive urbanization. Writing, one of Childe's criteria, did not exist in the early cities of the Central Andes, and in Mesoamerica writing remained relatively crude and there was little evidence of technologi-

cal progress during the definitive urban phase. Lack of technological sophistication also characterized the Indus Valley cities
which controlled an elaborate network of political and economic
relationships with subordinate farming populations. They never
did acquire the full complement of "bronze age" metallurgical and
toolmaking techniques, despite contacts with Mesopotamia dating
back to about 2500 B.C. Unlike Mesopotamia, Indus Valley urban
settlements were unfortified and their art was devoid of motifs
associated with war. Finally, the Indus capitals of Mohenjo-daro
and Harappa were both laid out according to a rigid gridiron pattern, with areas of uniform size and design reserved for granaries,
workshops, and housing, quite unlike Mesopotamia's irregularly
patterned urban centers. Even the elevated citadels which rimmed
the western edge of the Indus capitals bore little similarity to the
more formal temple and palace precincts typical of Mesopotamian
cities.

In China, a garden-type agriculture dependent upon artificial
irrigation and drainage and such simple implements as the hoe and
spade resulted in a pattern of urban settlement distinctly different
from that based on the extensive land cultivation of the Fertile
Crescent. The widely held notion that Chinese civilization was dis-
seminated by the plow is not substantiated by archaeological data
which provide no evidence of the existence of plows in China prior
to the fourth century B.C. Yet, the Yin Shang centers of the
Huangho Basin were definitively urban. Anyang, the most eastern
Yin Shang capital, demonstrated a unique arrangement with an extensive grouping of almost contiguous handicraft-farming hamlets
sharing a specialized ceremonial and administrative core, Hsiao-
t'un. Another unique feature of Yin Shang urbanization was its
ideographic script, unlike any of the forms of writing developed in
Mesopotamia or Egypt.

The fact that definitive urbanization has not been a uniform
process in the several areas of the world where it has occurred attests to the adaptive character of population concentrations as they
accommodate to particular sets of demographic and environmental
conditions. Consequently, the purpose of analyzing definitive urbanization is not to arrive at some universally applicable concept
of the city, but to gain a better understanding of that sequence of

social interactions which produces such a great variety of urban centers in time and space—a sequence which may be described as follows:

> When primordial urbanization becomes increasingly well established as the result of accelerated social inter-action, certain roles become more clearly defined and, hence, more specialized, notably those related to religion and war. Persons in religious roles, by performing rituals which elicit collective self-consciousness and afford the means of interceding with transcendental powers, provide the motivation necessary for the production and distribu-tion of an economic surplus. Interaction with foreign populations generally results in further enlargement of this surplus and, at the same time, enhances the role of specialized military and political leaders in the population. Palaces, citadels, residences, craftshops, storehouses, waterworks, roadways, and tombs become centralized around the temple area which, in some situations, is eventually enclosed by a wall. Such definitively urban settlements represent an additional and alternative form of collective adaptation to the environment—a veritable cultural innovation.

As the process of definitive urbanization crystallizes, cities serve as multifaceted, centralized foci of essential human services not only for their internal populations but also for populations re-siding in less advanced surrounding communities, giving them an opportunity for a richer, more diversified, and, hence, more stimu-lating life-style. Consequently, the contention of some urban sociol-ogists, several of whom are discussed in Chapter 2, that cities are intrinsically alien to, or at least incompatible with, rural communi-ties is not substantiated by tested ecological theories.

CLASSIC AND INDUSTRIAL DEFINITIVE URBANIZATION

Having differentiated the two stages in the history of world urbanization, the primordial and the definitive, it is important to focus upon the marked contrast in the occurrence and extent of de-finitive urbanization before and after the eighteenth century. To denote the contrast, Eric Lampard has used the terms "classic" and "industrial."[16] Under classic conditions, definitive urbanization exists when there is a progressively centralized series of interde-pendent communities, ranging from hamlets and villages to towns and capital cities, whose number and/or size does not change over long periods of time. This relatively static type of urbanism, which characterized Europe, Africa, and China from ancient through medieval and up to early modern times, is generally attributed to the restrictions imposed by an unspecialized rural economy and by the minimal amount of interregional trade. Similarly, the purpose of population migration was limited largely to the expansion of existing agricultural villages or to their consolidation into a more comprehensive network of communities. Historic examples of these processes were the development of an intensive rice culture in the Yangtze Valley and its integration, via canals and coastal waters, into the ancient north China system; the *Ostsiedlung* into the trans-Elbian lands under the Christian knights; and the occupation and settlement of lands in the Americas by Europeans in the sixteenth and seventeenth centuries.[17]

In contrast to classic urbanization, industrial urbanization manifests no regularities in form or balance over long periods of time. Rather, in its evolution since the Industrial Revolution, it has proven to be a dynamic process characterized by an increasingly rapid rate of incidence as well as by an increasing degree of specialization. Consequently, in technologically advanced societies, there is not the classic situation in which small towns predominate but one in which the proportion of the total population living in urban areas may range between 50 and 80 percent. Moreover, the most rapidly urbanizing areas are no longer necessarily those of greatest economic productivity. Modern methods of transportation and communication have made it possible not only for individuals to maintain contact without residential proximity, but also for large urban centers to extend their influence economically, socially, and politically far beyond their legally defined geographic boundaries. The relatively new concept of "urbanized area" connotes this possibility.

DEFINITIVE CITIES—
PREINDUSTRIAL, TRANSITIONAL, AND INDUSTRIAL

Gideon Sjoberg has delineated three categories of definitive cities: the preindustrial, the transitional, and the industrial.[18]

PREINDUSTRIAL CITIES

Historically, preindustrial cities have been predominantly governmental and religious centers. Their various ethnic and occupational groups are usually isolated from one another residentially, constituting relatively self-sufficient enclaves both economically and socially. Somewhat paradoxically, however, there is little specialization with respect to land use within these separated ethnic and occupational quarters, a particular household often serving residential, productive, and marketing purposes. Key positions in the educational, political, and religious structures are held by a small elite who are easily distinguished by their unique manner of dress and behavior. A broad gulf separates this class from the masses of lower-class people below whom, however, there exists a category of persons referred to as outcastes who perform essential but "unrespectable" services in the community. Typically, the elite reside in and around the centers of preindustrial cities, while the lower classes and outcastes live on their peripheries.

In preindustrial cities, the welfare of the family unit takes precedence over the interests of individual members, as exemplified by the predominance of arranged marriages. Moreover, the ideal family unit is the large extended type, with numerous relatives residing within one household and functioning as a social and economic unit. But this ideal generally is attained only by the elite. Lower-class families are much less cohesive and stable due to poverty and high morbidity and mortality rates. Besides serving as the principal socializing agent, the family is the center of leisure-time activities, especially for the women and children, who are permitted less freedom than adult males. Finally, and perhaps most important, the family is the chief determinant of one's occupation and, hence, of one's social class and style of life.

The technology of preindustrial cities is unsophisticated, and their economic organization is similarly uncomplicated. For example, a single craftsman not only carries out all stages in the "manufacture" of a given product but often sells it as well. "Practical" occupations such as manual labor and trade are relegated to an inferior position by the elite who assign these tasks to the lower class and outcastes. The elite are not even sufficiently concerned about commercial activity to establish minimum standards with respect to prices, currency, weights and measures, and the quality of consumer goods. Meager facilities for securing credit and investment capital are still other factors seriously restricting economic progress in the preindustrial urban setting.

While the political system in preindustrial cities tends to be highly centralized and bureaucratic in many respects, policies are more often an expression of the incumbent's personality than of rigid compliance with impersonal rules and regulations. On the negative side, however, this situation, together with the absence of a fixed-salary system, constitutes an inducement for bureaucrats to supplement their earnings by soliciting and/or accepting gratuities for the services they perform. The bureaucratic structure of the religious institution, as in the political area, is a powerful integrating and stabilizing force, for its highly specific norms and sanctions regulate almost every aspect of the urbanite's behavior. Since the urban elite have a monopoly on the highest ranks in the religious hierarchy and are the staunchest defenders of religious beliefs and practices, the preindustrial city is also the chief bastion of orthodoxy.

The formal educational structure, which serves primarily elite males and emphasizes religio-philosophical instruction, is still another factor that not only perpetuates and strengthens the religious heritage but reinforces and supports the elite's favored position in the social order of the preindustrial city. Experimental physical or social science is not encouraged and may even be said to be discouraged in the preindustrial city, as the members of the elite, the only formally educated persons, insist that the traditional knowledge in which they have been schooled must not be challenged or altered. Their depreciation of practical pursuits and manual labor results in further separation of the theoretical and practical aspects of learning. Not until the centuries immediately preceding the Industrial Revolution in Europe did the two aspects merge, making possible modern science and an industrial-urban social order.

TRANSITIONAL CITIES

Because the transformation of traditional cities into industrial cities takes place gradually, transitional cities are always hybrids demonstrating both industrial and preindustrial characteristics. Sociologists who study transitional cities in such developing areas as Africa and Asia usually ask two major questions: (1) Why are the societies in which these cities are located so anxious to industrialize? and (2) How do they seek to achieve this goal? The answer to the first question is the popular desire for "the good life," which connotes political freedom and economic prosperity for all segments of the society and the leaders' thirst for power and status. It is interesting that the leaders often are willing to sacrifice their traditional authority structures to achieve industrialization and a higher level of urbanization because failure to accomplish these objectives usually means either perpetuation of a nation's colonial status, or, if it has achieved independence, falling prey to the ambitions of another imperialistic power. The residents of economically backward or underdeveloped nations tend to be relatively weak politically because they are financially incapable of either mounting a revolution against oppressors or of defending themselves against aggressors.

Developing nations which pursue the communist ideal tend to emphasize heavy industry, while those emulating the democratic model not only tend to favor modern light industry, but may also strive to revitalize, or at least to maintain, the traditional handicraft industries. The two orientations differ significantly as to which segment of the society should bear the principal burden of making the transition from a traditional to an industrial urban nation. It is quite apparent that in the countries of Eastern Europe the Communists place the burden on the traditional elite and the peasantry. The former are relieved of their power and privilege, and the latter, at least in the initial stages of the transition, are denied satisfaction of many consumer needs so that the limited supply of capital can be invested in the manufacture of machinery, in the development of public utilities, and in the buildup of the defense industry. By contrast, the democratic ideal attempts to distribute the burden equally among the various socioeconomic classes and tends to encourage "a revolution of rising expectations" among previously poor and disadvantaged groups.

In most transitional societies there is considerable resistance, both covert and overt, to the introduction of new urban patterns, as illustrated by the vigorous opposition of the Catholic church to industrial urbanization in southern Europe and in Latin America. In other areas where it has not been predominant, it has simply attempted to influence the social structure of the new industrial cities. The principal source of resistance to industrial urbanization, however, are residents of small towns and villages, who benefit least from the emerging social order. In this regard, they have strong allies in the classical urban ecologists who favor the preservation of handicraft industries and other rural traditions in the developing countries and who recommend that urbanization be allowed to progress only to the extent of producing middle-sized towns. They regard the huge metropolises and megalopolises so characteristic of the technologically advanced nations as not only inefficient but pathological. It is important to point out, however, that the continued rural migration to large cities in most transitional societies seems to indicate a belief that urban communities can offer a more satisfactory style of life than small towns and villages. On the other hand, it could be just as convincingly argued that the ruralites migrate to cities primarily out of curiosity or because of extreme poverty and that they become disillusioned when, after living in an urban community for a period of time, their economic positions either remain unchanged or deteriorate. If ruralites could move to middle-sized rather than large cities, as classical ecologists have suggested, their expectations might be more easily and fully realized. In any case, the city makes social problems more visible, which is a negative feature for those with an antiurban bias, but a positive one for those who feel that social problems, like physical illnesses, must be diagnosed before they can be treated. It would be shortsighted not to recognize that most rural migrants to urban areas do eventually acquire the skills necessary for successful occupational performance and effective social interaction in an urban-industrial setting and do become socially mobile.

As stated earlier, transitional cities are hybrids which undergo several processes almost simultaneously: the persistence of certain traditional forms, the revision or modification of others, the disappearance of still others, and the gradual emergence of new forms. Consequently, it is not unusual for a time lag to result between the acceptance of new urban values and the development of institutional means for their attainment. In the economic area, for example, people who have been socialized to expect a higher standard of living than is immediately possible may become so dissatisfied that social and political disorder erupts. In a less explosive area—that of marriage and the family—Ronald Dore's research in Tokyo during the late 1950s revealed that, although many young people regarded romantic love as an ideal basis for courtship and marriage, the institutional means for implementing that ideal were not yet generally acceptable to their parents and elders.[19]

Another area of change in transitional cities is social class structure. Due to the fact that the elite dominate the educational system in traditional societies, they are the first segment of the population to become familiar with the scientific and technological bases for the transition which their societies are undergoing. Acceptance is another matter, however; a dilemma confronting many developing countries is how to socialize the educated elite to evaluate such practical pursuits as scientific research and industrial production as dignified rather than degrading. China's Communist leadership has been notably successful in this regard by requiring all students to participate in rigorous physical exercise programs and all intellectuals and professional persons to spend some time working on collective farms and in factories. In India, government planners are distressed by educated persons' aversion to practical pursuits, manual labor, and entrepreneurial activity, all of which are essential to industrial urbanization.

How to orient the lower class of a traditional society to industrial urbanization is an even more perplexing problem. In India, for example, just when many of the elite are discarding various features of the traditional culture, many disadvantaged groups whose economic position has become more secure due to industrial progress are beginning to develop a taste for them—especially those features related to the family and religion. Ernestine Friedl has observed, for example, that while the cities of Greece are modernizing and industrializing, contemporary Greek villagers still take the preindustrial city as their reference point.[20] As the influence of the mass media becomes increasingly widespread in transitional societies, such tendencies are being rapidly overcome, and some younger lower-class persons in transitional societies contiguous with technologically advanced nations (Mexico vis-à-vis the United States) have been socialized from childhood to accept industrial-urban values so that they experience no serious adjustment problems.[21]

Informal organizations play an important role in enabling persons in developing nations to adapt to industrial urbanization, for when migrants come to a city they tend to search out and associate with earlier migrants from their particular town or village and/or with persons of the same social class and ethnic and occupational characteristics. According to Sjoberg, such informal groupings in transitional cities perform at least three major functions: (1) they introduce the migrant from the villages to formal organizations, such as schools and unions, which assist him in adapting to the demands of the industrializing city; (2) they are the prime means by which the new urbanite sustains ties with rural traditions; and (3) they are the principal channels for the transmission of industrial-urban folkways from the city to the villages.[22]

Suzuki found from his research in Turkey that informal subgroups can also facilitate industrialization in transitional cities by fostering social stability among recent urban migrants, thereby promoting a more efficient labor force.[23] Other scholars, however, claim that they may have just the opposite effect, impeding industrial urbanization by sustaining migrants' ties with the rural past.[24] In fairness to the latter position, it should be pointed out that Suzuki failed to analyze his subcommunity within the context of the broader Turkish culture and neglected to state explicitly that the city in which he conducted his research was already semi-industrialized.

In terms of the above discussion, it is interesting to observe that, in several recently industrialized societies, organizations have been and are being developed specifically to sever the attachment of new urbanites to their rural background and to expedite their accommodation to, and assimilation of, industrial-urban norms. In the Soviet Union, for example, the Communist Party and labor unions have been the major agencies inculcating in workers such values as discipline, punctuality, and efficiency. Labor unions are also an important means of indoctrinating factory workers in India, and the Communist Party as well as urban communes have been utilized by China to socialize both long-established and recent urbanites to new health and sanitation standards. The formal education system, more than any other mechanism, however, is relied upon by all developing nations to orient their constituents to the new industrial-urban style of life.

Another factor which cannot be ignored if one would validly assess a society's transition from traditional to industrial urbanization is the use of nationalism in glorifying a society's history and traditions to give its people a sense of identity and of continuity, which facilitates their abandonment of an old social order in favor of a new one. This technique is especially apparent in the Soviet Union, where the government has consciously promoted a revival of the art, literature, and music of the Turkic people of central Asia at the same time that it has attempted to destroy their traditional economic, political, familial, and religious organizations. In Communist China and in India too, folk art, music, and literature are being given increasing support by the government and are, hence, growing in popularity and prestige as these societies continue to make the transition from traditional to industrial urbanization.

INDUSTRIAL CITIES

Unlike the preindustrial city, whose center is a political-religious complex, the industrial city has a commercial and/or industrial focus, and consistent with this emphasis is the fact that its commercial and industrial buildings have more stories than those of government and religion and that industrial urbanites adhere far less than preindustrialites to sacred values. Instead, practical values compatible with industrialization—notably, planning, speed, and efficiency—predominate and are embodied in such familiar urban phenomena as scientific research, regional planning agencies, rapid transit systems, and machine production. Unlike the preindustrial city, which has little or no land use specialization within its occupational and ethnic enclaves, the industrial city has legally defined residential, commercial, and industrial zones. Finally, in marked contrast to the preindustrial city, whose elite reside in and toward the center, the industrial city's core is characteristically inhabited by the most disadvantaged citizens, the privileged classes residing on the outskirts.

Of special interest to urban sociologists is the comparison of social stratification in industrial and preindustrial cities. While some sociologists contend that social mobility is at its peak under industrial urbanization, others perceive a firming-up trend in such industrialized nations as the United States and the Soviet Union. The first sociological position insists that the numerous jobs created by advancing technology could not be filled without the sanctioning of individual occupational mobility in the industrial city, and the second group, in the Durkheimian tradition, claims that the complex division of labor necessitated by industrial urbanization has produced greater rigidity in the social class structure. One explanation for these divergent conclusions is the fact that although the industrial city's poor are not as wretchedly poor and its elite are not as far removed from the common man as were their counterparts in preindustrial or transitional cities, an equal opportunity to enjoy "the good life" is still lacking. In spite of greater permissiveness with respect to such factors as dress, speech, and mannerisms, which facilitate a person's escaping from his categorical identity and expressing his individuality, the existence of "islands of residential segregation" in industrial cities is patent evidence of continued restrictions on mobility. Moreover, because of their leisure-time, educational, and financial implications, extensive participation as well as leadership in formal organizations are still largely a prerogative of middle- and upper-class persons in industrial cities. Lower-class persons tend to confine their involvement in formal organizations to churches, lodges, and labor unions, placing far more importance upon informal relationships with kin and friends. In other words, contradictory forces are simultaneously at work within industrial cities, some encouraging greater fluidity than that which prevailed under earlier urban conditions, and others encouraging maintenance of the status quo or even greater rigidity. To illustrate, while several low-ranking positions in the preindustrial city (physicians, managers of manufacturing or commercial enterprises, and entertainers) have risen considerably in status, and other high-ranking occupations (the clergy and certain categories of "intellectuals") seem to have fallen in status with the advent of industrial urbanization, the status of certain roles, namely, key government positions, has remained unchanged, continuing to carry prestige. One point over which there has been no controversy, however, is that there is a distinct difference between the method of exercising leadership under preindustrial urbanization and under industrial urbanization. Whereas the former appeals to absolutes and tradition, the latter appeals to popular consensus, which means that leadership under industrial urbanization is really more tenuous than that under preindustrial conditions.

As noted earlier in this chapter, in preindustrial cities only the urban elite can attain the societal ideal of a large, extended family residing within a single "household." In the industrial-urban context, however, this family pattern becomes dysfunctional and ceases to be an ideal. Instead, the conjugal family, which is more consistent with the new higher status and increased freedom of women and adolescents, becomes the ideal form. Another reason for the predominance of this relatively small, flexible family unit in industrial cities is its compatibility with a highly mobile labor force which inevitably loosens kinship bonds, forcing individuals to rely upon the conjugal family as their principal source of emotional security. But since emotional well-being is a very subjective and intangible goal, it is difficult for any particular institutional structure to assure it, as the proliferation of specialists providing counseling services today seems to prove.

While the conjugal family is epitomized in American cities, it is not only becoming increasingly prevalent in the industrial cities of such recently traditional societies as Russia and Japan, but a source of concern as well because of its functional connection with the development of a youth culture and the rising incidence of delinquency. The high standard of living in industrial cities makes it unnecessary for young people to work in order to help earn a livelihood for their families. Many jobs in an industrial-urban society cannot be performed by adolescents because they demand considerable formal education or specialized training. Leisure and affluence, in turn, facilitate the organization of youth gangs whose detachment and alienation from the adult world frequently lead to deviant behavior. Not unlike the United States, Russia has problems in its cities with young hooligans who lack dedication to Soviet ideas, and Japan has difficulty with its youthful beatniks and revolutionaries.[25] The "youth culture" has also contributed to the increasing acceptance of romantic love as the major basis for marriage in industrial societies. Thus, parents no longer arrange their children's marriages according to practical and prosaic considerations. Another conspicuous trend associated with the emergence of the conjugal family in industrial cities is the rising status of women, which finds expression in their increasing role as wage-earners and decision makers both in and outside the home. However, while the traditional strict dichotomy between male and female jobs is gradually disappearing due to recent fair employment legislation, covert sex discrimination still exists in industrial cities. Women's periodic withdrawal from the labor force on maternity leave and the popular perception of women as sex symbols account for much of this discrimination by employers.

A comparison of the political organization of the preindustrial or transitional society with that of the industrial-urban society suggests that democracy is an essential, but possibly insufficient, criterion for the stability of the latter society on both the local and the national levels, for it is through the democratic process that the industrial-urban system reconciles and unifies the divergent value positions of its many special interest organizations, professional associations, labor unions, and other groups. Even modern dictatorships have made limited concessions to the principle of "the consent of the governed," as exemplified by the increasing tendency of Soviet leaders to encourage "feedback" from their constituents by permitting them to criticize at least the lesser officials in "letters to the editor" columns in newspapers.[26]

Any analysis of the political structure of industrial cities would be incomplete without consideration of their legal systems. In contrast to preindustrial cities, where one is presumed guilty until proven innocent and where magical-religious rites are frequently employed to decide the issue, industrial cities demonstrate a growing trend toward universalizing and rationalizing the legal structure, a pattern which seems to be slowly developing even in the Soviet Union.[27] This trend may be ascribed in part to the improved educational and economic status of the common man and in part to the proliferation of occupational specialists and pressure groups in industrial cities whose varied and often conflicting interests must be adjudicated.

The economic organization of industrial cities also differs markedly from that of preindustrial cities. Labor legislation and more efficient production methods have shortened the work week and afforded the laboring classes more leisure time. But this efficiency has not been an unmixed blessing, for automation has reached the point in some industrial societies, notably the United States, where it is becoming increasingly difficult for unskilled and semiskilled persons to find work. Thus, the preindustrial city's elite and the industrial city's common man tend to share one

41569

thing—leisure. At the same time, the industrial city's highly skilled workers are typically overinvolved in their employment situation, often at the sacrifice of many other important life goals.

Another important economic distinction between the preindustrial and industrial cities is that in the former the division of labor is based almost solely upon product specialization and in the latter it is based upon an extremely wide range of specialized knowledge and skills. The intensive specialization of labor characterizing industrial-urban societies is a function of large-scale bureaucracy, just as are such activities as (1) intensive planning, (2) the preparation and filing of numerous lengthy reports, (3) the conducting of audits and investigations by experts, (4) the recruitment of workers on the basis of achievement rather than ascription so as to obtain the most qualified persons, and (5) the standardization of coinage, weights and measures, prices, and the quality of goods and services—all of which are lacking or rudimentary in the economies of preindustrial societies.

When the question is posed as to whether the industrial or preindustrial society's system of labor division fosters greater social unity, the data seem to support the Durkheimian position that since the industrial city's division of labor requires a greater degree of interdependence among workers than does that of the preindustrial city, the industrial city makes the greater contribution to social unity. At the same time, however, the industrial system's emphasis upon specialized knowledge and skills encourages the formation of vested interest or pressure groups, which compete for the considerable economic rewards available, a competition which sometimes precipitates open conflict. Offsetting this disunifying potential is the system of informal education via the mass media which promotes social unity by standardizing, to a great extent, the flow of information to all socioeconomic, racial, and ethnic groups. Moreover, the mass media are an indispensable factor in the life of industrial cities, for without them it would be impossible to disseminate tremendous volumes of essential information to large and sprawling populations.

Even more indispensable to industrial cities than the mass media is the system of formal education, for their very existence depends upon an adequate supply of systematically trained scientific specialists. Consequently, most developing nations today are undertaking a fundamental revision of their educational systems, shifting the emphasis from the humanities, which dominated their curricula for centuries under colonialism, to the sciences. These revisions include extending the opportunity for an education to a broader range of people, a trend which is producing significant social changes. Not only are more citizens prepared to exercise a leadership role, but the scientific orientation of their education induces them to question the validity of prevailing patterns of behavior and to seek alternative, and perhaps improved, approaches to accomplishing personal and social objectives. This is in stark contrast to the situation in preindustrial cities where the rule of the elite is absolute over the powerless masses and the traditional values, beliefs, and modi operandi are regarded as too "sacred" to be subjects for debate or change.

Another important concomitant of these educational revisions is the increasing secularization of industrial cities, which means that religious values are no longer of paramount importance and that behavior is regulated permissively rather than prescriptively. While religion continues to influence people's lives, it does so to a lesser degree than in preindustrial cities, as exemplified by the common tendencies to consider religion a private rather than a public matter, to confine religious values to limited areas of behavior, and to compromise these values when expediency seems to be the more practical and comfortable approach. There is considerable variation in the degree of secularization from one industrial city to another, however, depending upon its societal context.

A related religious issue is how people in industrial cities cope with the problem of meaning. Some have substituted scientism and nationalism for religion, as demonstrated by the Russian intellectuals' choice of nineteenth-century "scientific socialism" as the basis of their utopian model for industrial-urban living.[28] Nationalism has much in common with religion in the sense that it not only offers a reason for living and dying, but requires sacrifice. For the vast majority of people living in industrial cities, however, hedonism—the pleasure philosophy—has become the principal motivation for living, a trend which is due largely to the successful efforts of commercial advertising in creating an unending number of human "wants" which it proposes to satisfy by offering a similarly unending supply of tantalizing goods and services. The "new sexual morality" is still another expression of the hedonist mentality.

Throughout the preceding analysis of industrial cities, there has been an effort to stress their cultural uniformity based on the premise that the technological progress which created them presupposes a considerable number of structural imperatives. This premise is based on the readily observable fact of decreasing diversity in the organization of the basic social institutions as one proceeds from simple to technologically sophisticated societies. Granted that there are significant differences among industrial cities located in divergent societal and, hence, cultural settings, there are still more numerous and important similarities among them. Expressing the same point from a different perspective, the differences *among* industrial cities are much fewer and less significant than the differences *between* industrial cities on the one hand and preindustrial or transitional cities on the other. Thus, cities in Japan, Russia, and the United States have more traits in common than all three of them have relative to transitional cities in industrializing societies like India or in preindustrial societies like Cambodia.

Once industrialization laid the foundation for the modern industrial city during the eighteenth and nineteenth centuries, secondary economic growth soon transformed it into the metropolis. This process involved such complex functional and structural changes both within the industrial city and in its surrounding suburbs that R. D. McKenzie's pioneer study of the early 1930s dealing with urban communities referred to the metropolis as "practically a new social and economic entity." [29] Principal among these changes were the decentralization of numerous activities, the separation of residential and employment zones, a high rate of spatial mobility, and the extension of the city's social, economic, and political influence over a wide geographic area. Equally important, however, is the dependence of the industrial city upon its suburbs, as its contemporary fiscal problems dramatically illustrate. Consequently, the whole complex of interrelationships within a metropolitan area can be best described by the biological term *symbiosis*.

The metropolis may be defined as a multinucleated urban area within which the larger cities, characterized by functional diversity, exercise varying degrees and types of control over smaller, more narrowly specialized cities, many of which are politically independent in the sense of being incorporated. Such late nineteenth-century technological developments as the substitution of electric power for steam in industry, improvements in transportation, the invention of the telephone, and innovations in printing which made possible modern advertising and the expansion of newspaper circulation, actually created the metropolis. Certain of these developments enabled people and industry to move out from large industrial cities to smaller adjoining rural and urban communities where land was cheaper, taxes were lower, and the population was less congested, while other developments enabled them to keep in touch with life in the industrial city despite their spatial separation from it.

URBAN GROWTH

Having discussed the history of urbanization, the characteristics of preindustrial, transitional, and industrial cities, and the evolution of the industrial city into the metropolis, we will devote the remainder of this chapter to the important question: What are the sources of urban growth? Succinctly stated, there are only three sources: (1) an excess of births over deaths in the city; (2) the expansion of rural settlements which are reclassified as towns or cities; and (3) population migration from rural areas to the city, commonly referred to as the urbanization process. When today's advanced societies began to industrialize, urban mortality rates generally exceeded birthrates and rural-to-urban reclassification was a minor factor, so that the only important source of urban growth was migration from rural areas. Because the demand for agricultural products is relatively inelastic and as farm workers' productivity increased and capital costs rose due to technological advancements, urban commercial, manufacturing, and service establishments (the demand for whose products is elastic) began to absorb the superfluous rural laborers and to pay them higher wages than they had been earning as farmers. Consequently, a substantial portion of the agricultural population moved to cities. In the later industrialization stages of today's advanced societies, however, this trend has gradually come to an end because there is no longer enough farm population to furnish significant migration to cities.

With the rate of urbanization having diminished in the advanced nations, it is the underdeveloped countries, representing three-fourths of the world's population, that are mainly responsible for the rapid urban growth now characterizing the world as a whole. Among these nations, the pace of urban growth is still relatively slow in eastern and southern Europe, but in the rest of the underdeveloped world the proportion of the population living in cities is rising twice as fast as in the industrialized nations, even when allowance is made for the fact that many of the latter have broadened their definitions of urban places to include suburban and fringe areas. Even more impressive is the fact that urban growth in the underdeveloped countries is proceeding more rapidly than during the peak industrializing years of the advanced nations. This is a truly disconcerting trend because these nations, already densely settled, tragically impoverished, and with gloomy economic prospects, are expanding their urban populations by sheer biologic increase, not by rural-urban migration. Today in the underdeveloped nations the inhabitants of towns and cities are only slightly less fertile than their rural cousins, and the formerly higher death rate for city dwellers has been reversed on account of the disproportionate share of public health funds spent in the cities. Consequently, if a high rate of rural-urban migration were encouraged, their cities would grow at an even more disastrous rate than at present. Indeed, without encouragement, so many squatters from the rural areas have settled in all the major cities of the underdeveloped countries that it has become virtually impossible to provide services fast enough to take care of them.

Thus, while the rapid growth of cities by rural-urban migration had the effect of solving rural economic problems in the advanced countries, the growth of cities in the underdeveloped nations by natural increase has discouraged rural-urban migration, thereby intensifying rural economic problems, and has either left unresolved or aggravated the plight of those ruralites who have dared to migrate to urban areas despite the negative indicators. The possibility of expanding agricultural land and capital fast enough to accommodate the enormous natural increase in rural populations is even less, however, than the possibility of accommodating them in the cities. Consequently, as their rural populations continue to swell, increasing densities per unit of arable land are inevitable. A case in point is Venezuela whose farm population increased 11 percent during the period 1950-1961.[30] As a result, while there were only 64 males engaged in agriculture per square mile of cultivated land in 1950, there were 78 in 1961, compared with 4.8 males occupied in agriculture per square mile of cultivated land in Canada, 6.8 in the United States, and 15.6 in Argentina.[31]

Even in the advanced nations of the world today's cities are confronted with serious problems. Disaffection is present at both ends of the socioeconomic spectrum: among the underprivileged in-migrants from the relatively depressed and deprived hinterland, as well as among the affluent out-migrants residing in the wealthy suburban fringes, handicapping urban administrators' attempts to cope with problems of congestion and decay inimical to human comfort, health, and safety. Moreover, few people seem to understand that the pattern of tomorrow's cities is being formed by today's rapid population growth, which even urban planners continue to treat as something to be planned for, rather than as something itself to be planned.

We may well ask ourselves several questions. Shall cities in general be rebuilt and revitalized to perform their traditional role as centers of culture and prosperity? More specifically, shall the shantytowns on the fringes of cities in Asia, Africa, and Latin America be transformed into livable places providing adequate human services, or shall they continue to be human cesspools? Shall the cities of the industrial West be cleansed of the blight which has been accumulating in them since the beginning of the Industrial Revolution, so that they will be in a more favorable position to win back the more prosperous residents and industries whose tax revenue is essential to their financial stability? Or will they continue to sprawl out, increasing the trend toward megalopolis and consuming thousands of acres of valuable open space? Generations of scientific research and sophisticated planning have made it possible for man to land on the moon, but his approach to many urgent problems on the planet earth, among them population control and city planning, is more a reflection of the Dark Ages than of the age of invention and creative improvisation. We must begin to act now if the cities of the future are to respond adequately to the needs and enduring values of the people who will live in them. The current interest in the ecological approach to the study of urban communities in which more emphasis is placed on the social and cultural aspects than on others is indeed an optimistic trend.

Chapter 2

Major Sociological Perspectives on the Urban Community

It is generally conceded that Robert E. Park and Ernest W. Burgess established a field for the study of urban phenomena at the University of Chicago during the second decade of the twentieth century with their research focusing on the processes of personal and social disorganization in the inner city. While the sociological study of the city continues to be dominated by the crisis approach, stressing such problems as crime, poverty, racial tensions, pollution, traffic congestion, urban sprawl, irrelevant education, drug abuse, illegitimacy, venereal disease, suicide, and the financial difficulties of local governments, its theoretical perspective has broadened in recent years. First, there has been a shift of interest from the central city to the wider metropolitan area, contemporary urban ecologists being concerned primarily with regional networks and with the character of relationships between communities therein. Among the pioneers in this transition were Charles Merriam, Calvin F. Schmid, Roderick D. McKenzie, Graham R. Taylor, Nathan L. Whetten, Walter Firey, and Don Bogue. Second, sociologists now recognize that the city is a complex system of related elements—the physical environment, a heterogeneous population, and social institutions. Hence, three major theoretical perspectives have emerged in urban sociology: the ecological, the demographic, and the juridical. Finally, there has been increasing emphasis upon the comparative method in urban research.

The major theoretical perspectives derive their names from the particular variable or variables to which they give priority. For example, the basic tenet of the juridical perspective is that the city is predominantly a political entity which may produce marked alterations in the culture of a nation by generating and popularizing new social ideologies and social movements. As the principal source of creative intellectual endeavors and the major communications media, the city naturally stimulates significant types of social change. Moreover, throughout the world it is cities, not rural areas, which are the focal points of the bureaucratic, educational, economic, religious, and political organizations which regulate society.

The delineation of local power decisions as the crucial independent variable determining urban land use patterns has been one of William Form's most notable contributions to urban sociology.[1] This matter has been treated more fully, however, by Meyerson and Banfield who describe how certain land use patterns are the products of compromises among competing local interest groups. In their case study of how the Chicago Housing Authority selected public housing sites to comply with the provisions of the Federal Housing Act of 1949, Meyerson and Banfield commented as follows:

> From the standpoint of the Authority, the public interest was an amalgam of ends of various types and its corporate ends were, of course, assumed to be consistent with the public interest.... So the staff of the Authority supposed that in strengthening their organization and in furthering the cause of public housing they were serving the public interest. They also assumed that, when doing so would not entail large sacrifices in terms of the ends of their own organization, they ought also to serve the ends of other official and semi-official agencies. Thus, the Authority took into account the ends of the Board of Education, the Mayor's Commission on Human Relations, the Land Clearance Commission, and other agencies which had some legal or other claim to represent the community. The ends of these agencies, however, were often vague, inconsistent, and unstable, and sometimes they conflicted with other ends which had some claim to be considered in the public interest. These were practical difficulties, [but] the staff [of the Chicago Housing Authority] took

it for granted that to be in the public interest a housing
program ought to harmonize "as far as possible" with the
ends of these agencies.

In addition to its own corporate ends and those of
other public agencies, the Authority took account of certain ends which it imputed to the community as a body
politic. . . . The staff seemed to assume that there existed
a "creed" or "code" that was widely held and that actions
which ran counter to this code were not in the public interest. This "code" specified that racial amity and integration were very much to be desired, that waste was to
be avoided, that all citizens should be treated with rigorous impartiality, that the values of family, home, and
good citizenship should be furthered by public effort, and
that public officials should subordinate neighborhood and
private interests to the public interest. . . . The code which
the Authority imputed to the body politic was, of course,
more nearly the code of the upper social classes in
America (or at least the professional-intellectual groups
among them) than of the lower classes, [as it was more
nearly the code] of people who acted in representative
(and, hence, group- or community-regarding) roles than
of people who acted in private (and, hence, self-
regarding) roles. As Miss Wood [staff head of the Chicago Housing Authority] once told 350 civic leaders who
were gathered at a testimonial dinner in her honor, the
Authority always tried to express "the wish and the will,
the ideals, the objectives, the moral code of you, the
'good' people of the City."[2]

An especially striking example of how national power decisions can shape urban ecological structures is the South African
government's implementation of its apartheid policy by relocating
sizable numbers of "colored" persons in specially created new communities on the periphery of such large cities as Johannesburg.
Moreover, such political manipulation of land use patterns demonstrates the fallacy of the popular tendency to attribute all or most
changes in these patterns to economic and technological forces. Indeed, the South African government's relocation program, by forcing many workers to travel long distances to their places of employment, is actually thwarting the country's industrialization
process.

National political decisions help to shape not only a city's internal structure, but its growth as well. Indeed, historical evidence

indicates that the rise and fall of cities have been closely associated with and even determined by the rise and fall of empires.[3] Today, as well, many cities have come into existence as the result of deliberate social planning by national governments. In the Soviet Union, for example, Communist authorities have been vigorously promoting industrial urbanization at the expense of the rural-agricultural way of life through the conscious and systematic use of political power. The collectivization of farms and the mechanization of agriculture, for example, have made many farmers superfluous, forcing them into the urban labor market. As a consequence, the central government has secured greater control over the agricultural surpluses essential to the maintenance of an expanding urban population. Similarly, in developing nations such as India, the pattern of urban growth often depends upon the outcome of the struggle between two opposing political forces—those favoring a preponderance of smaller communities based on light industry and those preferring the large metropolises generally associated with heavy industry.

Despite the fact that international power struggles have been a major inducement to industrialization and urbanization in the underdeveloped areas of the world, sociologists have by and large ignored their significance in this regard. The motivation for the ruling elite in many underdeveloped nations fostering industrialization and urbanization, even at the risk of diminishing their own power on the domestic level, is twofold: first, to enhance their prestige in the eyes of world leaders and, second, to discourage the continuance or revival of colonialism in their respective countries. Japan's industrial urbanization, for example, was stimulated, in part at least, by the ruling group's external status and power considerations.[4] International power struggles which have terminated in armed conflict have made an even more indelible imprint upon urban centers, in both preindustrial and industrial societies, a fact which was strikingly illustrated by the effects of bombing in World War II on the cities of Western Europe and Japan. Certain cities such as Rotterdam and Berlin which have been completely rebuilt have entirely new ecological structures, and, of course, the divided city of Berlin has two distinctly different social structures since the erection of the wall in 1961. Domestic revolutions have produced similar effects on urban social structures, as demonstrated by the contrast between pre-Communist and post-Communist urban life in Russia and China, especially in the intellectual, economic, and political areas.

The political perspective has not been especially prominent in the writings of urban sociologists, however; the demographic and ecological approaches have been far more conspicuous. The demographic perspective is concerned mainly with urban population composition, distribution, and trends in terms of fertility, mortality, and migration, and with the balance between urban populations and three interrelated variables: total land supply, knowledge concerning land use, and the standard of living, all of which are determined by a society's technological sophistication and its system of wealth and income distribution.

The urban sociologist who has most effectively employed the demographic approach is Kingsley Davis. Of special significance is the distinction which he has made between the percentage of a society's population residing in urban areas and the growth of its cities—a distinction which clearly differentiates the character of the urbanization process in the past from that of the present. Cities have traditionally grown as the result of migration from rural areas, not only giving the migrants a "new lease on life" but relieving the economic problems of the hinterland. Today, however, especially in the underdeveloped areas of the world, urban populations are growing mainly by natural increase—the surplus of births over deaths—thereby stifling migration from rural areas and, hence, the economic advancement of these impoverished areas and their residents. Another important contribution of the demographic perspective in urban sociology is its demonstration of the rapidity and intensity of world urbanization, suburbanization, and metropolitanization. Research by the International Population and Urban Research Center at Berkeley, for example, shows that if the current rate of world urbanization continues over the next quarter century more than half of the world's population will be living in cities of 100,000 people or more by the year 1990.[5]

The principal advantage of the demographic approach to the study of urbanization is that it deals with quantitative data about the world's cities which have become increasingly available since the end of World War II, facilitating the intercultural analysis of urban life. It would be a grave mistake, however, if the sociologist were to study urbanization solely in demographic terms, for an urban area in a sociological context connotes much more than a large, heterogeneous aggregation of people. Whether the sociologist is focusing on communities with a population of five thousand, one hundred thousand, or one million inhabitants, he cannot adequately compare them cross-culturally on the basis of size alone; it is imperative that he analyze the *total social situations* within which they exist.

It is not surprising, therefore, that the most popular perspective in urban sociological research has been the ecological one, focusing upon the relationship between people and their habitat, investigating the reasons for the existence of given spatial distributions, and analyzing how these patterns affect social life. Thus, Stuart Dodd has observed that the ecological approach lends support to sociology as a positivist discipline, for when one considers populations exclusively in demographic terms, i.e., in terms of migration and mobility rates, he is soon impressed with the apparent absence of volition from behavior.[6] Moreover, extensive ecological studies supplement the demographic content of urban sociology by stressing the social and cultural aspects of urban life. Therefore, ecologically oriented urban sociologists fall into four categories depending upon the importance which they place on natural circumstances as opposed to cultural values in determining urban locations and structures: (1) classical biotic materialists; (2) socioculturists; (3) neoclassical physical materialists; and (4) social area analysts.

Robert E. Park and Ernest W. Burgess introduced the term "human ecology" to American sociology when in 1921 at the University of Chicago they launched a systematic effort to study human behavior in urban communities in terms of plant and animal adaptation, on the assumption that competition for scarce resources is the basic principle underlying both processes.[7] Relying heavily upon the works of such European sociologists as Simmel, Maine, Tönnies, Durkheim, and Weber, Park and Burgess and their fellow classicists studied biotic competition as a subsocial process through such concepts as dominance, succession, invasion, natural areas, and concentric zones, their central concern being the identi-

fication of the patterns and processes involved in the transition
from a preindustrial, agrarian, feudal society to an urban, industrial, capitalistic one.

These classical ecologists, often referred to collectively as the
Chicago School, reflected the popular trend during the late nineteenth and early twentieth centuries of merging two philosophical
systems—social Darwinism and classical economics. On the one
hand, Burgess, one of the two founders of the Chicago School, relied heavily upon classical economics, assigning the core or domi-
nant position to the central business district relative to the other
four zones in his concentric zone theory of urban ecology. Park, on
the other hand, demonstrated a greater affinity for social Darwinism, insisting that although geographic advantages and disadvantages initially determine the location of cities and their internal
structure, subtler influences tend eventually to control their population distribution:

> ... personal tastes and conveniences, vocational and eco-
> nomic interests infallibly tend to classify the population
> of big cities. In this way a city acquires an organization
> and distribution of population which is neither designed
> nor controlled. Each section of the city takes on the char-
> acter and the quality of its inhabitants, its differentiated
> and relatively segregated populations. Thus, what was
> initially a mere geographic expression is transformed into
> a congeries of neighborhoods with sentiments, traditions,
> and local histories.[8]

According to Park, human physical proximity not only facilitates
social contact and association, but eventually results in the emergence of a normative order. Consistent with Park's analysis, research by Willhelm and Sjoberg in Austin, Texas, has suggested
that certain subgroups in American cities, notably businessmen
with frequent and intimate relationships in retail associations and
service and social clubs, have incorporated subsocial or impersonal
forces into their value system which are frequently used to justify
the maintenance of the status quo in regard to such important urban patterns as zoning practices.[9]

At the University of Chicago, Park and Burgess headed an impressive group of sociologists (Walter Reckless, Robert Faris,
Warren Dunham, Paul Cressey, Frederic Thrasher, Theodore An-

derson, Harvey Zorbaugh, Ernest Mowrer, Louis Wirth, and Robert Redfield) in the ecological study of many American cities. This resulted in their concluding that certain social variables—social status, family types, age groups, and deviant behavior (divorce, desertion, illegitimacy, emotional illness, crime, and delinquency)—have a constant spatial distribution in all large urban communities.

Few theoretical orientations have had as powerful and pervasive an influence upon urban sociology, however, as Wirth's famous essay "Urbanism as a Way of Life," which views the city—typified by size, density, and heterogeneity—as the principal determinant of many kinds of social action. Redfield's book *Folk Culture of Yucatán* also designates the city with its heterogeneity and lack of isolation as a key variable, and, like Wirth's essay, perceives urbanism as a way of life characterized by secularization, secondary group relationships, voluntary associations, increased segmentation of roles, and inadequately defined social norms.[10] Indeed, Wirth considers these traits as inevitable accompaniments of urban development independent of the effects of industrialization, which helps to explain his negative view of all cities whether preindustrial or industrial. But Wirth's writings reflect the events of the 1920s and 1930s—World War I, massive foreign immigration as well as domestic migration, and the Great Depression—all of which subjected American cities to unprecedented pressures.

Though more of a moralizer than a scientist, the well-known and widely quoted Lewis Mumford shares Wirth's pessimistic view of American urban life. In his book *The City in History* (1961), Mumford ascribes most of the crucial problems facing our society today to the imbalance between nature and human culture. Perceiving the natural environment deterministically, Mumford contends that cities and their inhabitants cannot function effectively unless they accommodate their technology and social organization to it.[11] Reminiscent of Georg Simmel's evaluation of urban life as pecuniary, predatory, and impersonal, the negative attitude toward urban life which has dominated American urban sociology stems largely from the notion that the evolutionary development of the urban community has produced dislocations in traditional and valued institutions with deleterious and even disastrous consequences for the individuals involved.

The biotic framework of the Chicago School of Ecology came

under severe criticism with the publication of Milla Aissa Alihan's book *Social Ecology* in 1938 and Warner Getty's article "Human Ecology and Social Theory" in a 1940 issue of *Social Forces*.[12] In 1947, two other works questioning the validity of traditional ecological materialism appeared: Walter Firey's book *Land Use in Central Boston* and an article by A. B. Hollingshead, "A Re-Examination of Ecological Theory," in *Sociology and Social Research*.[13] Katherine Biehl, Beverly Davis, Otis Duncan, C. E. Gehlke, and Paul Hatt also became involved in the discussion, attacking as unrealistic the biological premises of the classical ecologists, urging that explanations for ecological data be sought mainly in terms of cultural values and social organization, and introducing a new "voluntaristic" approach to human ecology. They pointed out that even Chicago, where the classical ecologists most systematically applied their principles, had become the metropolitan center of the midwest chiefly through political action and aggressive business practices, for its location was no more favorable than that of Beloit, Kankakee, or Rockford. Geographic determination was thus shown to be an oversimplified explanation of urban patterns.

The American city is also more highly organized than most of the classical ecologists realized. Even slum areas possess intricate patterns of social interaction which are frequently overlooked by middle-class social scientists. Less excusable, however, is their ignoring or understating of the vital role which bureaucratic organizations play in the lives of American urbanites. Beginning with the studies of Miller and Swanson, however, an increasing body of research has corrected this shortcoming.[14] The limitations of classical ecologists' preoccupation with urban social disorganization and pathology are even more obvious when used as the frame of reference for cross-cultural research. Oscar Lewis's data from Mexico City, for example, have demonstrated that urbanization does not invariably result in the complete breakdown of the social and moral order.[15] Contemporary studies of urbanization in Africa also demonstrate that while its cities are undergoing change at an extremely rapid rate, traditional behavior patterns persist alongside the new organizational forms which have emerged.[16] Moreover, Le Tourneau's Fès and Miner's Timbuctoo with their rigid normative orders have proved erroneous Wirth's belief that even cities in preindustrial societies suffer the same kind and degree of social disorganization as do cities in industrial societies.[17]

Several generalizations emanating from the Wirth–Redfield perspective regarding rural-urban differences also need to be qualified. For example, certain institutional patterns characterizing American urban life are often falsely assumed to prevail in other urban settings as well. That this is not so is illustrated by the fact that the family in its most highly organized form—the large extended type residing under a single roof—is most characteristic of the urban elite in preindustrial societies, whereas in the United States it is most common among lower-class ruralites. Moreover, rural-urban distinctions are not nearly so clear-cut in the industrial societies of the Western world as in the preindustrial societies of the underdeveloped world. In other words, classical ecologists have failed to recognize that cities are shaped to a large extent by the broader societal and cultural context in which they exist. Recognizing that much of the ecological and social structures of cities is determined by external social forces, urban sociologists today treat the city as a dependent rather than an independent variable. While some cities in the past achieved political autonomy, most cities— certainly contemporary ones—have been mere subsystems of their respective societies and, as such, have been subject to their controls. However, despite the fact that the classical ecologists have been severely criticized in recent years, their works still exercise considerable influence over urban research, such as that by Robert Smith on preindustrial Tokyo and Marshall Clinard on the relationship between urbanism and criminal behavior.[18] Moreover, the theorizing of Wirth and Redfield is especially being perpetuated in introductory sociology textbooks, which may account for the prevalent use by today's activist-oriented students of such terms as "loss of identity," "alienation," and "anomie" in their castigation of America's urban milieu.

Turning next to the ecological conception of the urban community as a sociocultural entity, it is important to point out that here the city is perceived not as merely a large, dense population occupying a specific geographic area, but as an organized aggregation of individuals who agree on what cultural patterns they wish to support. In other words, socioculturists emphasize urban values, social stratification systems, and institutional controls which coordinate the behavior of sizable, heterogeneous, and functionally

differentiated populations. Radhakamal Mukerjee in India and
Theodore Caplow in France, for example, have demonstrated that
sacred and aesthetic values prevent land values from being decisive
in determining urban land use patterns.[19] In India, the caste quarters into which many cities are divided frequently have sections reserved for such economically useless purposes as religious shrines,
and in France the extensive space allocated to historic parks and
squares represents a similar ethic. In the United States, other sociocultural ecologists—Jonassen in New York, Myers in New
Haven, and Seeman among Utah's Mormons—likewise have conceded major importance to cultural values in accounting for the
spatial distribution of human activities.[20]

Utilizing data from Boston, Firey, more than any other socio-
culturist, has provided a firm empirical foundation for those re-
searchers who regard values as the key determinant of urban
ecological patterns. Dickinson's book *The West European City*,
Jones's book *A Social Geography of Belfast*, and von Grunebaum's
impressionistic essay on Muslim cities all support Firey's theory.[21]
Indeed, it is when vastly different societies are studied that the relationship between values and ecological patterns becomes especially clear in terms of the size, density, and expansion of their
urban centers. Of course, some societies possess value systems that
are much more permissive than others.

In addition to their influence upon the development of cities
in general, values largely account for the development of particular
types of cities such as Mecca, Benares, Jerusalem, or Rome, whose
long histories reflect the persistence over many centuries of greatly
divergent religious value systems. Still another example of values
motivating the development of particular kinds of cities is the recent trend, especially in underdeveloped countries, of building new
capitals to symbolize economic progress and political independence.
In a similarly specific context, Whyte and Meadows have inves-
tigated the relationship between different city planners' philoso-
phies and their proposals for rebuilding the core cities of our metropolitan areas and relieving their population congestion.[22] Inasmuch as purposive city planning is increasingly shaping urban
life in the United States and in Europe, including the Communist
bloc nations, we need many more studies such as that by Orlans on

a planned city in England and that by Marris on Lagos, Nigeria, specifying how values influence the planning process.[23]

The third category of ecologists, the neoclassical or physical materialists, reject the socioculturists' emphasis upon values as the prime determinant of urban land use patterns. Otis Duncan, Leo Schnore, Jack Gibbs, and Walter Martin, the most notable representatives of this ecological school, have been influenced not only by the Chicago classical ecologists, but by Durkheim, by the classical economists, and, to some extent, by the materialistic orientation of the Marxists. However, Duncan and Schnore differ significantly from Gibbs and Martin in both their theoretical premises and their methodology. Whereas the first two proceed inductively in an effort to establish the validity of their concept of "ecological complex," the latter start with the concept of "sustenance" and deductively arrive at their theory of urbanization.

The ecological complex of Duncan and Schnore has four functionally interrelated "external, " "physical," and "impersonal" components—environment, population, social organization, and technology—which are said to "absolutely determine" urban ecological patterns. While this theoretical framework readily lends itself to the organization of large amounts of quantitative census data, its contention that human ecology operates entirely on an impersonal basis fails to coincide with reality and must, therefore, be declared invalid. Duncan, for example, deals with the smog situation in Los Angeles as though a *population* automatically reflects the changing *physical setting* (environment) through a particular *social organization's* implementation of *technological devices* in a *unidirectional* fashion, whereas, in fact, serious *alternative responses* have been and are now being discussed by governmental agencies as well as by other social organizations.[24] In other words, disputes between various special interest groups in the population regarding the form and/or content of social organizations within Los Angeles for technological control of the environment are taking place. Thus, although Duncan began his investigation of the Los Angeles smog-control controversy inductively by collecting factual information about it, he apparently allowed deductive logic from untested assumptions (i.e., the impersonal determination of ecological matters) to invalidate his analysis of the data.

With Gibbs and Martin, the other two neoclassical ecologists mentioned, the emphasis is upon sustenance activities. Their major work, "Urbanization, Technology, and the Division of Labor," illustrates this in the following propositions set forth by the study:

1. The degree of urbanization in a society varies directly with the division of labor.
2. The division of labor in a society varies directly with the dispersion of objects of consumption.
3. The degree of urbanization in a society varies directly with technological development.
4. Technological development in a society varies directly with the dispersion of objects of consumption.[25]

From these postulates Gibbs and Martin deduce the theorem that the degree of urbanization in a society varies directly with the dispersion of objects of consumption.

Like Duncan and Schnore, Gibbs and Martin ignore values in analyzing formidable amounts of empirical data which they have organized with their ecological approach. In the work cited above, they write: "It may ... be true that, within certain limits, sociocultural values and ideologies influence urbanization and the division of labor. But we do reject these phenomena as possible explanations of the particular relationships observed in this study."[26] Even if one were to agree with Gibbs and Martin that values are irrelevant to the urbanization process, their contention that values are irrelevant to the division of labor is almost impossible to accept, for the question immediately comes to mind as to how the services of labor could be engaged unless certain values were shared among laborers themselves as well as between management and labor. Even in societies where labor's services are exchanged for goods rather than money, there must be some consensus as to what constitutes a fair exchange.

Two other neoclassical ecologists, Amos Hawley and William F. Ogburn, may be credited with stressing the role of technology in influencing not only the location of cities, but their internal arrangement as well. Yet, Ogburn's contention that "the placement of city populations, residences, and places within cities is *singularly* a function of local transportation, as cities themselves are the creation of long-distance transportation," is obviously a gross exaggeration; the same evaluation must be made of Hawley's assertion that "the scatter of population about urban centers is a *direct* response to the increased ease of movement."[27] Considerable data have been gathered in various parts of the world indicating that cultural values and power factors frequently modify and even negate the influence of technology on urban processes. Both the Dotsons' study of Mexican cities and Gist's survey of Bangalore, India, for example, suggest that sociocultural factors have retarded the suburbanization process in these industrializing communities.[28] It is also interesting to observe how the Berlin Wall, the creation of a political ideology, has superseded technological factors in determining migration and residential patterns in the divided city of Berlin.

The theoretical disregard by the neoclassical ecologists of the importance of social values results in their perception of both social action and social organization as preordained, inevitable, and unalterable phenomena, and of man as a passive creature manipulated by forces of change which they describe as "external physical" conditions. Operationally, however, neoclassical ecology is not really value-free, for in every society the external physical conditions—environment, population, social organization, and technology, which its proponents claim to be the determinants of ecological phenomena—have some meaning ascribed to them by human beings who deliberately alter that meaning from time to time. Consider, for example, the worldwide declining concern about controlling environmental pollution when compared to the increasing commitment to resolving the energy crisis. While both problems—environmental pollution and the energy crisis—have the same value implications with respect to population (namely, reduction of population growth), different social organizations have emerged in response to them (the Environmental Protection Agency and the Federal Energy Administration, respectively, in the United States) and some of the technology which has been developed to reduce pollution (motor vehicle emission control devices) is inimical to proposed energy conservation measures (e.g., the production of automobiles with improved gasoline mileage).

Social area analysts, the fourth and final category of ecologists, have added other geographic units to Burgess's classical concentric zones, namely, Hoyt's sectors, Ullman–Harris's nuclei, and Shevky–Bell's social areas. All three units reflect the theory that population homogeneity in terms of such socially significant

traits as skills, ethnicity, life-style, and migrant status, produces
a communality of interests which, in turn, constitutes an inducement of associations which presumably generate and support a normative social order. A major shortcoming of social area analysis,
therefore, is its almost complete lack of any systematic specifica-
tion of the mechanisms by which physical space influences social
space, a radical departure from the Park–Burgess Chicago School
of urban studies. Among the contemporary proponents of social
area analysis, only Scott Greer, in his book *The Emerging City:
Myth and Reality,* has attempted to analyze the role played by ecological space in setting the conditions for the development of a normative order.[29]

Like the classical Park–Burgess University of Chicago ecologists, Greer compares the modern urban milieu with preurban and
nonurban communities, explaining that the former presents special
or unique problems with respects to the maintenance of order. But
whereas the Park–Burgess group contended that urbanization invariably causes *organizational disruption or dislocation,* Greer
takes the positive position that urbanization involves simply *organizational transformation.* According to this viewpoint, before the
level of world urbanization reached the point where huge, heterogeneous populations amassed at certain locations, accompanied by
the proliferation of specialized functions to satisfy their varied
needs, there was neither a demand for, nor the possibility of, establishing social interaction patterns based solely upon communalities
of differentiated interests. Briefly, the marked transformation in
the human environment produced by the urban-industrial revolution has reduced the significance of and hence the necessity for the
spatially and socially inclusive community—the traditional ecological community which the Chicago ecologists and their devotees
have regarded as sacrosanct.

While Greer's concern for the problem of maintaining order
in the modern urban community has stimulated his interest in the
development of innovative social control mechanisms as well as in
the revision of traditional ones, he also recognizes the normative
significance of the many and varied communities of interest resulting from the multiplicity of specialized functions performed in the
modern urban setting. This is indicated by his statements that "the
highly differentiated set of activities necessary for [the persistence

of the city] requires complex and effective integrative mechanisms in order to produce predictability and structural stability through time. . . . Accordingly, much of the behavior of the urban population can be understood and predicted through knowledge of the group structures that absorb the energy of individuals and coordinate their behavior in time."[30]

There are, of course, geographically separated and socially distinctive categories of people in all urban areas which do not establish formal associations based upon spatial proximity or affinity of interests, but only a biased observer would focus attention upon such aggregations and consider them representative of all urban populations, ignoring the much greater incidence of social organization in cities. Moreover, the absence of formal social groups among certain segments of the population does not necessarily connote social disorganization, social pathology, or lack of informal organization. Indeed, kinship ties may be so strong among certain segments of the population as to make formal organization entirely superfluous.

The major theoretical orientations in the field of urban sociology having been discussed, the time has come to consider the recent trend toward comparative urban analysis, a trend which has already begun to supplant the formal testing of sociological theories as the principal basis for data collection. A major obstacle to cross-cultural urban research, however, is the difficulty of securing standardized data; United Nations agencies must be given credit for most of that which is available. Hence, until recent years American urban sociologists have treated the ecology of the city largely in terms of the United States, which accounts for their extremely limited explanatory models. As Bellah has observed, "Since the generation of Weber and Durkheim, macroscopic urban problems involving comparative and historical research have been somewhat slighted as microscopic urban research has come to the fore."[31]

Another formidable barrier to cross-cultural urban research is the restrictions placed upon the activities of social scientists by government leaders in many countries. Fortunately, however, the range of freedom for social research seems to be increasing rather than diminishing in most parts of the world. Data on the world's cities, while not uniform in quantity or quality, are nevertheless expanding rapidly, and as an increasing number of societies become industrialized and urbanized this situation will undoubtedly improve. Because government administrators in both urban-industrial and developing nations must depend upon such data for rational planning, the establishment of urban research on a solid cross-cultural basis constitutes a major challenge. Chapter 4, which deals with urban planning policies and programs in Western Europe, is intended as a partial response to this challenge. Since a review of social thought concerning the ideal city from antiquity to the present should logically precede a discussion of such practical considerations, however, this will be the subject matter of Chapter 3.

Chapter 3

Concepts of the Ideal City: From Antiquity to the Present

THE IDEAL CITY: FROM CONCEPT TO REALITY

Throughout history men have envisioned ideal communities or utopias, the majority of which have been conceptualized in terms of the city. Following a long but sporadic series of utopian works initiated by Plato's *Republic* in the fourth century B.C., a strong resurgence of conceptions describing the ideal community largely in economic, political, religious, and social terms occurred in Italy and England during the sixteenth and seventeenth centuries. Around 1516, for example, Thomas More created an imaginary island with fifty-four city-states, each having 6,000 families and a maximum population of 40,000 people, which he named Utopia. Albrecht Dürer's "City of Tomorrow" was likewise conceived early in the sixteenth century. Designed as a guild city, with each trade having its own separate section or district, the City of Tomorrow was laid out according to a gridiron pattern with streets and buildings arranged in straight lines, the entire community being protected by heavily fortified walls.

A utopian community similar in design to Dürer's City of Tomorrow was described by Johann V. Andreae during the early part of the seventeenth century. Named Christianopolis (1619), this fortified city's central focus was a religio-economic complex consisting of a temple and marketplace. Still another early seventeenth-century utopia was Tommaso Campanella's City of the Sun (1623) consisting of seven concentric circles, a pattern which was revived in the twentieth century by Park–Burgess and by Homer Hoyt in, respectively, their concentric zone and sector analyses of urban communities.

In general, however, seventeenth-century utopian writers were much less concerned about the physical design of their communities than about their economic and political systems, as dramatically illustrated by Francis Bacon's *New Atlantis* (1627) and James Harrington's *Commonwealth of Oceana* (1658). Since there was little possibility of their imaginary communities coming to life in the immediate future, to go into detail regarding their layout would have been an exercise in futility. Indeed, during the next two centuries not only were no utopian communities erected, but utopian thought itself came to a sudden halt. Not until the late nineteenth century, after the Industrial Revolution had created slums in the large cities of all industrial nations, was there a revival of utopian ideas emphasizing both physical and social environmental factors. Representative of the utopian thought of this period were Samuel Butler's *Erewhon* (1872) and Edward Bellamy's *Looking Backward* (1888).

Twentieth-century utopias, in contrast to the small communities envisioned by earlier utopian writers, have sometimes consisted of entire countries or hemispheric blocs as illustrated by Aldous Huxley's *Brave New World* (1932), James Hilton's *Lost Horizon* (Shangri La—1933), Austin T. Wright's *Islandia* (1942), Burrhus F. Skinner's *Walden Two* (1948), and George Orwell's *1984* (1949). The latest crop of these utopias, which may be classified in the science-fiction category, seems to be moving away from an earlier technological orientation toward social science, contending that a better urban future must be based upon a thorough understanding of contemporary social problems. Contemporary urban planning is incorporating many of these utopian ideas—namely, that it is possible and worthwhile to manipulate the environment, that the good man is a reflection of a decent and healthy environment, and that a work-oriented neighborhood or town is desirable. The major reasons for urban planners' drawing upon the resources of utopian thought have been succinctly stated by Thomas A. Reiner:

1. A careful study of the ideal-community literature has contributed much toward the identification of areas of agreement as well as disagreement within the planning profession. Both are necessary, for any art which lacks a systematic body of criticism lacks vitality and potential for growth.

2. The ideal community, by presenting a synoptic view of the urban environment, reflects the importance of interaction between specialists in the planning field and those in related professions.

3. A significant indicator of a field's maturity is the degree to which succeeding generations of its theorists build upon the body of earlier ideas and experience. Similarly, the extent of the application of accumulated knowledge by its practitioners is a clue to the field's progress. Thus, familiarity with ideal-community proposals suggests a wide range of approaches and solutions which can enhance the creativity and effectiveness of the planning profession.[1]

In short, utopian thought can make an invaluable contribution to the planning profession not only by suggesting new directions for research but also by proposing innovative schemes for implementation.

The correlation between model and real communities is not a new trend. Plato's *Republic*, for example, is generally believed to have been patterned after a utopian experiment in Sparta, and the close resemblance between More's *Utopia* and the Incan empire has caused some critics to speculate whether, perhaps, its narrator was someone who had traveled extensively in Peru. These two cases are unusual, however, in the sense that a real community inspired the ideal; in the history of utopian thought the relationship has generally been reversed. During the nineteenth century, for example, thousands of Americans left their homes to join groups whose purpose was the establishment of various types of utopian communities. Some of the group leaders were religious zealots who convinced their devotees that the only way they could maintain the integrity of their faith was to isolate themselves from nonbelievers and persons with different religious beliefs; others were intellectuals who wanted to experiment with a life-style based on a new system of values, such as a "classless society" in which there would be no status distinctions, in which material goods would be de-emphasized and shared equally, and in which communal sex would be practiced; and still others viewed the founding of a utopian community as a way to get rich quick at the expense of their naive subjects. John Reps has described the quest of these groups as follows: "Marching across the continent with the planners of cities dedicated to Mammon—the grid surveyors, the town speculators, the creators of railroad towns, and the other men of affairs—were the reformers, the utopians, and the pariah religious sects in their restless quest for kingdoms of paradise on mortal earth."[2]

The most successful of the religious groups were the Rappites, separatists from the German Lutheran Church whose leader, George Rapp (1757–1847), came to America in 1803. He purchased 5,000 acres of land in Pennsylvania which subsequently became the community of Harmony, where he and his followers awaited Armageddon. New immigrants from Germany were the only source of membership once the community had renounced marriage in 1807. Despite this fact and its poor location, Harmony prospered and was a community in the fullest sense, offering employment not only in agriculture but also in several factories and mills. In 1815 the Rappites moved to a site above the mouth of the Wabash River in Indiana and built the community of New Harmony, where within five years they cultivated 3,000 acres of land. When the urge to move sparked Rapp once again in 1825, the New Harmony community was sold. Subsequently, the Rappites established a new community at Economy, eighteen miles from Pittsburgh, which prospered despite internal dissension and Rapp's death in 1847 until the Rappite society itself dissolved in 1905.[3]

The New Harmony, Indiana, settlement of the Rappites had been sold in 1825 for $150,000 to Robert Owen, the English factory owner who had made such a success of the New Lanark textile mills near Glasgow, Scotland. After having published a pamphlet in England called *Discourses on a New System of Society* (1813) Owen had decided to implement his ideals in the United States. He believed that industrial societies could be reformed if new communities were constructed for a maximum of 1,200 persons each. Inhabitants would share the products of their cooperative agricultural and industrial labor on the basis of need alone. Thus in 1825 Owen brought to New Harmony 900 settlers—a heterogeneous group of enthusiastic radicals, lazy theorists, and freeloaders whom Owen successfully welded into a genuine cooperative society for a few years, but dissension eventually arose over whether the form of government should be town-meeting democracy or socialism. By 1827 Owen admitted the failure of his venture, the chief reasons being the settlers' lack of preparation for communal living (their selfishness and lack of cooperation) and a shortage of skilled craftsmen. In other words, failure to regulate either the number or the type of members and lack of economic self-sufficiency doomed the colony from the beginning.[4]

Owen's French contemporary Charles Fourier (1772–1837), in an effort to reorganize society along socialistic lines, founded about forty "phalanxes" in the United States during the 1840s, the most successful being Red Bank, New Jersey, and Brook Farm, Massachusetts, but the majority survived less than a year. Each "phalanx" was a vast hotel-like building (surrounded by agricultural land) which housed 1,600 people and contained all the necessities of life. Etienne Cabet (1788–1856), another Frenchman and founder of the Icarian Society, sent a group of his followers to Texas in 1848 to establish a communistically organized community, but upon their arrival they discovered that their leader had been exploited by the realtors from whom he had purchased land for the settlement. Indeed, there was no land for the money he had paid. Subsequently, Cabet moved northeastward with his group to Nauvoo, Illinois, where he planned to build a community with broad streets enhanced by beautiful monuments and with residential superblocks containing neighborhood units. Cabet's plans were never implemented, however, because his authoritarian personality caused so much tension and open conflict in the community that he was finally removed from leadership in 1856.[5]

The Oneida (New York) community, a communistic religious settlement founded by John Humphrey Noyes (1811–1886) in 1848, featured a conventional gridiron street pattern, its colonists devoting their pioneering energies to social rather than ecological creativity. Their system of "complex marriage," for example, advocated complete freedom of sexual intercourse for pleasure but attempted to restrict intercourse for conception to eugenically "fit" persons. In spite of the Oneida colony's economic success and internal harmony, it was this unorthodox marital system which eventually elicited so much outside opposition that Noyes was forced to move to Canada in 1880, whereupon the community lost its unique character.[6]

More than two hundred other utopian communities were founded in the United States during the nineteenth century by such fanatically religious groups as the Altruists, the Straight-Edgers, the Society of the Woman in the Wilderness, and the Spirit Fruit Society, all of which became extinct when the founders died or left, not only because the followers were overly dependent upon the charisma of their leaders, but being too idealistic to realize that not everyone is motivated by brotherly love and good will, they made themselves easy targets for exploitation by unscrupulous business-men and bigots. The constituents of these communities were sorely lacking in organizational skills, scientific know-how, and effective defensive tactics—traits with which, incidentally, most of the nine-teenth-century utopian settlers were not well endowed.

A revolutionary concept of urban design advanced in 1882 by the Spanish engineer, Arturo Soria y Mata, was the "linear city" consisting of parallel residential zones extending two hundred yards on either side of a long traffic corridor from which service roads branch off at right angles into the various neighborhoods. Beyond the residential areas is a greenbelt of wooded and agricul-tural land. However, because of the unfortunate association be-tween the linear-city idea and the cluttered, sign-ridden highways constituting the major arteries leading into and out of our major cities, Soria's innovative concept has not been widely implemented. Probably the best example of its application is Islamabad, the new capital of Pakistan designed by the prominent Greek architect-engineer, Constantinos Doxiades. On either side of Islamabad's broad axial boulevard are communities patterned in a gridiron which can be extended longitudinally to accommodate population growth. Doxiades has named his version of Soria's linear city "dynapolis," contending that congestion and strangulation can be obviated by preventing cities from expanding in more than one direction.

The most successful utopian urbanologist in terms of having his ideas concreted was Ebenezer Howard (1850–1928), whose fa-mous book *Tomorrow: A Peaceful Path to Real Reform* (first published in 1898; republished in 1902, and since as *Garden Cities of Tomorrow*) was the catalyst behind Britain's new towns movement begun in 1946. Written as a commentary upon the disastrous consequences of the Industrial Revolution for England's largest cities, Howard's book reflected the influence of Henry George's thought concerning the disposition of unearned increments in land values, of Buckingham's 1849 industrial town model ("Victoria"), of proposals for land nationalization (Spence and others), and of the suggestion by economist Alfred Marshall that London's population could be reduced by moving whole neighborhoods as a unit to the country.[7] These influences were especially apparent in Howard's proposal that the congestion in England's metropolitan centers be relieved by directing their surplus populations into garden cities lying within a twenty-five- to thirty-mile radius of these large centers and separated from them by an inviolable greenbelt. The garden cities were to be model communities whose land use would be controlled by the central government to assure the achievement of a socially healthy environment. Thus, in Howard's words, "there are not only two alternatives, town life and country life, but a third alternative in which all the advantages of the most energetic and active town life, with all the beauty and delight of the country, may be secured in perfect harmony."[8]

Built from scratch on large tracts of cooperatively purchased rural land, Howard's garden cities would each have a maximum of 30,000 residents to facilitate both intimacy and heterogeneity, occupational opportunities proximate to workers' homes for a wide range of skill categories and in sufficient number to promote economic self-sufficiency, and a surrounding greenbelt which would not only provide agricultural products and recreational space but promote internal unity by its "girdling" or containment effect. It was Howard's dream that the growth of all metropolitan areas would eventually be controlled by such garden cities whose accessibility would be assured by the development of efficient rapid transit systems.

Not just an idealist like most of the utopian thinkers who preceded him, Howard practiced what he preached. In 1903 he organized a company which he named First Garden City, Ltd., to build Britain's first garden city, Letchworth, whose 3,800-acre site thirty-five miles north of London he purchased by floating a public stock issue. Because only £100,000 of the £300,000 authorized issue was sold by the end of the first year, the board of directors was forced to mortgage the remainder of the £160,000 site cost. Another source of discouragement was the town's slow population growth so that after ten years it had only 8,000 inhabitants.[9] Yet, Sir Frederic Osborn recalls that when he came to Letchworth as its housing manager in 1913 "the whole place was imbued with a constructive spirit. Clubs sprang up for everything from music and drama to politics and gardening. Everybody knew everybody else, . . . and class and income barriers were at a minimum. . . . Its residents were a true cross section of the British population."[10] Moreover, Raymond Unwin's innovative plan for Letchworth which substituted superblocks and cul-de-sacs for the conventional gridiron street pattern made the town extremely attractive from a physical standpoint. Finally, great care was taken not only to preserve the natural setting when streets and buildings were constructed but also to enhance it by skillful landscaping. Behind each cottage in Letchworth, for example, was a garden for the enjoyment of the adults and a playground for the children, so that a ratio of fourteen acres of open space per 1,000 residents was achieved at the same time that a low density of twelve persons per built-up acre was maintained.

Despite its early problems with finances and population growth, Letchworth today has 30,000 inhabitants, and shortly before the town was taken over as a publicly owned corporation by an act of Parliament in 1963, the stockholders' £400,000 investment had increased in value to £3,728,000. In 1961 alone the dividend amounted to a 32-percent return on the original investment, proving that new towns return immense profits over the long run though seldom over the short run.[11] Perhaps even more important, Letchworth set a precedent for new town design which has survived to the present day.

Long before Letchworth had proved to be successful, Ebenezer Howard and his colleagues tried to convince the British government to adopt and implement their garden-city concept on a scale sufficient to relieve the country's serious problem of population congestion. "We asked for one hundred new towns in 1918," recalls Sir Frederic Osborn, "but all we got was one and we had to build it ourselves."[12] In 1918, Howard, Osborn, and two associates formed Welwyn Garden, Ltd., and chose a 2,378-acre site twenty-one miles north of London on which to build the new town of Welwyn, setting a target population of 36,500 inhabitants. Consistent with their Georgist economic philosophy, the company issued £250,000 worth of shares bearing a maximum annual dividend of 7 percent, any additional profit being reserved for the welfare of the new town residents. Unfortunately, however, due to the adverse economic conditions prevailing at the time—the post–World War I recession—only £90,000 worth of shares were sold.[13]

Consequently, as at Letchworth, Welwyn's developers had to resort to borrowed funds and cash advances to pay the £105,000 price for the land and the cost of installing the expensive infrastructure. Nevertheless, they adhered to their original intention of controlling land use in the town by leasing sites for development rather than selling them. This idealistic policy resulted in their being forced into bankruptcy during the Great Depression when the original £1 shares depreciated to two shillings. Then in 1948 the British government assumed control of Welwyn under the provisions of the 1946 New Towns Act, thereby terminating the landownership rights of the town's creditors. In the process, however, the government paid £2,315,000 for Welwyn's assets, £1,395,000 more than the combined original investment of £119,500 by the stockholders and £800,000 by the debenture holders. Not only were Welwyn's financial difficulties similar to those at Letchworth, but its growth problems as well; by 1947 it had reached a population of only 18,000 inhabitants, one-half its 1920 goal. Moreover, as at Letchworth, there was considerable opposition to the construction at Welwyn from people living in the vicinity.[14]

Today, however, Welwyn is a prosperous town with about 43,000 inhabitants who, by virtue of the fact that one-third of the town has been allocated to open space, live in a parklike setting surrounding the green central mall which, because of its size and well-manicured appearance, is commonly referred to by the residents as Little Versailles. Other aesthetic features of Welwyn are the way its streets curve gently to accommodate stately trees and the way its homes are clustered about cul-de-sacs on nearly every block. In common with Letchworth and all of Britain's post–World War II new towns, Welwyn's housing stock is a mixture of dwellings built by private commercial developers, by nonprofit cooperatives and by the government, which has facilitated the socioeconomic heterogeneity of the town's population. Moreover, Welwyn is self-sufficient economically, for less than 10 percent of its working population commute to London.

The first section of this chapter has demonstrated how ideal communities have served throughout history as models for many individual and corporate efforts to modify and improve man's physical and social environments. Some of these ideal communities have almost prophetically anticipated certain problems facing today's major cities—urban sprawl, traffic congestion, pollution, lack of an aesthetic living environment, and ghettoization of the poor and other minorities—and have constituted very practical solutions for them, Ebenezer Howard's garden city being the best example. For the urban planner, therefore, the best of the ideal communities are not only examples of how broadly an unfettered mind can think and dream, but they contribute to the systematic destruction of the belief that all that is with us today is of necessity given, permanent, and at least bearable, if not good.[15] In other words, these communities encourage constructive criticism of the existing environment and of the society which has produced and maintained it, a matter which will be more fully explored in the second section of this chapter.

CONCEPTS OF THE REAL CITY

Two broad evaluations of the real city are discernible within the past two hundred years: from the eighteenth century's philosophy of Enlightenment evolved the view of the city as virtue, and from the urban-industrialism of the nineteenth and twentieth centuries, an antithetical conception of the city as vice. In all three centuries, ideas about the city have been inextricably linked with prevailing values regarding the nature of man, society, and culture.

EIGHTEENTH-CENTURY CONCEPTS
OF THE REAL CITY

Voltaire (1694–1778) first praised the city in terms of his view of London. He regarded it as the "Athens of modern Europe" by virtue of its epitomizing such values as freedom, commerce, and art—political, economic, and cultural values which he attributed primarily to the city's "respect for talent." It was not long, however, before Voltaire began generalizing these positive traits to all modern cities. Another factor characterizing urban life which, according to Voltaire, made it the "cradle of civilization" was its ardent pursuit of the seemingly antithetical goals of industry and pleasure. Moreover, he regarded the contrast between rich and poor in cities as the initial basis of social progress. Voltaire savored rich men's lives of refined sensuality: their trips in handsome gilded carriages across imposing city squares to "assignments" with actresses, to theater performances, and to lavish meals. According to Voltaire, such bon vivants created work for countless artisans through their sybaritic mode of existence. "They not only provide employment for the poor, but become models to emulate. Aspiring to the life of civilized ease led by their betters, the poor are encouraged to industry and parsimony, and thus improve their state. Thanks to this happy symbiosis of rich and poor, elegant ease and thrifty industry, the city stimulates progress in reason and taste and thus perfects the arts of civilization."[16] Voltaire was convinced that in the final analysis social progress depended on the city's diffusing "reason and taste" to all classes of people.

While Voltaire credited the nobility with civilizing the city, Adam Smith (1723–1790) maintained that the city, in turn, civilized the rural nobility, "leveling them and elevating burghers and tradesmen to produce a nation orderly, prosperous, and free."[17] As an economist and moralist, however, Smith was not as strongly pro-urban as Voltaire, placing primary emphasis upon the mutually beneficial relationship between the city and the country in terms of the latter providing the former with raw materials in exchange for manufactured goods, a transaction which he regarded as the "backbone of prosperity." Moreover, Smith maintained that "to cultivate the ground is the natural destination of man" and that the psychic satisfactions of the planter surpass those of the urban merchant or manufacturer. "The beauty of the country, . . . the pleasures of country life, the tranquility of mind which it promises, and . . . the independence which it . . . affords, . . . more or less attract everybody. . . . The city stimulates; this country fulfills."[18]

To Adam Smith the area of the world which was most conducive to the enactment of the ideal urban-rural relationship was North America, "where primogeniture restricts neither personal freedom nor economic progress." [19] Smith hoped that the principal by-product of this economic relationship would be that all or most city dwellers would eventually accumulate enough savings to move to the country and engage in farming. In his opinion this was the ultimate source of personal fulfillment. Thus, this great advocate of laissez-faire economics set the stage for that romanticization of rural life which was to permeate English social thought during the nineteenth century.

Even during the eighteenth century, however, while the virtues of the city were being extolled, antiurban sentiment began to manifest itself. Two prime examples were Oliver Goldsmith's condemnation of urban capital for its materialistic influence on the countryside and the contention of the French physiocrats that national economic prosperity depends more upon the promotion of agricultural than industrial productivity. Other factors which reinforced this trend were the growing popularity of pantheism, which substituted the worship of nature for the worship of a personal God, and the increasing alienation of the intellectual classes as traditional social patterns deteriorated. Consequently, by the end of the eighteenth century the "spendthrift rich" and "industrious artisans" of Voltaire and Smith had become Wordsworth's "getters and spenders," equally wasting their talents and resources and equally alienated from nature, and the "rationality of the civilized city" which Voltaire valued so highly had imposed "mind-forged manacles" on both nature and man, according to the poet William Blake.[20]

NINETEENTH-CENTURY CONCEPTS
OF THE REAL CITY

Two factors account for the fact that as the eighteenth century progressed into the nineteenth the city became increasingly associated with vice. First, the acceleration of the urbanization rate as the industrialization process secured a firmer grip on the country aggravated what had been a relatively minor degree of urban physical and social deterioration. Second, the residual effects of the Enlightenment's perception of the city as the prime source of wealth and culture intensified the disillusionment of many objective observers of the city as they watched its development during the nineteenth century. There were two categories of critical response to the industrial-urban scene: (1) archaists such as Coleridge (1772–1834), Ruskin (1819–1900), Gustav Freytag (1816–1895), Dostoevsky (1821–1881), and Tolstoy (1828–1910) who unequivocally repudiated the industrial age and its creeping trend toward megalopolis, advocating a return to agrarian and small-town life, and (2) futurists such as Engels (1820–1895) and Marx (1818–1883) who formulated programs to reform rather than abandon the scene.

The influence of archaistic thought even among the nineteenth-century urban bourgeoisie was clearly evident in the lack of a distinctive urban architectural style during this period. For example, the designers of three British rail stations in London apparently felt compelled to look to earlier historical periods for inspiration: those of Euston Station to ancient Greece; those of St. Pancras Station to the Middle Ages; and those of Paddington Station to the Renaissance. Difficulty in accepting nineteenth-century urban society as well as in perceiving the future except in terms of the past was also evident in the Paris of Napoleon III and in Kaiser Wilhelm's Berlin. Counteracting this trend, however, were Marx and Engels, the most prominent futuristic urban critics of the nineteenth century, who, while demonstrating in their early writings a definite predilection for the medieval craftsman who was his own "boss," owned his own tools, and performed all stages in the productive process, never advocated a return to earlier social patterns or the espousal of some utopian concept of community life. Indeed, while rejecting the industrial city existentially, Engels affirmed it historically: "Only the proletariat... herded together in the big cities is in a position to accomplish the great social transformation which will put an end to all class exploitation and all class rule."[21] Engels viewed life in the industrial city as an essentially maturing experience whereby peasants and small-town artisans must lose their feelings of inferiority and gain self-confidence in preparation for developing a proletarian consciousness. He contended, however, that eventually under socialism the "intimate connection between industrial and agricultural production and as uniform distribution as possible of the population over the whole country... will... deliver the rural population from isolation and stupor and bring the blessing of nature into city life."[22]

TWENTIETH-CENTURY CONCEPTS
OF THE REAL CITY

A new generation of urban critics, the fatalists, has emerged during the twentieth century. According to the fatalists, since the industrial city has destroyed the credibility of all traditional creeds which once provided the basis for social integration, the sensuous and sensual participation in modern urban life is the only rationale for human existence. Thus, while the futurists had sought to reform urban life through organized social action, the fatalists, considering its plight irreversible, have simply resigned themselves to it by developing a philosophical position compounded of despair, hedonism, and stoicism. This negative concept of the city reached its fullest theoretical expression in the thought of Oswald Spengler (1880–1936) and its fullest implementation under the National Socialists in Germany during the 1930s. Spengler hated the city so intensely that he hoped it would eventually destroy itself, for he had witnessed its exploitation or "milking" of the countryside and had observed the restlessness and instability of the urban masses due to their lack of social consciousness.

Putting Spengler's views of the city into action, the Nazis launched their regime by announcing as one of their major policies the relocation of Germany's urban population on the "holy German soil" and by selecting medieval Nuremberg as the setting for their annual party congress. Somewhat ironically, however, the Nazis' program of city building reinforced the very traits of the city which Spengler despised so greatly, unless one takes the point of view that the Nazis were thereby helping to fulfill Spengler's desire for the city's demise. Thus, the Nazis exemplified the industrial city's apparent devotion to technology over aesthetics by cutting down the beautiful trees of Berlin's Tiergarten to make way for a wide boulevard—the "Achse"—where "rurally regenerated" Hitler youth were free to ride their motorcycles. They accentuated the urban loss of individuality by subjecting the residents to frequent mass political demonstrations and by forcing them to comply with rigorous and inflexible regulations in practically every area of life. It would seem, therefore, that a grave inconsistency existed between the Nazis' ideological commitment to the values of small town and rural life and their practical commitment to industrial urbanism with all its vices.

The United States has also had its gloomy urban critics, the most prominent being Lewis Mumford (1895–), whose broad historical perspective on the city, whose admiration for the human scale of the medieval city, and whose unrelentingly sarcastic commentary on the modern commercial and industrial city can only be appreciated by reading his major works—*Technics and Civilization* (1934), *The Culture of Cities* (1938), and, most important, *The City in History* (1961). Four major values underlie Mumford's work and constitute his criteria for the "good city":

1. *Private and Public Man*: Insisting that there should be a balance in everyone's life between rest and privacy on the one hand and action and communion on the other, Mumford contends that the good city facilitates the achievement and maintenance of such a balanced life.

2. *City and Country*: Mumford believes that everyone should have some experience with farm life, preferably during his younger years, in order to gain a broader awareness of the world and to become refreshed physically and mentally. In fact he feels so strongly about this that he favors the government's making such experience compulsory. Yet he does not consider the country superior to the city; rather he regards these two environments as constituting an ecological unit; the mutually beneficial relationship cannot be ignored without dire consequences for both areas.

3. *Community*: Mumford believes that ideally the residents of a community should share certain values and have a strong identification with the larger community, or at least with their particular neighborhood, as people once did during the Middle Ages. Until such a state of affairs returns, however, Mumford advocates maximizing government land and property ownership to better assure its use in the public interest.

4. *Organic Growth*: Mumford believes that the city may be compared to a living organism with definite growth and expansion limits which, if exceeded, result in illness or even death. Therefore, he advocates the control of urban growth in the interest of a healthy and viable community life.

Mumford's greatness is not as an original thinker but as a

synthesizer and elaborator of European thought regarding the city which he almost exclusively has championed in the United States. The three men whose ideas have most influenced his urban philosophy are Patrick Geddes with his concern for regional planning, Ebenezer Howard with his garden city movement, and Piotr Kropotkin with his strong pleas for the decentralization of urban populations and facilities.

Kropotkin (1842–1921) based his firm convictions about urban decentralization on his prediction that technological progress would soon reach the point where industries would no longer be dependent upon coal for power or railroads for transportation, giving them greater flexibility with respect to location. Moreover, he foresaw the time when mass communication and transportation systems would make it unnecessary for human beings to "huddle together" in huge urban aggregations in order to maintain contact, but rather would give them the option of living in smaller communities where they could participate more personally and, hence, more meaningfully in community organizations. It was this orientation which motivated Mumford and his associates who worked together in the Regional Planning Association of America during the 1920s to promote the decentralization of cities and the dispersal of business enterprises and populations into smaller urban units.[23]

Whether or not Mumford is correct in his assertion that Patrick Geddes (1854–1932) was more knowledgeable about urban development than any of his contemporaries, Geddes was indisputably one of the most powerful influences upon applied sociology during the first quarter of the twentieth century. His extensive community studies and his exhaustive research on slum problems in Edinburgh during the year 1866 were largely responsible for convincing social reformers and social workers that social action without a basis in careful research is not only a dangerous but a wasted effort. Mumford, however, was most impressed by Geddes's conviction that the region is the ideal social research and planning unit; indeed, when the late President Kennedy recommended the establishment of a new cabinet post for urban affairs, Mumford opposed the suggestion with the argument that it would federalize city planning and decision-making rather than maintain these functions at the regional level where they belong. Mumford's commitment to regionalism has been documented by Roy Lubove who credits him with introducing into the United States knowledge of the French regionalist movement of 1850–1860 through the Regional Planning Association of America.[24]

Mumford conceives the role of regional planning as that of decentralizing overpopulated areas, revitalizing old centers, and creating balanced new centers for social, commercial, and industrial activity so that no one particular size or type of community would dominate a region. According to Mumford, exactly the reverse situation prevails today, the modern industrial metropolis dominating its region by encouraging population congestion through its maintenance of inflated land values and the concentration of economic, recreational, and cultural facilities through power politics. Consequently, outlying communities are usually no more than sprawling dormitory suburbs or villages with such minimal facilities that their residents either are doomed to a monotonous and drab existence or are forced to commute long distances to the metropolis, often daily, contributing to the traffic jams and air pollution which constitute two of our nation's most serious urban problems. Hence, Mumford rejects small towns and suburbs with their too low population densities, unbalanced populations (largely white middle class), and incomplete social and economic life, as well as the giant metropolis with its too high density, equally unbalanced population (largely the poor and minorities), and overly intense civilization. The regionalism to which Mumford aspires would result in the "conscious redirection and collective integration of all those activities which rest upon the use of the earth as site."[25] According to him, the regional planning process ideally involves four elements: (1) the surveying and careful planning of all land uses and the implementation of comprehensive conservation programs which effectively prevent and/or eliminate all forms of pollution; (2) the study of "people needs" and desires with respect to all the basic areas of life; (3) the evaluation by planning experts of alternative proposals in terms of their human, spatial, temporal, and financial implications; and (4) informing and involving the public during the final review, decision-making, and implementation phases. Moreover, Mumford would put responsibility for rural and urban planning under one planning body in order to avoid an "inorganic" or fragmented approach to this very important function.

Throughout his life Mumford has been an admirer of Ebenezer

Howard, two of whose ideas he has propagandized for over forty years, namely, that there are natural limits to urban growth and that the physical features of the urban environment ought to incorporate the best of the rural and urban settings. In 1928, two of Mumford's associates in the Regional Planning Association of America, Henry Wright and Clarence Stein, built Radburn, New Jersey, incorporating these and others of Howard's ideals regarding community structure. Mumford, Wright, and Stein were all firmly committed to Howard's belief that the best way to cope with the problems of urban congestion and physical and social decay is to build new towns in clusters, distributing among them the present functions of the metropolis and separating them by protected greenbelts so that all the advantages of the metropolis could be retained while preserving as much open space as possible.

Although Radburn failed to develop into a genuine new town (it lacks both industry and commerce, depending upon nearby New York City as an economic base) and went through difficult financial problems during the Depression, it became a popular residential community following World War II. According to a recent evaluation by the urban sociologist Alvin Boskoff:

> [Radburn has demonstrated] that suitable, orderly neighborhoods could be achieved without the drab uniformity of "packaged" suburbs, and yet with adequate provision for future growth. It is no surprise, then, that the essentials of Radburn are already "classic" and that several European cities have adopted these features in constructing extensive additions to established communities.[26]

Three important qualities of an ideal community are exemplified by the Radburn plan: the superblock, the continuous park belt, and a distinct separation of residential areas from vehicular traffic. Thus, the basic structural determinant in Radburn is not the street but the superblock, constituted internally by a series of dead-end streets terminating in a public park and surrounded by avenues for vehicular traffic. Underlying this plan is the contention that streets constitute an advantage only for real estate interests which have traditionally evaluated a piece of land mainly in terms of its street frontage. Mumford has expressed his negative view of the street as an instrument of commercial exploitation as follows:

"The rectangular street and block system, projectable indefinitely toward the horizon, [is] the universal expression of capitalistic fantasies."[27] Another feature illustrated by Radburn and viewed favorably by Mumford is the use of community centers to provide a focus for neighborhood spiritual and cultural life, a function performed by the church in earlier times. Mumford also approves of the fact that these community centers are within short walking distance of all the residences, for he contends that "spatial nearness [is a prerequisite] for all primary forms of intercourse."[28]

Yet, Radburn as an ideal community has not had much influence on urban planning in the United States. Although isolated elements, such as the superblock, have been incorporated into many modern housing developments, a total new-town complex such as that envisioned by Howard and Mumford was not attempted by builders in this country until about ten years ago, and these innovators were few in number. Because town-building in the United States is largely carried out and managed by a combination of private corporations, it is extremely difficult to implement a nation-wide new towns program such as those in Great Britain, the Netherlands, and Sweden (described in Chapter 4) which have been not only initiated but heavily financed by the respective central governments.

As an urban historian, Mumford has been severely criticized for his extreme antiurban bias, an accusation which seems to be confirmed by the fact that he has resided most of his adult life in Amenia, a small town in upstate New York. In response, Mumford admits to having evaluated the industrial city in an extremely negative manner, but he justifies his appraisal thus: "No small part of the urban reform and correction that has gone on these last hundred years, and [especially] this last generation ... has only continued in superficially new forms the same purposeless concentration and organic de-building that prompted the remedy."[25] It is not surprising, therefore, that Mumford has also been critical of such contemporary "solutions" to urban problems as urban renewal with its program of slum clearance and rebuilding which has produced many splendiferous civic and cultural centers across the country. More basic than Mumford's concern for the structure of the modern city, however, is his concern for the welfare of the individual living in this setting. Motivated primarily by values emanating from nineteenth-century utopianism, Mumford has always rejected the political absolutism and laissez-faire economics epitomized by the modern metropolis because they exploit the urban masses. Yet many of the cities most admired by Mumford are products of totalitarian regimes of one kind or another. For example, Greek cities were ruled by less than one-eighth of the population, medieval cities were dominated by the church and the nobility, and the Dutch and Italian cities of the Renaissance were the creations of small but powerful commercial groups. Even the new towns in Britain which represent the best expression of Mumford's ideas on city planning are directed by autonomous public authorities largely immunized from the intense pressures of community opinion.[30]

CRITERIA FOR THE IDEAL CITY OF THE FUTURE

Classical ecologists explained human behavior as the direct result of physical environment; for example, slums were said to "breed" crime and vice. More recent research, however, attributes both conventional and deviant behavior primarily to the influence of the social environment—the totality of human relationships, both formal and informal, which an individual experiences during his lifetime in the family, in school, at work, in the church and neighborhood. The man-made or man-modified physical environment itself is now considered primarily an expression of societal values. The physical environment, in turn, influences the social environment by curtailing or encouraging human relationships and, by virtue of the paucity or abundance of aesthetic features, affects human happiness. While the steadily rising incidence of violence, crime and delinquency, racial and class tensions, alcoholism, drug addiction, mental illness, and other symptoms of anomie in our society today must be ascribed primarily to the malfunctioning of our social institutions, the situation is aggravated by the character of the physical environment in certain parts of our cities—especially that offer the best chances of achieving "the good life" which, ac- many poor families are forced to live due to lack of money and mobility. Let us then discuss those qualities of the urban environment that offer the best chances of achieving "the good life," which, according to Aristotle, is the main reason that men stay together in cities.

A WIDE RANGE OF CHOICES

The principal motivation for the migration of millions of ruralities to urban areas throughout the world is not so much the glamor of city life as the alleged improved opportunities for making a living. In terms of this objective, a wide range of choices with respect to employment is certainly a major criterion for a good urban environment. But just as important a consideration is the city as a good place for living "the full life" in terms of location and type of residence, shopping facilities, educational, cultural, and recreational opportunities, medical services, voluntary associations, and personal contacts.

A large stumbling block in the way of these objectives in the United States today is the increasing tendency toward territorial segregation by class which is to a great extent motivated by racial prejudice. The obvious solution is to make housing available to all classes and races in all sections of our urban areas, but this would require much more extensive government subsidization of housing than at present to cover the difference between prevailing rental and purchase prices and the amount low-income families could afford. More important, however, is the increased amount of government power that would be required to prevent racial prejudice from defeating such a plan. Such a modus operandi would, of course, meet with strong resistance under our representative form of government, at least for some time into the future. Consequently, in our effort to eradicate slums and improve the housing conditions of the poor, we have resorted to such palliatives as "urban renewal" which not only reduce the already short supply of low-cost housing but also destroy the meaningful social interaction patterns in low-income neighborhoods, a fact which even many professional planners tend to ignore. As a result, the families and individuals displaced by urban-renewal programs have the choice of paying more money for housing which is frequently no better and sometimes worse than that which has been bulldozed or of moving elsewhere, and, at the same time, they no longer have the psychological support of familiar faces, facilities, and institutions—a far more essential element in their lives than in those of middle- and upper-class people. Much of the money spent on urban renewal would be far more beneficially used for the rehabilitation of deteri-

orated homes in low-income neighborhoods so that even some
higher-income persons might be induced to live in these areas. At
the same time, lower-income persons should be given access to
neighborhoods from which they are now excluded by means of such
government-assisted mechanisms as suggested above. Still another
example of an unwarranted limitation of choice in our society is
the dearth of public indoor and outdoor facilities for recreational
and cultural activities, a fact which few visitors from Western
European countries fail to observe and criticize.

ACCESSIBLE AMENITIES

A wide range of choices with respect to any category of facilities in an urban area is quite meaningless, however, unless these
facilities are also accessible. For example, although many American
cities have large parks, they are frequently not centrally located
and are, therefore, inaccessible to the people who need them most—
the poor who live in dark, crowded, deteriorated dwellings and who
cannot afford commercial recreation. A similar comment can be
made with respect to public playgrounds and swimming pools; they
are most numerous and best equipped where they are needed
least—in high-income neighborhoods. There is also a great need for
more small open spaces and recreational areas immediately behind,
beside, or in front of apartment buildings and other dwelling units
to maximize their accessibility for preschool children, the aged, and
the handicapped. One of the major attractions of the new town concept is the fact that it proposes to make the full range of human
amenities accessible to people's residences, including jobs and shopping and service facilities, thereby minimizing the need for the
automobile with its attendant costs in terms of time, money,
frayed nerves, pollution, and loss of life. Yet, since most urbanites
demand mobility beyond the limits of their home community, accessibility to mass-transit facilities should be another important objective of every urban area which aims to promote the good life.

VEHICULAR AND PEDESTRIAN SAFETY

Because most vehicular accidents result from rear-end colli-
sions, sideswiping, and impacts at intersections, the construction
and use of separate thoroughfares for different kinds of vehicular
traffic is an essential condition for a safe urban environment. In

addition, however, there is an urgent need to encourage the development and widespread use of mass-transit systems and to curtail that of the automobile as a safety measure for both drivers and pedestrians. Prior to the advent of the automobile, city streets and squares were reserved primarily for pedestrians and an occasional horse and carriage so that children could play and adults could shop, stop to chat with friends, or sit down on benches or around the edge of a fountain or monument to relax or just to watch passersby with little fear of being killed by a vehicle.

The restoration of at least some of these areas of the city to their original purpose can be achieved by the complete separation of vehicular and pedestrian traffic in time, horizontally or vertically. Separation in time, as practiced today in Lima, Peru; Stockholm, Sweden; and Copenhagen, Denmark, for example, means that at certain times of the day major shopping streets are closed to all motorized vehicles except taxis. Radburn, New Jersey, pioneered both the horizontal and vertical separation of pedestrian and vehicular traffic in the United States by providing service access roads at the rear of dwelling units, pedestrian walkways at the front of residences, and tunnels beneath arterial streets for the protection of pedestrians.

While the success of shopping centers throughout the world can be attributed in large degree to their separation of pedestrians and vehicles, the lesson they teach has not been applied in the United States to the extent observed in Europe. In the interest of pedestrian safety, much broader application should be made in the central business districts (CBD) of our large cities of the most feasible solution, namely, the vertical separation system which accommodates pedestrians on arcaded sidewalks either above or below vehicular thoroughfares.

HUMAN COMFORT

The principal objectives of planning for human comfort are freedom from pollution, a favorable microclimate, and an optimum spatial environment.

Freedom from Pollution

With the sophisticated technology available today, noise pollution should be drastically reduced and the concept of "waste dis-

posal" should be replaced by the concept of "recycling." Despite the
cost of pollution in terms of human health and comfort, the maintenance of personal and public property, the conservation of our
natural resources, and the appearance of our physical environment,
the businesses and industries which emit pollutants while render-
ing services and manufacturing products usually do not find it
"financially feasible" to control these emissions or to make them
usable. The government, then, has a moral responsibility to require
them to do so and to subsidize the cleanup or recycling program;
it must formulate, enforce, and finance such programs, for the
public welfare is at stake. This approach is an essential prerequisite to restoring the urban environment to its time-honored status
as the best place to enjoy the good life.

A Favorable Microclimate

The term *microclimate* refers to the impact of general climatic
conditions in a large geographic area, such as a region, on the climate of a relatively small subunit, such as a particular urban area
or section thereof. While it is obvious from this definition that
some cities would have fewer microclimatic problems if they were
located in a different region, there are many means by which they
could ameliorate these problems within their present environment.
For example, water and plants, especially trees and shrubs, can mit-
igate extremes of temperature and absorb dust and soot as well as
noise, and the location and shape of buildings can greatly influence
the movement of air, thereby creating or preventing violent gusts
or complete stagnation.[31] However, any city which intends to
offer an equal opportunity for the good life to all its citizens must
be concerned not solely with general microclimatic conditions, but
with the microclimate of specific neighborhoods. While the affluent
can afford to live in homes which profit-motivated builders pur-
posely construct in sections with the most favorable microclimate,
the poor are forced to live in ghetto areas where no one but the
government wants to build houses and where microclimatic conditions are generally unfavorable to health and happiness.

An Optimum Spatial Environment

The contemporary trend toward housing an increasing proportion of the urban population in apartment buildings, as well as the

tendency for big businesses to erect skyscrapers in the central business district, has made most of our large cities look like steel and concrete "jungles." Indeed, it is difficult to find any large areas in our central cities which have been allocated exclusively to nature. Moreover, many private as well as public buildings use artificial rather than live trees, plants, flowers, and grass for decorative purposes. The entire visual scene reflects a value system which places a higher premium on monetary and power considerations than on human happiness. Another negative aspect of the urban spatial environment which militates against its being conducive to the good life is the high density prevailing in many residential and employment situations. For some urbanites, physical proximity to other human beings may compensate for lack of intimacy, but this is not generally true. Moreover, while extreme social isolation may be deleterious to mental health, too much social interaction can be equally devastating, causing anxiety, nervousness, and lack of time and privacy for independent thought and activity.

An ideal urban spatial environment should also feature a reasonably wide variety of land uses and building types. All too often, however, traditional zoning regulations prevent a well-designed mixture of land uses and buildings of various heights and styles such as one observes in many European new towns. They are pleasing places to be in, and are a reflection of imaginative planning that produces an attractive and stimulating urban environment, in contrast to the monotonous and boring one which results from compliance with conventional zoning practices. Moreover, the planned town facilitates the urbanite's identification with his community because he can take a genuine pride in its uniqueness and beauty.

VITAL URBAN CENTERS

Most of the major problems confronting the modern metropolis—decaying buildings, traffic congestion, crime, and racial tensions—are concentrated in our central cities. As a result, many urbanites have abandoned downtown businesses in favor of suburban facilities where there is more free parking space, where they feel safe from personal attacks, and where the physical environment is more aesthetic. Consequently, some central-city merchants have gone out of business, others have stayed but offer low-grade goods and services and hire security officers for protection, and still others have opened new outlets in the suburbs. There are those individuals and groups who feel that our central cities should be allowed to die a slow death on the premise that they have outlived their usefulness, that they are too expensive to salvage, or that the people still living in the central city aren't really important enough for planners to be concerned about the quality of their physical and social environment. But, there are other more humane, optimistic, and tradition-respcting individuals and groups who recognize the fact that no great civilization ever survived without care and concern for its great cities. The truth of this aphorism can be witnessed today by the tremendous expenditures in time and money devoted to the rehabilitation of such great European cities as Paris, Stockholm, Amsterdam, and Vienna. Fortunately, positive forces have prevailed in many American cities, too, as exemplified by the successful central-city redevelopment projects undertaken in recent years in Cincinnati, Philadelphia, Pittsburgh, and New York City, to mention only a few. As a result of such projects, three basic features of central-city redevelopment schemes are now considered of paramount importance: the continued concentration of major urban functions in the core of the central city but with improved accessibility; new pedestrian precincts in the form of malls connected with underground parking facilities by ramps and escalators; a focal complex of restaurants, cafes, recreational and amusement facilities; and open spaces such as parks and squares to provide an atmosphere of fun, excitement, relaxation, and beauty.

With the prospect of urbanization and urban growth continuing far into the future, the concept of the city as primarily a place for making a living is gradually giving way to that of the city as a place for living. A concomitant trend has been increasing concern and care for the urban environment as exemplified by the relatively recent public interest in the "ecology movement" and its crusade against various forms of pollution and defacement of the landscape. As a nation, we are gradually coming to an acceptance of the principle that only if the res publica is given top priority can a humane urban environment be created and maintained. It is

this principle which has motivated Western Europe's most successful urban planning programs, notably in Great Britain, the Netherlands, and Scandinavia—programs which are being studied and
emulated today by countries throughout the world, including the
United States. These will be discussed in Part II.

Part II

The Urban Habitat: Practical Perspectives

The ideal urban environment cannot be translated into reality without planning. It is this practical approach to urban ecology which is now our theme. Since Western Europe has both a longer urban history and greater experience in urban planning than the United States, its planning policies and programs are treated in Chapter 4; those of the United States, in Chapter 5. A plea is made in Chapter 6 for the creation of a more humane urban America through the formulation of a national urban policy, in which the construction of new towns around central cities* and the revitalization of central cities themselves by building new towns in-town as well as by more traditional means would play a prominent role.

---

*Used here to indicate a city of 50,000 or more people that constitutes the hub or one of the major foci of a standard metropolitan area which also includes suburban and rural communities dependent upon it.

Chapter 4

Urban Planning Policies and Programs: The Experience of Western Europe

In general, all Western European countries have witnessed the same types of social change in recent years. First, the basic shift of family activity from production to consumption has led to the increasing employment of married women. Second, significant increases in leisure time have produced rising demands on recreational facilities and increases in weekend and vacation-period traffic. Third, the increased number of aged persons, a phenomenon experienced by most Western European countries earlier than in the United States, helps to explain why their programs adapting various physical and social structures to this condition are further advanced than ours. Fourth, the increasing mobility of Europeans has had considerable impact on population distribution, the more dynamic urban centers attracting the most jobs and people, thereby causing a shortage of urban land which makes decisions regarding its use complex and difficult. This scarcity of urban space has been the greatest single force influencing planning in Western Europe. Fifth, and another potent factor influencing planning activity, has been the steady rise in per capita income, a trend which is expected to continue well into the future as indicated by the following statement of a Netherlands delegate to a United Nations seminar on the future of urban settlement:

> Within a generation, the lower-income groups will be
> in a position to afford what the middle-income groups
> can today.... They will demand more spacious and better
> equipped dwellings, more space about the house, in many
> cases a weekend house in the countryside, better facilities
> for recreation and sports, more roads and parking space
> for their cars, clean air, pure water, and quite a lot of
> things we can hardly imagine [today].[1]

Sixth, many of the social and economic changes cited above have
been strongly influenced by technological changes, including the
following: improvements in transportation, which have influenced
drastically the location of commerce, industry, and residential
areas; the elevator, which has permitted more intensive use of land
for commercial and residential buildings; and, conversely, new
production and assembly techniques, which have led to lower factory buildings and greater demands for industrial space.

TRENDS, OBJECTIVES, AND MEANS

European planning is evolving rapidly. While there has always been substantial consensus among Europeans that excellence
in the design of the physical environment is a prerequisite of the
good life, planning efforts in the past were directed largely at the
solution of particular problems. Today, however, they are more often of a comprehensive nature and reflect the conscious efforts of
the governments to: (1) establish an optimum relationship between rural and urban areas, among cities and towns located
within the same region as well as in different regions, and among
the several regions within a nation; (2) preserve and promote contact with nature within the urban environment; (3) maintain the
historic character of villages, towns, and cities, taking into account
the requirements of population expansion, economic growth, and
technological change; and (4) guide future urban growth toward
optimum-sized cities.

Implied in the first objective above is a second directed toward
a growing recognition of the need for regional planning and
a national urban policy, because dynamism and growth in one or
more areas which may be rural, urban, or both exert a pull for
capital and labor which results in stagnation or decline in other
areas. Simply stated, urban centers and regions cannot be treated
as islands unrelated to one another and isolated from the national
economic system. Hence, the basic aim of current European re-

gional policies has been defined as follows: "to promote the fullest development of the country's total resources by suitable guidance of investment, region by region, over a period of years."[2] The goals of national urban policies in Western Europe including those specified above as the second, third, and fourth objectives of the comprehensive planning trend, may be more broadly stated as improvements in the physical environment of families so as to enhance their social lives, an increase in the production and consumption of goods and services, and the physical modification of urban areas to better fit them for the needs of the future. To accomplish these goals, Western Europe has focused largely on the planning and development of (1) urban extensions, (2) satellite communities, (3) new towns, and (4) urban growth centers. But regardless of the means employed in a particular instance, social and economic considerations play as prominent a role as the physical component. Specific applications of each method will be examined later in this chapter.

A prominent difference between the countries of Western Europe and the United States is that, in the former, the central government plays an extremely influential role in economic, physical, and social planning. Although the citizens of Western European nations have the political power to change this situation, they have chosen to continue and even increase the role of government. In the area of housing, for example, the involvement of European governments has increased substantially since World War II, and an anticipated continuation of shortages and greater expectations will make reversal of government intervention very unlikely. Moreover, as a general rule central governments in Western Europe not only require their local governments to prepare comprehensive development plans for their respective jurisdictions, but require that they submit these plans to the central government for approval. Then to facilitate implementation of the approved plans, central governments usually offer local governments various forms of financial assistance or subsidies.

PLANNING POLICIES AND PROGRAMS
IN THE NETHERLANDS

In terms of organization for and achievement in national physical planning, probably no country has been as successful as the Netherlands. Despite the scarcity of land in the country, effective land use legislation has made it possible to accommodate twelve million people residentially, and at the same time to have sufficient space for many other purposes. The first urban planning legislation in the Netherlands was the Housing Law of 1901, which despite its name had nothing to do with housing. Instead, it required city councils in municipalities with a population of 20,000 or more and those in municipalities whose populations had increased more than 20 percent in five years to prepare plans for the construction of canals, squares, and streets. Since that time, however, Dutch planning legislation has undergone several major revisions in the interest of modernization and greater efficacy. The major provisions of the current legislation, including the most recent revisions in 1965, are as follows:

1. Each municipality must draw up a town plan for its territory outside the built-up area, indicating for all the land whether it will be open for building and, if so, *what* may be built.

2. The municipal authorities are entitled to apply a system of permits to any activities causing a change in the land, such as excavations and reclamation projects.

3. Building, regardless of its purpose, is allowed only after permission has been obtained from the municipal authorities, a building permit being granted only if a building plan is in conformity with the town plan for the area where the building is to take place.[3]

As this list of provisions indicates, not only is every major municipality in the Netherlands required to prepare a land use plan for the entire area under its jurisdiction, but all building and other relevant projects must be carried on within the context of this plan. Consequently, land use is so well controlled in the Netherlands that high building densities have been achieved without congestion and large cities have been prevented from sprawling out haphazardly into adjacent rural areas.

One of the major reasons for the success of planning legislation in the Netherlands is its relatively simple administrative structure. Since the Housing Act of 1901, planning initiative has begun at the municipal level, there being approximately 950 municipalities distributed among the 11 provinces in the country. And because planning is carried out at the grass roots level, it tends to be highly responsive to the needs of local citizens. Nevertheless, it is always closely coordinated with regional planning which is the responsibility of the provincial governments. Indeed, prior to implementation all municipal land use plans must be approved by the relevant provincial authorities. The Physical Planning Council at the apex of the administrative structure formulates national planning policies which are implemented by the Minister of Housing and Physical Planning, who is empowered to impose binding directives upon the provincial or regional planning authorities, just as the latter are empowered to do in relation to the municipal planning authorities (see Chart 4.1). In summary, the Netherlands has a comprehensive land use planning program operating at the national, provincial (regional), and local levels which requires by law that municipalities assume responsibility for the planning specifics in their respective areas, giving them considerable freedom of choice in determining these specifics as long as they do not conflict with national and regional planning objectives.

Planning legislation in the Netherlands also provides for citizen participation in the planning process by offering three opportunities for registering complaints if there appears to be a conflict between private and public interests in regard to a particular proposal. The first level of appeal is at the municipal level when the proposal in question is presented for public appraisal. If, upon raising an objection to the proposal a citizen is dissatisfied with the municipal council's response, he can register his complaint with the provincial authorities who eventually render a decision in the case after consulting with the Civil Service Department. The third and final recourse for appeal is the Crown, the titular head of the central government (see Chart 4.2). In practice, however, little use is made of this grievance procedure because the average Netherlander trusts the judgment of the officials he elects. Moreover, because the civil service has a long tradition of expertise and integrity regardless of its political orientation, it also enjoys the confidence of the citizenry in such matters as land use planning. For example, land expropriation by the municipal government to implement town plans (such as those for Bijlmermeer southeast of Amsterdam) is so generally accepted that it is the rule rather than the exception. Of course, "reasonable monetary compensation" is offered the landowner in all expropriation cases, but regardless of this fact, it seems that the long history of fighting to keep out the sea has instilled in the Netherlanders a respect for the value of land in terms of the public welfare—in marked contrast to the individualistic and exploitative attitude toward land which still prevails in the United States.

In spite of its excellent reputation for land-use planning, however, the Netherlands is still confronted with several serious problems in this regard. One is the concentration of all kinds of industry around the western port areas, so that the time is rapidly approaching when the government may have to force some industries to move in order to make room for others which absolutely depend upon the proximity of deep navigable water. Similarly, the population of the country tends to be concentrated in these areas, resulting in extremely high residential densities. This, in turn, produces a yearning for a weekend or summer home in the woods, beside a lake, or even on the water in the form of a houseboat which, if unrestrained by government action, could soon result in the gradual disappearance of open space for public use and in the defacement of the country's most beautiful natural areas. Finally, although Netherlanders do not have as high a percentage of automobile ownership as some European nations like Great Britain, Sweden, France, and Italy, the increasing trend in this regard is threatening the country with urban sprawl, not to mention traffic problems.

The Netherlands' chief source of hope for a solution to these problems is the Zuyder Zee project, begun in 1918, whereby the Zuyder Zee or South Sea, which was in open communication at its northern end with the North Sea, was dammed off and henceforth became known as Yssel Lake, or Ijsselmeer, deriving this name from the Yssel River which flows into it. The overall effect of building this dam could be summed up as "coastline shortening," a principle that has long been well understood and applied in Dutch hydraulic engineering. When the barrier dam was completed in 1928, the government began the second phase of the project, namely, reclaiming the water-logged land behind it to form five "polders."⁴ While the primary objective for these polders at that time was to serve as agricultural land so that the country could be more self-sufficient agriculturally, today they are viewed primarily as areas vital to residential and industrial development which will help to relieve the congestion on the west coast as well as in the Amsterdam area. Lelystad, a sizable new town named for the renowned engineer

Lely, who devoted his life to the reclamation of the Zuyder Zee, is already in the process of being developed approximately in the middle of the project and will become the capital city. As indicated above, the central and deepest part of the former Zuyder Zee is now a huge freshwater lake—Ijsselmeer. This body of water, together with the smaller freshwater lakes between the reclaimed areas and the "old land," not only is useful in preventing salty seawater from forcing its way through the weak soil, the sluices, or open river mouths into the farmland, but also constitutes a valuable source of drinking water and provides a place for recreational activity. Thus, a land reclamation project originally intended for a single purpose has become the object of integrated planning to provide a new living environment in the Netherlands.

APPLICATION OF THE URBAN EXTENSION METHOD
OF PLANNED EXPANSION
IN THE AMSTERDAM METROPOLITAN AREA

The conviction that Amsterdam must scientifically plan its expansion became a firmly established principle in 1928 when the City Council decided to set up a town development section as a distinct entity within the Department of Public Works. During the early years of its existence, this section's most important task was the preparation of a General Extension Plan, the first in the history of the Netherlands based on scientifically calculated population projections. Completed in 1935, the General Extension Plan was approved by the Crown in 1939, and thereby obtained the force of law.[5] Extensive additions have been made to the built-up area of Amsterdam since World War II in accord with this plan, the new town of Bijlmermeer ten miles southeast of Amsterdam being one of the most recent (see Chart 4.3). Begun in 1968, Bijlmermeer was expected to have 100,000 residents by its completion year of 1976.[6] The grasslands of a few years ago on which Bijlmermeer now stands have been transformed into an enormous sandy plain traversed by high and low dikes on which a unique traffic system has been built. Six-lane highways leading to the national road system and providing quick access to Amsterdam have been constructed on the highest dikes. Approximately ten feet below on the lower dikes are four-lane roads which connect the main highways with the town's parking facilities. Finally, there are the ground-level roads for the exclusive use of pedestrians and cyclists.

More than 90 percent of Bijlmermeer's housing consists of prefabricated eleven-story apartment blocks (nine stories atop two floors reserved for public facilities) constructed according to five different plans by private, nonprofit building societies which are subsidized by the National Ministry of Housing (see endsheets). Hence, there are five distinct neighborhoods or districts in Bijlmermeer, each with fifteen flats or about forty-five persons per acre. Over half—about 5,800—of the 10,000 flats already constructed in Bijlmermeer have four rooms and a kitchen, 2,000 have three rooms and a kitchen, 1,500 have two rooms and a kitchen, and, for larger families, there are approximately 550 five-room and 30 six-room apartments. Not only do all flats have a full balcony, but there are a sufficient number of elevators in each apartment block so that no tenant must walk by more than three flats on the way to his own. Rents vary from 178 to 350 guilders ($50 to $100) per month, depending upon the size of the tenant's flat.[7]

On the first public-facilities level or ground floor of each apartment block are huge storage and waste-disposal rooms. "Indoor streets," constituting the second public-facilities level of each apartment block, not only provide tenants with access to the elevators and enable delivery men and salesmen to take their merchandise on electric trolleys up the elevators to all nine apartment unit levels, but they house the mailboxes and panels of the internal telephone system and afford community rooms for group activities. These "streets" are connected by covered bridges with those in the adjoining apartment blocks and with the parking garages adjacent to each residential district, the roofs of which provide parking space for visitors' cars. Car owners must pay about $15 per month in addition to their apartment rent for space in these garages which have been constructed on the basis of 1.5 cars per family.[8] Bus stops and the city railway station, however, are within a quarter mile of those residents who do not own a car or who prefer to use public transportation to commute to and from work in Amsterdam.

Each of Bijlmermeer's five neighborhoods or districts has its own school complex providing both private and public nursery school and primary education in the immediate vicinity of the apartment blocks. North of Bijlmermeer, in the Venser Polder, sites have been reserved for the building of Catholic and Protestant post-primary schools, a technical school, and a "college" of domestic science,[9] but the public post-primary educational establishments already in existence occupy a central location in the town. Bijlmermeer is unique among Europe's residential areas in having reserved so many acres of land (2,225) for recreational use. Its apartment blocks occupy a park-like setting surrounded by beautiful lawns, attractively grouped trees, shrubs, plants, and flowers, and artificial lakes for fishing and canoeing. More than seven hundred park benches will eventually be provided for young lovers and tired strollers, and here and there kiosks will be built for the sale of soft drinks, ice cream, and other sweets. In addition, there will be some sixty children's playgrounds, about twenty areas for football and basketball games, and ten roller skating rinks. A huge shopping and cultural center housing a theater, a swimming pool, and branches of many renowned Amsterdam stores is also planned for Bijlmermeer. In addition to this main center, however, five smaller neighborhood centers will be built to provide daily necessities for Bijlmermeer's residents.[10] Businessmen are being induced to come to Bijlmermeer by offers of low rent in the present temporary central market and choice of location in the new centers when they are completed. There will be no factories in Bijlmermeer itself, but industrial sites are now being prepared in the immediate vicinity of the new town, and large areas between Bijlmermeer and Amsterdam have been reserved for service industries.[11]

PLANNING POLICIES AND PROGRAMS IN SCANDINAVIA

PLANNING LEGISLATION IN SWEDEN

Industrialization in Sweden occurred relatively late, around 1850, at which time only about 10 percent of the country's population resided in urban areas or in what today would be considered small towns. Nevertheless, Sweden's first planning legislation, the Building Act of 1874, was about twenty-five years ahead of similar legislation in other European countries which had become industrialized earlier; its scope was rather limited, dealing mainly with safety and hygiene considerations. In 1931, however, a new piece of legislation was passed, the Town and Country Planning Act, which introduced the following planning innovations: (1) the national government could authorize a site-development plan against the wishes of a municipality; (2) local authorities were granted broader rights to purchase land in order to implement an authorized plan; and (3) a new instrument, the rural development plan, was instituted to regulate land use in the countryside.[12] Unfortunately, the large-scale land use planning anticipated by the Town and Country Planning Act never occurred because the law failed to prohibit private landowners from subdividing their properties, thereby seriously restricting the ability of local governments to assemble large tracts of land or unduly protracting the implementation of plans for such tracts. Consequently, the 1931 planning act was superseded by another in 1947 which has served as Sweden's principal planning instrument to the present day, although several amendments have been made to it in recent years.

In Sweden, a constitutional monarchy dating back to 1809, legislative authority is vested in the Crown and in Parliament, but the chief executive is the prime minister. The king chooses his ministers from the party or coalition which controls the legislature (Riksdag). Ministries in Sweden are governmental units concerned primarily with national policy questions. They prepare government bills, issue regulations, and consider appeals. Acting within the policy framework set out by the ministries are the national boards which administer government programs. Thus, the Ministry of Physical Planning and the National Board of Urban Planning are the primary agencies responsible for planning in Sweden. In addition, the national government influences municipal planning through monetary and other economic policies which set priorities for construction activity.[13]

A major distinction made by the Town and Country Planning Act of 1947 is that between "comprehensive" regional and master planning and "detailed" rural and site development planning. When, as frequently happens in Sweden, several municipalities combine resources for planning purposes, the process is referred to as regional planning. The Crown, which is the titular head of the central government, exercises great control over this type of planning, sometimes requiring a group of municipalities to develop a regional plan and stipulating its scope. Even after the plan has been approved by the Crown, however, it is regarded as merely a guide for the development or redevelopment of an area rather than as an inflexible planning instrument, although the 1947 Act clearly specifies that such development activities must be carried out within "a reasonable period of time."[14] While regional planning involves cooperation among several municipalities and is not required by the Crown in all areas of the country, master planning involves single cities and townships. Virtually all cities and many townships are required by the 1947 Act to formulate master plans "to the extent necessary for normal planning," and these plans may become coercive in whole or in part by order of the Crown. In most instances, however, after municipal council approval of a master plan, local planning authorities are given considerable freedom to determine the nature of detailed rural and site-development projects based on the master plan. Moreover, while these projects must be submitted to the Crown for approval, they are rarely rejected.

Unlike the Town and Country Planning Act of 1931, that of 1947 not only prohibits private landowners from subdividing their properties but requires them to secure a permit before building on their land to insure that such construction will not be alien to the public interest in terms of designated economic, sanitary, and social criteria. The Nature Conservation Act of 1965 supplements these restrictions by prohibiting construction of any kind in rural areas specifically designated by the government as valuable for their scenic qualities.[15] Since such areas are reserved indefinitely for public use, however, the government compensates the owners for the heavy financial loss they incur by refraining from developing the land. Still another restriction on the use of private property imposed by the 1947 Town and Country Planning Act is the provision empowering government authorities to expropriate the land required to implement their development plans within "reasonable time and cost," in which cases compensation to the landowners is determined by special expropriation courts. Contrary to the situation in the Netherlands, however, land expropriation is not frequently employed to facilitate planning in Sweden because of the many legal conditions surrounding the practice.

Generally speaking, Swedish planning legislation has been fairly effective, but it has had several major weaknesses, including inadequate provisions for regional planning and overreliance upon local-government responsibility for planning, which have had some unfortunate consequences in terms of the allocation of land for industrial and recreational purposes. It is hoped that a more comprehensive approach will result from the new planning instrument recently drafted in Sweden—the national plan.

APPLICATION OF THE SATELLITE-COMMUNITY METHOD
OF PLANNED URBAN EXPANSION IN SWEDEN AND FINLAND

During the late nineteenth and early twentieth centuries, the
city of Stockholm purchased extensive tracts of peripheral land in
an effort to stem the tide of Swedish emigration to the United
States by offering inexpensive home ownership on municipally
owned land. But the decision of the Stockholm City Council in 1941
to build an underground rail transit system influenced suburban
development more than any other factor. Subsequently, the 1952
master plan for Stockholm provided for the future growth of the
city in a succession of satellite communities with fairly high population densities which would be separated from each other by narrow greenbelts.[16] To date, about twenty satellite communities, each
planned for 10,000 to 30,000 inhabitants, have been constructed
northwest and south of the central area of Stockholm (see Chart
4.4). Thus, whereas in the United States central-city administrators
view with alarm the increasing movement of people, business, and
industry to the suburbs, the city of Stockholm is actually encouraging such movement, planning for a reduction from 27 percent to 17
percent in the proportion of Greater Stockholm residents living in
the central city by the year 2000.[17]

All of Stockholm's satellite communities have been laid out in
roughly the same pattern: their shopping centers and high-rise
residential buildings are clustered around the rail transit station;
two-story flats form the second residential "ring"; and single-
family detached dwellings are located on the periphery. They also
follow a common residential construction pattern, namely, about
a fifty-fifty split between units erected by commercial contractors
and those erected by nonprofit cooperatives and city-owned corporations. Residential financing in Stockholm's satellite communities, however, is a much more complex matter than their layout and
construction patterns. Since apartments constitute the major portion of new residential construction in these communities, their
financing will serve as an example of the system as a whole. Commercial contractors, nonprofit cooperatives, and public corporations are all treated alike in regard to financing the first 70 percent
of their construction costs; that is, private banks usually finance
60 percent of the cost through a first mortgage and an additional
10 percent through a second mortgage, both at the prevailing inter-

est rate of 7 to 7.5 percent. It is in regard to financing the remaining 30 percent of the construction costs, however, that nonprofit cooperatives and public corporations have the advantage over commercial contractors. Whereas for the nonprofit and public builders the government will finance 95 and 100 percent of the remaining costs, respectively, it not only requires commercial contractors to finance the remaining costs through a third bank mortgage but controls the rents which they charge as a condition for the "privilege" of securing this mortgage.[18]

In many ways, Stockholm's satellite communities are similar to the British new towns discussed later in this chapter in that they have been built primarily to relieve the congestion of the central city and to provide for orderly expansion of the metropolitan area, other considerations being the need to upgrade blighted areas, the housing shortage, and the limited land available for development within the city limits. Unlike the British new towns, however, they are not intended to be self-supporting; although they have some industrial facilities, about 80 percent of their residents work elsewhere, mainly in downtown Stockholm.[19] Incorporated into Stockholm's local government, the satellites are closely controlled during as well as after their development, which accounts for their great success in terms of design, the provision of subsidized housing, a wide variety of community facilities, and a high level of social services. They have proved to be extraordinarily imaginative answers to the problem of urban congestion.

The Example of Farsta, Sweden

In 1954, the Stockholm City Planning Department prepared a master plan for Farsta (see Chart 4.5), a satellite community located about nine miles south of Stockholm. Two years later, on October 12, 1956, the Stockholm Real Estate Department commissioned a group of six Swedish contractors, known collectively as AB Farsta Centrum, to plan and build the town center. By April, 1958, two large chain stores, Tempo and Kvickly, had signed for space in Farsta Center; the prestigious Stockholm department store, Nordiska Kompaniet (NK), and the Martin Olsson Supermarket held out until 1959. By October 23, 1960, the town center—an open type characteristic of the 1950s—was completed and formally opened.[20]

Today, in addition to the larger stores mentioned above, Farsta Center contains about thirty smaller business and service establishments, including a liquor store, a restaurant and cafeteria, a bakery, a pharmacy, a beauty and barber shop, a medical center and dental clinic, a youth center, a social service agency, a cinema, a community hall, a post office, a police station, a car repair shop, six banks, a news and ticket office, a library, a kindergarten, and two churches. A fountain, a pond, flowers, trees, shrubs, and benches adorn the pedestrian mall, the underground area of which is reserved for service traffic. At the end of this pedestrian mall, rather than beneath it as in most Stockholm suburbs, is the station for the rapid rail-transit line (see Chart 4.6). Consequently, everyone leaving and entering the station must pass through the town center. There are 1,700 outdoor parking spaces and 250 underground spaces at Farsta Center, for in addition to approximately 60,000 local residents, it serves an estimated 200,000 persons from surrounding areas who can reach it within fifteen minutes by automobile.[21]

The development of Farsta Center by AB Farsta Centrum is a good example of successful cooperation between Stockholm's municipal administration and private enterprise. After witnessing the commercial success of Vallingby's town center, completed in 1954 by a municipal development and management company,[22] AB Farsta Centrum convinced Stockholm's city administrators to entrust them with the planning and construction of the projected Farsta Center. Not only did they succeed in accomplishing their goal but they did so with minimum financial risk, as most of the large retail and commercial establishments which became occupants of the center purchased their properties soon after completion. At the same time, the city of Stockholm profited both politically and economically from the private development of Farsta Center, because it not only demonstrated the city's willingness to regard private enterprise as a partner, but it enabled the city to utilize its financial and manpower resources elsewhere.

Similarly, when Farsta was being developed (1956–1965) and the demand for housing was great, even though the city of Stockholm had at least four public companies engaged in home construction according to municipal specifications under a cost-plus or fixed-price agreement, contracts were also awarded to several cooperative societies and commercial builders whose motivation and modus operandi differed considerably from that of the public companies.[23] Commercial contractors, while enjoying recognition for performing services in the public interest, are primarily interested in making money and usually enlist the aid of large, private financial institutions in the construction of residential areas. Cooperative building societies, on the other hand, are private, nonprofit organizations, often composed of special interest groups, which finance their construction operations from the pooled investments of their members augmented by funds borrowed from major lending agencies such as Ekkronan in Stockholm.*

---

*In Sweden most responsibility for housing resides in the Ministry of Labor and Housing, but certain housing responsibilities rest with the Ministry of Social Affairs and a few with the Ministry of Education and Ecclesiastical Affairs. There are several national boards for special purposes which while they operate outside the ministries are under their general supervision. One of these is the National Housing Board which is responsible for the implementation of Swedish housing policy via twenty-four regional boards, one for each of the countries in Sweden. From these regional boards responsibility for administering housing policy falls on the municipalities. While the national and regional housing boards are responsible for policy guidance and economic contributions in the form of loans and allowances, the municipalities are responsible for the planning and production of residential construction on an adequate scale. However, municipalities directly build a relatively small percentage of Sweden's housing, a substantial portion of which is constructed by so-called public utility housing companies or foundations which are, in effect, arms of the municipalities. To be recognized as public utilities and to qualify for the maximum government loan of 100 percent, these organizations must be nonprofit in character and must operate in close cooperation with the local authorities. The municipality appoints more than half of their board members, the remaining board members consisting of persons independent of interest in commercial builders. There are more than three hundred public utility housing enterprises in Sweden, most of them belonging to a national association called SABO (Swedish Public Utility Housing Enterprises) which promotes housing construction by its members throughout Sweden, provides its members with various administrative and financial services, helps members conduct surveys, and negotiates with public authorities and other organizations on behalf of its members.

The next most important housing producers in Sweden are the nearly three thousand cooperative organizations in the country which are guided and assisted by two national organizations—HSB and Svenska Riksbyggen. Cooperative housing in Sweden operates in a manner similar to that in the United States and the role of HSB and Svenska Riksbyggen is similar to that played by the Foundation of Cooperative Housing (FCH) in the U. S. The HSB, for example, plans the housing, negotiates with the government for financing, and sets up a small board to represent the ultimate cooperators. After the housing is completed, the real cooperative is formed as the housing units are occupied.[24]

There are two types of dwelling units in Farsta: rented apartments and single houses which are largely privately owned. Fifty percent of all the apartment buildings have been constructed by public corporations; 30 percent, by commercial contractors; and 20 percent, by nonprofit cooperatives. Securing a cooperative apartment, for example, requires a down payment of $1,000 and annual rent of $1,500 to $2,000. Single houses, on the other hand, are either public-corporation or commercial-contractor units, the former having an average sale price of $30,000 and requiring a $5,000 down payment, and the latter having an average sale price of $40,000 and requiring a $10,000 down payment.[25] While the exterior of some housing in Farsta is red brick, more often it is stucco, but drabness has been avoided by the liberal use of colored trim. The rocky, hilly, forested landscape also lends beauty to Farsta's residential areas. Another interesting feature of Farsta's housing is that all units are heated by power emanating from the Agesta Atomic Power Plant located three miles from the town center. The reactor is built into a 100-foot rock excavation and is surrounded by thick concrete as a protection against radiation.[26]

Residences in Farsta tend to be clustered, with multistory apartment buildings which constitute 62 percent of the dwelling units concentrated around the town center, and single-family row and detached houses, which constitute the remaining 38 percent of the living units located further out in three distinct neighborhoods. This accounts for Farsta's high average population density of sixty persons per acre (see Chart 4.7). Child welfare facilities and pedestrian safety features figure prominently in Farsta's residential areas; there is a supervised playground and day-care center in each neighborhood, and all footpaths cross vehicular traffic routes on a separate level.

At present, all the adults in 40 percent of Sweden's households are gainfully employed, which accounts for the tremendous demand for services such as day nurseries, central systems for cleaning and laundering, restaurants which also provide precooked meals for taking out, and nursing personnel to take care of the temporarily ill. In addition, 20 percent of the Swedish households consists of retired persons, many of whom require domestic help and care. Life in a subdivision of single-family houses is scarcely geared to meeting the needs of such households. For them, the greatest convenience is offered by the apartment house with a population sufficiently large to sustain service facilities within the building itself. Another factor conducive to concentrated building in Sweden is the climate; where densities are high, it becomes economically feasible to install streets and footpaths which are heated from below to rid them of snow and ice. Moreover, more and more Swedes—and indeed Scandinavians generally—are opting for two dwellings in preference to one, resulting in a pattern whereby families alternate living between an urban flat and a country bungalow. Summing up, the compact satellite with its relatively dense building pattern seems to stand the best chance of survival in Sweden.[27]

Only 25 percent of Farsta's residents are employed locally; most of the remaining 75 percent commute to jobs in Stockholm, just twenty minutes away by subway. One explanation for this situation is that industrial development has proceeded slowly in Farsta due to its alien topography—steep rocky hills and narrow valleys—making factory sites small and expensive. The best ground in Farsta in terms of facilitating construction work has been leased to government agencies such as the Telecommunications Administration which employs some 4,000 people. The city of Stockholm has not constructed factory shells or provided railway spurs for freight-car service in Farsta, for the attendant influx of new employers and their employees to the community would aggravate the already acute housing shortage. Government administrators have rationalized Farsta's paucity of job opportunities by contending that, with increased car ownership and the expansion of the municipal transit system, workers' mobility has increased to the point that local employment is no longer necessary. Recently, however, the Folksum Insurance Company established an office in Farsta which employs about 1,000 persons, significantly increasing the town's occupational opportunities.[28]

The Example of Tapiola, Finland

Regarded by some community planners as the most beautiful satellite town in the world is Tapiola, situated on the Gulf of Finland six miles west of Helsinki (see Chart 4.8 for diagram). Its name, derived from the Finnish legendary forest sprite, Tapio, is extremely appropriate in terms of its extraordinarily beautiful setting amidst a lush evergreen forest. The prime mover behind this project since its inception in 1951 has been Heikki von Hertzen, a former banker who purchased the 670-acre site in the rural commune of Espoo for $700,000. The purchase was made on behalf of the Finnish Housing Foundation, Asuntosäätiö, a nonprofit corporation which von Hertzen formed by combining five district organizations—the Confederation of Finnish Trade Unions, the Society of Civil Servants, the Central Association of Tenants, the Mannerheim League, and the Finnish Association of Disabled Civilians and Ex-Servicemen—with the Finnish Family Welfare League of which he was at the time managing director.[29]

Immediately following its organization, the Finnish Housing Foundation launched a project regarded by many experts as a utopian dream—that of building an entirely new community for a population of 17,000, constructing not only commercial and industrial facilities and some housing but also a complete network of public utilities and facilities. Its prime objective was to build a town dedicated to man—his homelife, his leisure and recreation, a place where children could grow up in beautiful and safe surroundings and where traffic facilities would be subordinated to pedestrian needs. It is not surprising, therefore, that von Hertzen was forced to begin his project with a short-term loan from an anonymous source and that, even later, when he was successful in securing bank financing, it was for short terms, five to thirteen years, at 7.5 percent interest. In addition to the plan's ideality, von Hertzen's project to heat all dwelling units in his garden city by a remote central heating system seemed financially unfeasible. Another objection raised by experienced community developers was that the proposed density of thirty persons per acre was too low in terms of the area's harsh weather because services such as the heating of streets and footpaths from below would be economically unfeasible. People also thought that the one-third of the residents who were to be children and young people, in combination with the climate, would soon make a shambles of the town's parks, lawns, and flower beds. Reflective of practical problems once construction began is the fact that von Hertzen had to constantly supervise the contractors lest they cut down trees unnecessarily when making a street or laying the foundation for a building.[30]

Tapiola's dwelling units have been constructed in three distinct neighborhoods separated from each other and from the town center by a greenbelt of parkland. Of the 4,600 units, 20 percent are apartments and 80 percent are single-family terrace and row houses.[31] One of the major principles followed in the planning of Tapiola has been the consistent interspersing of multistory and low residential buildings for variety's sake as well as to create an atmosphere of spaciousness. The quality of Tapiola's housing, like that in Finland generally, ranks among the best in the world because of the creativity of Finnish architects, the country's bountiful and high-quality timber, and the long experience of Finnish builders in constructing buildings capable of withstanding unusually harsh climatic conditions. Moreover, the architectural style of Tapiola's residential buildings is well suited to the topography of the site, which may be described as gently rolling, rocky, and heavily forested. The buildings, together with artistic landscaping and the creative use of such "public furnishings" as benches, street lights, and directional signs, have produced a truly aesthetic environment for Tapiola's residents. Finally, each residential neighborhood in Tapiola has been laid out in such a way that housewives need walk no more than two hundred yards from their dwelling units to a small shopping center for the purchase of such daily staples as bread, butter, milk, and fish, and children never need to cross a vehicular thoroughfare as they walk to school. Playgrounds for preschool children are, in most instances, immediately in front of the dwelling units to facilitate parental supervision.

Ninety percent of Tapiola's housing is owned on a cooperative basis, prices ranging from $6,000 for apartments and $10,000 for town houses to a low of $15,000 and a high of about $60,000 for single-family detached homes. Under this system, a tenant secures ownership of his dwelling unit by obtaining a twenty-two-year loan at about 7 percent interest from a private financial agency to cover the first 40 to 45 percent of the purchase price. A second forty-four-year loan at 1 percent interest for five years and at 3 percent thereafter is then secured from Finland's State Housing Board to cover an additional 30 percent of the purchase price. Thus, only 25 to 30 percent of the purchase price of a dwelling unit must be paid by the owner. The 10 percent of Tapiola's residents who choose to rent rather than purchase a dwelling unit are restricted to apartments, the monthly rate ranging from about $40 to $125.[32] A distinctive feature of Tapiola's housing situation is government subsidization of 40 percent of the dwelling units for low-income families to facilitate a heterogeneous population in the community. Consequently, a wide range of educational backgrounds, occupations, and incomes is represented among Tapiola's residents. One recent survey found that 36 percent of the town's residents hold university degrees and are either executives or professionals; another 26 percent are owners of small firms, foremen, and office workers; and 38 percent are blue-collar and service workers of various kinds.[33]

Visitors are usually surprised to discover that so many people of low income live in Tapiola and that they have been successfully integrated residentially and socially with white-collar workers, professional people, and executives in business and industry. A factor contributing to this besides the government's housing subsidies is Tapiola's community paper, *Tapiola Tanään* (Tapiola Today). Published weekly by the Finnish Housing Foundation, it not only welcomes all newcomers and provides advice intended to facilitate their adjustment, but it keeps all residents well informed about activities in the town. More important, however, the Housing Foundation has provided the most aesthetic and humane surroundings possible for all of Tapiola's residents. Still another factor facilitating integration of the various socioeconomic groups in Tapiola is the active leisure-time organizations in the town and the adequacy of public places for them to meet in the neighborhoods as well as in the town center. To mention only a few, there are scout troops, choral societies, chess, bridge, camera, and fishing clubs, two Lions Club chapters, and the Tapiola Guild which promotes the common interests of the inhabitants.

The Finnish Housing Foundation has also set as one of its major goals the development of Tapiola into a thriving self-contained community, which means that efforts are being made to create 6,000 jobs in the area, making it possible for 80 percent of the gainfully employed population to find work locally. These employment outlets will be classified as follows: 2,870 in industry, service, and traffic; 1,720 in offices; 860 in shops, restaurants, and hotels; and 550 in schools and various social centers.[34] There are two small industrial areas in Tapiola, one separating the northern and western neighborhoods and one at the northernmost extremity of the town. The first contains Tapiola's central heating plant, a "small-industry house" built by the Housing Foundation which is occupied by thirty different small-scale industries, the Weilin and Göös Printing Factory which is one of the most modern in northern Europe, a large furniture shop, a gasoline station, a car-repair shop, and a service station. The second industrial area, which is only partially completed, contains a large packaging firm.

Another factor contributing to Tapiola's goal of self-containment is its town center; architect Aarne Ervi won first prize for its design in an open architectural contest conducted in 1953. Three promenades, one from each neighborhood, lead to this versatile administrative, commercial, and cultural center, located within 1.5 kilometers of all parts of Tapiola. An exclusively pedestrian precinct separated from the surrounding neighborhoods by greenbelts, the town center has both open and enclosed sections, includes children's play areas as well as "parking" stalls for baby carriages and dogs, and will eventually accommodate 1,000 cars in its underground garage. Other notable town-center facilities are the thirteen-story administrative office tower, Keskustorni, a landmark in Tapiola with its enclosed rooftop restaurant and terrace cafe; the shopping center Heikintori, a "department store" consisting of sixty-five specialty shops; and a social center, including a tourist office, a meeting hall, smaller rooms for leisure-time activities and evening classes, a young people's cafeteria and discotheque, restaurants, cafeterias, coffee bars, and kiosks (ice cream wagons), open until late in the evening.

Around the artificial square lake, with its beautiful fountains, in front of the town center are located a church with a parish hall and youth center, a glass-enclosed swimming pool with an ancillary outdoor facility, a terraced Greek-style theater for dramatic productions, a health center, and a sports hall with a bowling alley, "keep-fit" school, and gymnasium. In addition, construction of a tourist hotel has already commenced on the southern side of the lake, and a theater and concert hall, as well as a library and music college, have been planned for an area between the western side of the lake and the Keskustorni tower. Future plans include an exhibition hall for the fine arts, a secondary school for nine hundred pupils, and several technical schools. The lake itself, which was formerly a gravel pit, not only is an aesthetic feature of Tapiola that also can be fished, but serves as a cooling mechanism for the town's central heating system.[35]

Despite all the initial opposition to Heikki von Hertzen's proposal to build Tapiola, the garden city, it has proved to be an exemplary community, physically, socially, and economically, as demonstrated by its international reputation for beauty, the long waiting lists of prospective tenants, the successful integration of its heterogeneous population, and its assurances of economic self-sufficiency for the future. Tapiola has been so exemplary that von Hertzen and his Finnish Housing Foundation have been employed to plan several "growth centers" throughout Finland to prevent Helsinki from becoming a megalopolis.

ECONOMIC GROWTH CENTERS

Economic growth centers have emerged as a central concept in regional and national economic and physical planning policy in most European countries. There is, however, a wide range of opinion in regard to several crucial issues relating to growth centers such as (1) the criteria for identifying an urban settlement with growth potential, (2) the minimum-size population of a viable growth center, (3) the minimum level of public facilities and services required to attract and sustain efficient enterprise, (4) the types of subsidies that are justified to help give areas a new direction and momentum, and (5) the period of time required before centers can be expected to become self-supporting. Should public investment merely seek to remove existing deficiencies, for example, in transport, communications, energy, and water? Or should it go further and provide special facilities to help ensure the profitability of future enterprises which might be set up?

The wide difference in prevailing views on these questions stems partly from differences in objectives. In most countries, the concept of growth centers originally developed as a means of eliminating local unemployment and poverty; consequently, sites for such centers were chosen on the basis of indexes such as high unemployment rates, declining industries, and low incomes. While the concept of the growth center has remained essentially local in some countries, in others it has been greatly broadened to assume an important role in regional and national economic and physical planning. Antoni R. Kuklinski, for example, distinguishes between the concept of growth poles on a national scale as a tool in promoting basic changes in the distribution of population and economic activities, and the concept of growth centers on a regional scale as a tool of economic and social transformation in rural settlements and small towns.[36]

PLANNING POLICIES AND PROGRAMS IN GREAT BRITAIN

It was not until after World War II that the British passed legislation which became an effective instrument of economic and social planning. In 1947, Clement Attlee's Labor government enacted the Town and Country Planning Act in an effort to bring about some degree of balance between economic conditions in the north and south of England. Since the 1930s the north had been a depressed area with high levels of unemployment and extensive emigration to the south. Recognizing that the only way to balance standards of living and production levels in the two areas was for the government to determine the direction of economic growth in the country, the Labor government used the Town and Country Planning Act to secure exclusive control over all land use and to expropriate privately owned land, when necessary, to implement this objective. Moreover, in compulsory land purchase cases it attempted to minimize the differences in the price per acre paid to individual landowners so that one would not suffer and another prosper from the government's decision to purchase land in one area to discourage economic development and in another area to encourage it. Three basic objectives underlay the Labor government's policy: (1) to curb the rate of population and employment growth in London and the southern counties; (2) to increase the scale of economic activity in the northern part of Great Britain; and (3) to change the form of growth in the largest metropolitan regions, particularly around London and in the southern counties.[37] In executing this policy the government required every owner of developable land to submit a claim estimating the difference between the current-use and potential-use values of his land. When all these claims were adjusted by the central government, a total "development value" of £300 million was determined, this amount being paid to the landowners before July 1953. Thereafter, all land value increments resulting from various development projects were claimed by the government.[38]

Although the conservative Tories upon their return to power in 1959 eliminated the most objectionable feature of the 1947 Town and Country Planning Act by substituting the traditional "fair market value" principle for the "standardization of price per acre" principle in determining government compensation for land expropriation, they retained its control of land use which has ever since remained undisputed by the vast majority of British citizens.[39] The Labor Party returned to power five years later (in 1964), at which time it furthered the progress which the Tories had made in promoting industrial development in the north by requiring permits for all new factory construction as well as for additions to existing plant facilities in excess of 1,000 square feet (increased to 3,000 square feet in 1966) in London, the midland, and the eastern and southeastern regions. Next, to encourage economic development and industrial modernization in the north, the Labor government doubled standard incentives for investments in new plants and equipment. Then, to accelerate the effect of the new investment incentives and to encourage labor-intensive rather than capital-intensive industries, the Labor government set up for a period of seven years a system of supplementary grants intended to reduce labor costs by about 5 to 10 percent.[40] Finally, in April 1967, Parliament established by law a National Land Commission which was authorized not only to expropriate developable land, but to impose a 40 percent tax on any profit derived by private landowners from the sale of their properties. While this was a heavy tax, it was certainly less offensive than the Labor Party's usurping the total profit from such sales during its previous administration.[41]

That Britain's post–World War II land-planning policies have enjoyed considerable success is indicated by the fact that the north has been steadily improving its economic position relative to the south. There is some concern, however, about the gradual economic decline of the areas between the northern development region and the prosperous southeast and midland regions.[42] As stated above, however, there has been little debate about the theoretical feasibility of the British government's policies to control land use. Indeed, when the Tory government returned to power under Prime Minister Heath in 1971, it combined the old ministries of Transport, Housing and Local Government, and Public Building and Works into one superagency, the Department of the Environment, which has powers to control the use of all land where Britons live, work, and recreate.

THE APPLICATION OF THE NEW TOWNS MECHANISM IN GREAT BRITAIN

It has become almost axiomatic that in democratic societies social problems must reach a dire state before the majority of citizens become sufficiently aroused to demand action. Thus, it is not surprising that forty-three years elapsed between Ebenezer Howard's private development in 1903 of his garden city, Letchworth (which demonstrated the measures needed to stop urban sprawl in England), and the British government's passage of the New Towns Act in 1946. At the time of the passage of the New Towns Act, the Minister of Town and Country Planning made the following statement: "More damage has been done, both to our towns and to the countryside, through sporadic and ribbon development since 1909, the date of the first Town and Country Planning Act, than in any period preceding it."[43]

About the time Ebenezer Howard wrote *Garden Cities of Tomorrow* (1888), the development of electric trains and automobiles made possible the mass exodus from decaying industrial cities to the suburbs, a trend which was naturally encouraged by real estate developers who were shrewd enough to use Howard's term, "garden city," to describe just about any type of community with a small population. Following World War I, there was such a drastic housing shortage in Britain that the government hurriedly constructed several million homes with little or no regard for their quality or location, thereby aggravating the prewar trend toward haphazard, unplanned urban development. Consequently, already by the year 1920 slums had become so prevalent that Parliament appointed a committee headed by Neville Chamberlain to advise the Minister of Health on how to eradicate this problem. Chamberlain's committee suggested what Howard had proposed over thirty years before—that the central government finance the construction of self-sufficient garden cities, either around existing towns or on new sites in the economically depressed and sparsely populated areas of northern England, Scotland, and Wales, to stimulate the decentralization of London and the surrounding area.

The recommendations of Chamberlain's committee went unheeded, however, until 1937 when Chamberlain became prime minister and appointed a Royal Commission headed by Sir Anderson

Montague-Barlow to study London's population trends. The Barlow Commission came to the same conclusion in December 1939 as had Chamberlain's earlier committee, that London was overcrowded and that the solution lay in the government's financing the construction of self-sufficient new towns. Unlike the Chamberlain Committee recommendations, however, those of the Barlow Commission were eventually implemented (in 1946) due in large part to the tremendous devastation which bombing had wrought in Britain's large cities between 1940 and 1946. Five years after the publication of the Barlow Commission's report—in 1944—Sir Patrick Abercrombie presented his plan for Greater London, proposing that the city's population be reduced by 1,125,000 and that 250,000 of this number be relocated in ten new towns to be built beyond the London greenbelt as authorized by the Greenbelt Act of 1938.[44]

The next step was to determine how the new town proposal would become a reality. This became a project for a committee headed by Lord Reith who was Britain's wartime Minister of Works and Buildings. Upon investigating the opinions of local government officials, private builders, and financial experts regarding this matter, there seemed to be a consensus that only the central government could effectively execute a new towns program. Consequently, the Reith Committee recommended the formation of a development corporation for each new town designated by the Minister of Town and Country Planning, a corporation which would have the authority, if necessary, to purchase the sites required for their work. Other principles specified in the Reith Committee report which have guided Britain's new towns movement to the present day are that sites be located at least twenty-five miles from London, that the greenbelt be preserved as an inviolable area, and that economic self-sufficiency be a key feature of every new town.

The Reith Committee report set the stage for passage of the New Towns Act of 1946 which authorized the formation by the Minister of Town and Country Planning of the corporations which would build the towns. The law also afforded Britain's prospective new towns very favorable financing arrangements: sixty-year loans from the British Treasury for both housing and commercial facilities, the interest rate varying from 3 percent when the first new town corporation was established for Stevenage to a peak of

9.25 percent late in 1969, the rate in the mid-1970s hovering between 8 and 9 percent.[45] When compared with private financing in Britain, where interest rates are considerably higher than in the United States, and even when compared with private financing in the United States, the loans and interest rates offered to the new-town development corporations by the British Treasury constitute a substantial government subsidy.

Each of the development corporations which supervise the construction of Britain's new towns consists of a chairman, a deputy chairman, and up to seven directors, all private citizens who, in turn, have their own professional staff headed by a general manager. Their development plans must be submitted to the Department of the Environment for approval, whereupon the corporations not only develop specific new-town sites but install most of the public facilities—roads, water and sewer systems, and waste disposal plants—which local governments provide in privately developed communities. Moreover, they build most of the dwelling units which are, as everywhere in Britain, heavily subsidized, making possible extremely low rents. In the earliest new towns, for example, the average house still rents for $50, including service rates. Consequently, new-town corporations derive the bulk of their profits from the sale of their shopping center buildings, leasing the land on which they stand for ninety-nine years rather than selling it, a practice which they also follow with regard to purchasers of factory buildings. However, since most new towns have difficulty attracting even one department store until their population approaches 60,000 people, a new-town corporation sometimes enters a partnership with a firm operating such a business whereby the corporation agrees to build the firm's store and to charge low rent for its use in return for a share of the profits until an agreed-upon volume of business is achieved. Such arrangements have generally succeeded because new-town shopping centers eventually serve several hundred thousand people from areas surrounding the new town site.[46]

With approval from the Department of the Environment, the corporations can sell land to the small percentage of private home builders, to churches, and to bodies of local government (county councils) which, incidentally, build the schools, libraries, health centers, fire stations and magistrates' courts in new towns. While privately built homes in a new town may be sold without restrictions, corporation-built homes may be rented or sold only to persons who have a job there. However, this limitation has not caused any home occupancy problems because about 65 percent of the employees, especially the younger and more skilled, follow their employer when he moves to a new town. Hence, new town populations tend to be heavily weighted with young married couples in the middle-income bracket and, conversely, there is a conspicuous absence of unemployed and indigent persons.[47]

The construction of Britain's new towns has occurred in several stages. By 1950, the Labor government had planned and launched fourteen new towns which it hoped would siphon off approximately one million people from the congested cities of England, Scotland, and Wales by 1965. To absorb London's surplus population the government had planned seven new towns—Basildon, Bracknell, Crawley, Harlow, Hatfield, Hemel Hempstead, and Stevenage—and had taken over and enlarged Howard's garden city, Welwyn; Glasgow's population congestion was relieved by East Kilbride; it was hoped that residents of the scattered mining towns in northeastern England and in Scotland would be attracted to the more integrated industrial new towns of Peterlee and Glenrothes, respectively; and Newton Aycliffe in northeastern England, Cwmbran in Monmouthshire, Wales, and Corby in the midland of England were designed to inject improved housing and community services into already established industrial areas. But with the designation of Corby as the fourteenth new town in April 1950, a Conservative government returned to power and, except for Cumbernauld east of Glasgow, no new towns were started during the entire decade.

During the 1960s, however, a succession of British new towns emerged which were planned on a far larger scale than the new towns of the 1940s, several of them involving considerable expansion of existing towns and villages. In 1967, for example, Milton Keynes, located forty-eight miles from London in north Buckinghamshire, was designated as a new town with the expectation that it would grow into a regional city of 250,000 inhabitants, including 150,000 Londoners, by the end of the century. Consisting of 22,000 acres, Milton Keynes incorporates several fairly large existing towns such as Bletchley, Wolverton, and Stony Stratford. Similarly, Peterborough, a community of 86,000 people, was designated in 1968 for planned expansion to accommodate an additional 100,000 people, mainly from London, by 1980. Two other existing towns, Northampton and Ipswich, each with a population of some 120,000, are expected to accommodate an additional 70,000 Londoners by the same date.[48] (See map of Britain's new towns, Chart 4.9.)

The advantages of using an already going town as a nucleus for large-scale expansion include: the existence of an established and experienced administrative organization to work in cooperation with the new town development corporation; public services, shopping centers, and other facilities being already operative so that greater emphasis can be placed on the home building program; and existing industries needing only an opportunity to expand. The recent emphasis in Britain on larger new towns may be ascribed to greater individual mobility which has accompanied increased automobile ownership, making it possible for a community to expand without forfeiting its sense of cohesiveness or unity. In other words, the automobile makes all parts of a large new town as readily accessible to car-owning residents as all sections of the smaller new towns are to their residents by walking. Thus pedestrian scale as a prime feature of new town design is being de-emphasized. Moreover, larger new towns can offer a greater variety of employment to their inhabitants and can economically provide a wider range of urban facilities.

The Example of Cumbernauld, Scotland

Traditionally, one of the largest areas of urban congestion in Great Britain has been Glasgow, Scotland. In 1946, the Clyde Valley Planning Advisory Committee in Scotland recommended to the Secretary of State the enlargement of certain small towns and the establishment of several new ones to relieve Glasgow. In the next year, East Kilbride, a town of 2,500 persons eight miles southeast of Glasgow, was designated for expansion to accommodate approximately 50,000 people. While the 18,000 homes subsequently built in East Kilbride provided for substantial migration from Glasgow and while the Glasgow City Corporation built some 36,000 homes within its own boundaries between 1947 and 1955, there was still a shortage of at least 100,000 houses in Glasgow in 1951 when census data revealed that its average population density was four hundred persons per acre. Consequently, in 1955 the Clyde Valley Planning Advisory Committee recommended the expansion of two towns about fourteen miles northeast of Glasgow—Cumbernauld with 1,300 inhabitants and Condorrat with 1,200—to accommodate 50,000 persons.[49] This figure was revised upward to 70,000 inhabitants in December of that year by agreement of the Glasgow City Corporation and eighteen local authorities in the designated area, including Dumbarton County Council[50] (see Chart 4.10). As of 1975, about half of this new target population had been reached.

The 4,150 acres in the eastern portion of Dumbarton County designated as the site for the new town of Cumbernauld occupy a strategic location between the firths of Forth and Clyde in the heart of Scotland's industrial belt. Only 2,783 of the 4,150 acres can be used for the town's development, however, including 582 acres of open space, because of the area's hilly, rocky land and rugged climate. Consequently, in contrast to the neighborhood system characteristic of most new towns, the general concept of a town which has evolved in Cumbernauld is that of a compact urban center located astride the broad hogback of the principal hill—an oval 930-acre site some two miles long and one mile wide—which will eventually contain schools, shops, and some industry for 50,000 persons housed at a net density of eighty-five persons per acre. Residential facilities surrounding the hilltop will eventually accommodate an additional 20,000 people.[51]

The Cumbernauld Development Corporation has designated the town center, a vast, concrete, multipurpose building which is within walking distance of most residents, as the vital pivot of its new town (see Chart 4.11). Nevertheless, small stores designed to meet the daily needs of relatively remote residents have been provided at a ratio of about one for every four hundred dwellings, and small shopping centers are planned for the Abronhill and Condorrat districts at the east and west extremities of the town which are farthest from the town center.[52] The overall plan of the eight-level town center shows two parallel parts divided by a "spine" road which joins A-80 (the main highway from Glasgow to Stirling between which Cumbernauld is located) at either end of the center and at the same time provides access to the two lowest levels of the structure which are devoted entirely to transportation and contain a bus station, docks for loading and unloading trucks, and parking stalls for 5,000 cars. Customers may proceed by escalators, elevators, stairs, or ramps from these transportation areas to the pedestrian levels of the center, and goods are conveyed by hoists into the storage areas of the shops on the north and south sides of the building.

Cumbernauld's town center was erected in three stages. The first involved the construction of the core of the building which contains a wide variety of shops, a supermarket reputed to be the largest in Scotland, six banks, a post office, a first-class hotel called The Golden Eagle, a health center, a library, a public hall, thirty-five luxury penthouses, a rooftop restaurant, and a bowling alley. The second stage of the center's development extended this midsection of the structure in two directions to provide a long mall containing shops, a cinema, a dance hall, a sports center, a swimming pool, and a technical college. The third phase involved the provision of additional shops, cultural and entertainment facilities, and local government offices.[53]

Because of its hilltop location Cumbernauld's town center can be seen for many miles from the surrounding countryside. On the northeast side it resembles a geometric arrangement of rectangular masses, while on the southeast side it appears to be an irregular grouping of buildings topped by five train coaches, which are actually penthouses. It was this innovative design, along with the center's multilevel integration of so many public facilities and its separation of pedestrian and vehicular traffic, which in 1967 won for Cumbernauld the distinction of being the first recipient of America's R. S. Reynolds Award for Outstanding Community Architecture.[54]

A considerable diversity of housing has been provided in Cumbernauld—two-story terrace houses with and without gardens, a few low-rise buildings (four or five stories high), and twelve high-rise apartments (one twenty stories high and eleven twelve stories high) which accommodate only about 3 percent of the residents. This housing pattern was partly influenced by the nature of the soil, particularly on the north side of the town, which requires expensive foundation work for the construction of buildings higher than two or three stories. One justification for having built the apartment towers was that the extra cost of their foundations would be spread over a large number of dwelling units and another was that some new towners desire the quietude, privacy, and good view afforded by high-rise dwelling units. Cumbernauld's apartment towers are located mainly around the core of the town, producing a density there of about 120 persons per acre, while there is a density of about 70 persons per acre on the southeast slope of the main hill and on the more level land of the site where 97 percent of the town's population resides.[55]

The officials of the Cumbernauld Development Corporation are frequently asked by urbanologists to what extent the town's relatively dense housing pattern meets the stated needs of the residents, most of whom are young married couples with children (it is almost axiomatic in all parts of Great Britain that the majority of families express a desire for a two-story house with a garden, even though such a dwelling is a dream that many of them will never realize). Since it was so expensive to build high-rises in Cumbernauld, and since the risk of monotony with a predominant two-story dwelling pattern would have been negligible due to the town's hilly site providing variations in height and diverse views between houses, it is perhaps unfortunate that so large a proportion of the dwelling units are flats in fairly high buildings.

The generally favorable attitude toward Cumbernauld's housing facilities was clearly illustrated by a survey conducted in 1967 by the Sociology Department of the University of Strathclyde. Seventy-five percent of the people queried stated that they had "bettered themselves" by moving to Cumbernauld and "a better house" was by far the most frequently cited reason, with "a better chance for the children" and "better living conditions" being the next most frequent responses. Of the 107 respondents who did not feel that they had bettered themselves by moving to Cumbernauld, only 22 were discontented with their dwellings. Moreover, in spite of the very small size of the gardens provided with some of Cumbernauld's two-story terrace houses, the survey revealed that of the residents who had a garden or patio, 80.2 percent considered its size "just right" and only 15.5 percent considered it "too small." These "favorable" statistics may be accounted for by an additional finding of the survey, that 55.3 percent of the gardens or patios are used mainly for drying clothes, while, due to long periods of cold weather only 11.6 percent are used primarily for "sitting out."[56]

The Cumbernauld Development Corporation gives priority in rental housing to: (1) persons designated by the City of Glasgow Corporation as "overspill population," provided they have secured a job in Cumbernauld, (2) persons displaced by Glasgow's urban redevelopment projects irrespective of whether or not they have a job in Cumbernauld, and (3) key employees of Cumbernauld's industries and other organizations. After these persons have been housed, the remaining dwellings are rented to other applicants from Glasgow and the surrounding areas. Once accepted, a tenant must remain in his original home there for at least one year before electing to move elsewhere in the town, and then he or she must choose a more expensive dwelling unit.[57]

Only 2 percent of Cumbernauld's residents are home owners. At one time development corporations were allowed to offer 100 percent mortgages for all but the most expensive houses at an interest rate below that charged by building societies, but in 1966 the Ministry of Housing and Local Government brought this arrangement to an end by informing development corporations that they could only be "lenders of last resort" and by requiring them to raise their interest rate to the building-society level. Consequently, most people who buy homes in Cumbernauld and other British new towns with mortgages from building societies and insurance companies are high-income persons who benefit significantly from the tax relief on interest payments, which is equivalent to an annual subsidy of 41 percent of the interest for persons paying the full standard tax rate. Persons with low and even average incomes find it difficult or impossible to qualify for a full mortgage on most new town homes because there are very few older or cheaper houses available.[58]

According to officials of the Cumbernauld Development Corporation, an active social life prevails among the residents, a factor which they attribute in part to the dense housing pattern. However, while there are over 150 voluntary associations in Cumbernauld covering a wide range of interests, there is a serious shortage of suitable premises in which to carry on and expand activities. The Development Corporation, the Dumbarton County Council, and various churches in the town all provide meeting rooms, but these are always heavily booked. This situation may explain why 199 of the 495 Cumbernauld households (40 percent) visited by the sociological research team of the University of Strathclyde in 1967 complained of a lack of adult activities in the town; 51 percent stated that there was a dearth of recreational areas for young people.[59] However, certain groups have not only demonstrated extraordinary imagination but have expended considerable time, money, and effort to adapt existing facilities to their needs. Three examples are the conversion of some farm buildings at Garnhall into riding stables, the use of the old Forth/Clyde Canal for boating events, and the renovation of three old cottages as small theaters for the performing arts.

Other indices of the existence of a strong sense of community in Cumbernauld are the recent organization of the Civic Trust to coordinate the social welfare projects of all the voluntary associations and the formation of a twenty-member elected Town Council, with which the Development Corporation maintains a high-level liaison in addition to its periodic meetings with tenants' organizations in various districts of the town. Religious and educational organizations in Cumbernauld include eight churches operated by the Church of Scotland, the Scottish Episcopal Church, the Roman Catholic Church, the Baptist Church, the Congregational Union, and the United Free Church; eleven primary schools and three secondary schools; and a technical college designed for 10,000 students which was completed in 1973.[60]

In addition to the fact that Burroughs Machines gave Cumbernauld a tremendous head start toward industrial development by its decision to establish operations on the site several years before construction of the new town began, the Cumbernauld Development Corporation has been waging a continuous and enticing campaign to attract more industry since its appointment in 1956. First, building grants are offered under the Local Employment and Industrial Development acts to industries providing new jobs. New firms may receive grants covering as much as 35 percent of the cost of plant construction, and existing firms may receive grants covering 45 percent of the cost of expanding their plants and equipment. Second, the Cumbernauld Development Corporation builds factories to the specific requirements of industrialists for sale or lease (all leases are for ninety-nine years) on attractive terms. Third, the corporation regularly constructs so-called advance factories in anticipation of a demand for them by a wide variety of large and

BIJLMERMEER, THE NETHERLANDS
Construction began in 1968 under the auspices of Town
Development Section, Department of Public Works, Amsterdam.

Bijlmermeer: Panoramic view

Bijlmermeer: Pedestrian underpass

Bijlmermeer: Athletic field

Bijlmermeer: Tot lot near apartment building

Bijlmermeer: Play area

Bijlmermeer: "Streets" or corridors
in apartment buildings

Bijlmermeer: Pedestrian and cyclist pathways

Bijlmermeer: Train from Amsterdam

Bijlmermeer: Pedestrian arcades from garage to apartments

Bijlmermeer: Town center (2 views)

FARSTA, SWEDEN
Project begun in 1965 by AB Farsta Centrum under the auspices of
the Stockholm Real Estate Department.

Farsta: Housing and landscaping (2 examples)

Farsta: Town center

Farsta: Rapid transit train and bus stop

Farsta: Pedestrian underpass

Farsta: Folksum Insurance Company, employing over 1,000

Farsta: Athletic field

Farsta: Pedestrian overpass from town center to residential area

TAPIOLA, FINLAND
Project begun in 1951 by Heikki von Hertzen's
Finnish Housing Foundation.

Tapiola: Keskustorni Administrative Tower, town center

Tapiola: Panoramic view of Tapiola from Keskustorni Tower

Tapiola: Indoor and outdoor pools, Greek theater, fountains, artificial lake

Tapiola: Town center (2 views)

Tapiola: Housing (3 examples)

CUMBERNAULD, SCOTLAND
Designated as a new town in 1955 by Britain's
Department of the Environment.

Cumbernauld: Town center

Cumbernauld: Old town of Cumbernauld adjacent to which new town,
   Cumbernauld, has been built

Cumbernauld: Pedestrian underpass

Cumbernauld: Housing

Cumbernauld: High-rises and open space

CRAWLEY, ENGLAND
Designated as a new town in 1947 by Britain's
Department of the Environment.

Crawley: Town center (2 views)

Crawley: Housing (2 examples)

Crawley: Park

Crawley: Plant in the industrial area

Crawley: Industrial area

Crawley: Single-family housing

Crawley: Row housing

Crawley: Crawley Technical College

small manufacturing operations, as well as buildings which can be used as storage and distribution depots.[61] In 1961 the Development Corporation began constructing "advance" office buildings in order to encourage a broader employment base in Cumbernauld, and recently plans were revised to increase the proportion of office and service employees from 30 to 50 percent.[62] This is an interesting development in terms of the 1967 University of Strathclyde survey which indicated that more than half of the women not already gainfully employed in Cumbernauld would work if employment were available.[63]

As a consequence of all these incentives to industrial and commercial development, there are currently ninety highly diverse firms in Cumbernauld (employing over 8,000 people), including those devoted to the manufacture of office machines, window frames and doors, jointing materials, steel building components, parts for the motor industry, electronic components, paint, carpets, packing cases, shirts, and ladies' underwear, and those concerned with the storage, distribution, or service of compressed-air equipment, earthmoving machinery, floor coverings, pharmaceutical products, surgical supplies, and food.[64] About 50 percent of Cumbernauld's household heads are employed by these industries, the remaining 50 percent commuting largely by public transportation to jobs in surrounding communities, primarily Glasgow.[65]

Anyone visiting Cumbernauld for the first time is certain to be impressed by the quietude and tranquility prevailing in this new town due to the proximity of the countryside in all outward directions, the extensive grassy areas surrounding the buildings, and the fact that none of the dwelling units faces a main road. Conditions are conducive to a family-oriented residential atmosphere. Another impressive fact about Cumbernauld is that nearly 450,000 trees have been planted by the Development Corporation over the past ten years on the premise that landscaping is one of the most essential elements in new-town design. Still another significant condition is that all pedestrian paths leading to the town center, along which are located schools, churches, and recreational centers, are protected from the traffic on intersecting distributory and access roads by attractive bridges and underpasses, an important result of which is that Cumbernauld's pedestrian-auto accident rate is less than 20 percent of the national average in Scotland. Finally, besides building over 1,000 dwelling units annually in the new town, the Development Corporation has renovated the interiors and exteriors of many buildings in the contiguous old village of Cumbernauld, where the population has increased from 800 to 3,000 since the new town was developed, resulting in some new residential construction in the village as well.[66]

The Example of Crawley, England

Crawley, a 6,047-acre site approximately thirty miles south of London at the juncture of the counties of Surrey, West Sussex, and East Sussex and encompassing the villages of Crawley, Three Bridges, and Ifield, was designated as a new town by the Ministry of Housing and Local Government on January 9, 1947. The only one of the eight English new towns located south of London, Crawley, whose original inhabitants numbered only 10,000, has a target population of 80,000.[67] Unlike Cumbernauld, Crawley is divided into neighborhoods, all of which are located within a mile and a half of the town center, and most of the housing is single-family dwellings. To the ten original neighborhoods, whose names are Langley Green, Ifield, Gossops Green, West Green, Furnace Green, Northgate, Southgate, Tilgate, Pound Hill, and Three Bridges, an eleventh—Broadfield—was recently added in the southwest corner of Crawley (see Chart 4.12).

Designed to be largely self-sufficient, each of Crawley's neighborhoods contains within short walking distance of all its residents a primary school, a church, a community meeting hall, several (seven to twenty) small businesses such as grocery stores, bakeries, meat shops, and pharmacies, and a pub. The neighborhood pubs have highly descriptive names such as "The Maid of Sussex" in Three Bridges, "Dr. Johnson" in Langley Green, "The White Knight" in Pound Hill, "The Apple Tree" in West Green, "The Black Dog" in Northgate, "The Pelham Buckle" in Ifield, "The Downsman" in Southgate, and "The Windmill" in Gossops Green. Approximately 20,000 students attend Crawley's twenty-seven primary and secondary schools, the latter being situated along the neighborhood peripheries just off the main roads. Crawley's twenty-two churches represent nine denominations: Church of England (eight churches), Roman Catholic (five), Baptist (two), Congregational (two), Methodist (one), Plymouth Brethren (one), Free

Church (one), Mormon (one), and Jehovah's Witnesses (one).[68] Within each neighborhood one of the most positive features of the residential areas is the layout of the streets in such a way as to avoid monotony. Some roads curve and wind, while others are cul-de-sacs around which houses are grouped in the form of a square, irregular rectangle, or triangle.

There are four major criticisms of Crawley's otherwise excellent neighborhood plan. One is that the main London-Brighton road passes through Crawley on the west, separating the three neighborhoods of Langley Green, Ifield, and Gossops Green from the rest of the town. Moreover, the hazard presented by the seventy-mile-an-hour traffic on this bypass is aggravated by the fact that there are only two pedestrian bridges and one underpass across the road. Over the next five years, however, a second London-Brighton road will be constructed east of Crawley to reduce the traffic load on the older road. A second negative feature of Crawley's neighborhood layout is the segregation of the Pound Hill neighborhood by the high railway embankment on the east side of town. Third, the Broadfield neighborhood currently being developed southwest of Crawley for a population of 14,000 will extend well beyond the area designated for the new town, encompassing parts of the rural districts of Cuckfield and Horsham. This is a regrettable situation because it does not conform to the principles upon which Crawley was established; Broadfield sprawls across the greenbelt as originally conceived and constitutes more of a small town joined to Crawley than a neighborhood proportionate to the other ten, none of which has a population in excess of 9,500.[69] A fourth criticism relates to Crawley's residences in that several neighborhoods have an insufficient mixture of dwelling types. The concentration of larger homes built for owner-occupancy by the Development Corporation in West Green and by private builders in Ifield, Gossops Green, and Furnace Green, for example, has resulted in the segregation of executives and professionals from the majority of the new-town residents who, in turn, tend to regard these neighborhoods as socially exclusive. On the other hand, some neighborhoods have too high a concentration of small houses for rental by lower income groups. A more heterogeneous housing pattern would have afforded greater variety in the social as well as in the architectural aspects of these neighborhoods. It is unfortunate, too, that Crawley's footpaths and streets cross at many points without the protection of a bridge or tunnel and that its roads cannot adequately handle present traffic demands.

Both the Development Corporation and the New Towns Commission have found the cost of constructing and administering apartment towers substantially greater than that for individual houses. And, in accord with the wishes of the majority of Crawley's residents, they have concentrated on building a great variety (nearly 250 different styles) of largely brick homes with gardens, ten to fourteen units per acre. Consequently, 90 percent of Crawley's dwellings are single or semidetached houses, 75 percent of which have three bedrooms; 15 percent, two bedrooms; 5 percent, one bedroom; 4 percent, four bedrooms, and 1 percent, five bedrooms. Some of the one- and two-bedroom houses are bungalows for the elderly. The remaining 10 percent are one and two bedroom or combination bedroom and sitting room flats.[70]

Besides Crawley's 12,000 rental units owned by the New Towns Commission, there are about 2,000 rental units owned by the Urban District Council and 3,000 privately owned dwellings.[71] Crawley has a higher rate of home ownership—about 20 percent—than any of Britain's thirty new towns because it is the second oldest among them, having been so designated almost twenty years before the Ministry of Housing and Local Government restricted the mortgage-granting powers of development corporations and their successors, the New Towns Commissions (detailed above). While all of Crawley's privately owned homes have garages, and the rented units have group garages, one of the town's major problems at present is a shortage of about 1,000 automobile shelters (despite the fact that the ratio of garages to dwelling units has increased from 1 to 12 to 1 to 3 since construction of the town began in 1947).[72]

Rents for different types of accommodations in Crawley are shown in Table 1. The sale price of the average three bedroom home in Crawley is about $15,000, and the purchaser must usually make at least a 5-percent down payment. While both privately owned and corporation owned dwelling units in Crawley and in the other British new towns have always been eligible for government subsidies in the form of reduced tax rates and rents, respectively, these subsidies were, until recently, granted to the sponsors of the dwelling units rather than to their occupants, with the result that in some

Table 4–1
Weekly Rent Ranges in Crawley[73]

Size of Dwelling	Rent Ranges in Shillings*
Bedroom–sitting room flat	28–34
One-bedroom bungalow	40–46
One-bedroom flat	34–39
Two-bedroom flat	39–46
Two-bedroom house	42–56
Three-bedroom house	42–71
Four-bedroom house	54–70
Five-bedroom house	67–76

*1 Shilling = approximately 13¢.

cases tenants most in need of financial assistance received the least.[74] Since liberalization of its housing subsidy program in 1971, however, the government has been giving rent rebates directly to needy families living in corporation owned dwelling units (see explanation of the Greater London Council's new rent-rebate scheme, Chart 4.13).

Crawley's vital pivot, as in all new towns, is its town center (see Chart 4.14), the heart of which Queen's Square, a fairly large paved space with one vehicular thoroughfare, Queensway, passing through the center and joining another, Broadway, on the west side to form a "T." Since the town center is within walking distance of all parts of Crawley, it is unfortunate that it was not planned as a completely pedestrian precinct. Queensway could have terminated east of the main block of shops and Broadway could have terminated in a cul-de-sac at the end of the shopping blocks both north and south of Queen's Square. The main square is closed to vehicles on Fridays and Saturdays, however, and proposals are currently under consideration for a general rearrangement of traffic in the area which would lead to a greater separation of people and vehicles at all times. In general, Crawley's town center has a pleasant appearance: groups of trees and flower tubs occupy two corners of Queen's Square; plenty of seating is available for shoppers' relaxation; there is a Victorian bandstand and an attractive fountain designed by Bainbridge Copnall; and the latest addition is a clock tower donated by the New Towns Commission whose bells chime hourly the music from the film *Genevieve*. Grouped around these facilities are over 150 shops.

A pedestrian mall, Broadwalk—opposite Queen's Square on

the other side of Broadway—leads to Old High Street, the center of town life in Old Crawley where for centuries a market has been held near the medieval church and inn. On the perimeter of the town center large car parks have been provided for the approximately 25 percent of the patrons at any given time who come from outside Crawley.[75] Several new facilities are similarly located, including an entertainment center with a cinema, bowling alley, and ballroom; the main post office; the Telephone Exchange Building; the town hall; the College of Further Education with over 4,000 students; a swimming pool; Crawley Hospital; a library; fire and police stations; and the bus and railway stations. Above the railway station is a large office building from which British Railways derives considerable revenue, but as yet no parking garage has been constructed to accommodate the tremendous amount of automobile traffic generated by this complex. Still another unfortunate planning error in Crawley was the designation of an extensive area between the railway and bus stations for commercial development. This would have been a superb site for the proposed arts pavilion because of its proximity to the railway station, preparing the way for Crawley's becoming a regional cultural center. However, it appears that this objective has been subordinated to economic goals.

It is a basic principle of new town policy in Britain that work as well as housing must be provided to insure that new towns do not merely become dormitory suburbs of the cities whose overspill population they are designed to accommodate. A number of the older new towns can now rely to a considerable extent on the continued expansion of the industry already established in them, and some of the new towns most recently designated contain substantial existing centers of employment.

One of the most important tasks of a development corporation is to attract to its town a number of industrial and commercial companies. Under the central government's policy for the location of industry in the country as a whole, industrial development is guided by the Department of Trade and Industry to areas where it is most needed in the local and national interest; in carrying out this policy, the department gives high priority to the new towns. All the new towns are able to offer special advantages, such as the allocation of houses for a firm's employees and space for expansion, and on the whole, costs are lower than in crowded urban areas.[76]

Crawley's beautifully landscaped industrial area is located north of the town center adjoining the London-Brighton road and railway. Diversification is by design one of the main characteristics of this area, insuring a variety of jobs and full employment for most residents. Some ninety firms, including those engaged in light engineering, electronics, metalworking, woodworking, printing, plastics, pharmaceuticals, foods, and clothing, employ approximately 20,000 persons, nearly 10,000 of whom are not Crawley residents. About 3,000 of Crawley's residents—mainly professionals, married women, and single girls—work in London because of the lack of suitable employment in Crawley or because they prefer to spend their days in a bustling big-city environment.[77] Two methods have been used to finance Crawley's industries. The larger firms have invested over £10 million in the construction of buildings erected on sites leased from the Development Corporation or the New Towns Commission for ninety-nine years, while smaller firms requiring lesser amounts of standardized space have leased factories built by the two agencies.[78] A large office building, a service garage, and five banks are also located in Crawley's industrial area.

The population of Crawley has immigrated mainly from South London, and decentralizing industrial firms have brought as high as 90 percent of their employees with them. The population is highly stable (fewer than 0.2 percent per year return to London) since most residents prefer living in a house with a garden to living in a flat. Residents consist largely of married couples twenty to forty years of age who find Crawley's country air healthful for their children as well as for aged parents.[79]

The success of any community, however, depends heavily on widespread participation in, and satisfaction from, its leisure-time activities. There has been some criticism among Crawley's residents that social, recreational, and cultural activities take place too exclusively within neighborhoods rather than on a combined neighborhood basis. Provision for clubrooms and a multipurpose hall for cultural and special interest activities in Crawley's town center would not only insure sufficient support for these activities by making them accessible to residents from every neighborhood, but would contribute significantly to community cohesiveness. A circular bus route enabling people from the various neighborhoods to travel together to town-center social activities is also an urgent need. As one of the town residents, a sociologist, has commented: "One must either have his own means of transport or enjoy long evening walks, because public transport facilities do not encourage travel between neighborhoods. Bus service is provided between each neighborhood and the town center ... but there is no route around the town." [80]

AN EVALUATION OF BRITAIN'S NEW TOWNS

Britain's new towns, two of which have just been described in detail, have become internationally famous. Thousands of urban planners, architects, and builders have visited them; countries in every part of the world have imitated them in varying degrees; and innumerable journal articles and books have assessed their significance, some positively and others negatively. Several reasons account for this widespread interest in Britain's new towns.

1. They have proved that there is no intrinsic incompatibility between individual freedom and private property rights, on the one hand, and society's right to plan for the common good, on the other. As this chapter has shown, Britain has used the power of law and direct government action rather than persuasion and financial incentives to produce its new towns. In the process it has reduced congestion in the largest cities, provided a more humane living environment for nearly a million people, and distributed economic opportunities more equitably throughout England, Scotland, and Wales without depriving any group of its fundamental right to enjoy "the good life."

2. Britain's new towns have set an example for the world that orderly urban organization can be more than just a dream, that it can become a successful reality. Their superblock neighborhood plans, their neighborhood shops supplementing the town center facilities, their aesthetic mixture of housing styles and low densities, their cul-de-sac streets and separation of pedestrian and vehicular traffic, their beautiful landscaping and plentiful open space, their heterogeneous populations (with respect to race, age, and socioeconomic condition), their special housing provisions for the elderly, their economic self-sufficiency, and their successful blending of public and private development are all innovative features which not only make Britain's new towns model communities for other

countries to emulate, but highly desirable residential environments for British citizens. Indeed, the population turnover in Britain's new towns has been less than 4 percent.[81] But perhaps the most convincing evidence of the success of Britain's new towns to critics with a free enterprise bias is that the oldest ones have been financially profitable, and most economists are convinced that the others will in time repay the enormous investment which the government has made in them.

3. Today, with the worldwide interest in ecology, Britain's new towns have become especially interesting as concrete examples of how complex and technologically sophisticated societies can house their large populations comfortably and accommodate their numerous industrial and commercial establishments in the most modern facilities without abusing nature and without wasting open space. Indeed, despite its being an island with a relatively high population density, about 80 percent of Britain's land is still farmland, forest, and open space.[82]

4. Britain's new towns also adhere to the principle enunciated by Aristotle that "cities ought not to grow beyond what their bones and sinews were devised to support," for each of them is surrounded by an inviolable greenbelt which has prevented them from sprawling over into the countryside as most American cities have done. Indeed, in the United States our major cities have been sprawling so far that the phenomenon of megalopolis is observable in about thirteen areas across the country. Metropolitan areas distances apart are converging to form one continuous strip of urban development with little or no open space to relieve the monotony or to refresh the human spirit.

Yet, Britain's new towns have been criticized on several grounds.

1. Some urban planners contend that Britain's earliest new towns have too much open space, causing them to have more of a rural than an urban atmosphere.

2. Another objection which applies mainly to Britain's earliest new towns and which their planners admit is a valid criticism concerns street and parking inadequacies, the latter seen both in the residential areas and at the town centers. This situation can be explained by the planners' failure to anticipate fully the tremen-

dous increase in automobile ownership that occurred after 1950.

3. During the past quarter century since the British government began building new towns, only 2 percent of the population—about 1 million persons—has moved to them.[83] This is largely due to the fact that too few new towns have been built in Britain, and as a result they cannot adequately relieve the congestion and poor housing conditions prevailing in the large cities. As Prime Minister Harold Wilson commented during ceremonies at Stevenage marking the twenty-first anniversary of the British government's new-town building program:

> It is sad that more of our people . . . cannot enjoy the quality of environment found here and in our other new towns. The need for more new towns remains as urgent as ever. The new towns program will take on a new dimension in the 1970s. By concentrating our efforts on bigger schemes, we can achieve a faster and more economical rate of building. Because the pull of the great conurbations now extends far beyond their boundaries, we are thinking in terms of locating new towns much farther out—not 20 or 25 miles, but 60 or 70 miles. There is a growing recognition that even a regional new town approach to the problems of dealing with population growth and dispersal will not be sufficient. We have to think in terms of a need for new, even larger, planned urban areas —city regions, each to provide for many hundreds of thousands of people.[84]

4. In terms of architectural design and construction quality, British new-town housing is inferior to most housing in the United States. This comparison is not really a fair one, however, because the bulk of British new-town housing is low-cost public housing, while most housing in the United States is relatively expensive private housing. More important, however, when British new-town housing is compared with the housing available to the average citizen in Britain's large cities, it represents a considerable improvement and, in some instances, luxury.

5. Probably the best-known criticism of new towns is the depression of their housewives and the boredom of their teenagers, both popularly referred to as the "new-town blues" syndrome. Housewives complain about physical and social isolation

and the young people about the dearth of excitement and recreational activities. In response to these criticisms, some new-town proponents and officials claim that it is "normal" for people to complain when they move to any new environment because of the many adjustments which must be made and because of a lingering nostalgia for the life left behind, but, in time, the normal person is as happy or satisfied (sometimes even more so) in his new environment as in the previous one. In fact, considerable psychological research supports the theory that a planned living environment is more conducive to good mental health than an unplanned one. Moreover, there is a tendency for some new town residents to remember only the positive features of their previous environment—the large number of cinemas and other recreational facilities, neighbors known since childhood, and the big-city noise and hustle-bustle—and to forget the squalor of their former homes and neighborhoods, the crime in the streets, and the long, tiring trips to work each day.

THE USE OF URBAN GROWTH CENTERS
IN BRITAIN AND SCANDINAVIA

Five years after the beginning of the new towns program in Great Britain, an alternate called the "growth center program" was initiated, the principal differences between the two programs being the structure and scale of operations and the financing. The growth-center scheme consists of an agreement between a large city and a smaller municipality whereby the latter, with financial aid from the former, undertakes the large-scale development of housing, factories, and offices for people and firms relocated from the large city, but the expansion is not of such a magnitude as to transform the smaller town completely (as is the case when new towns develop around an existing village or settlement.) Two of the new towns in the northeast of Britain, Newton Aycliffe and Peterlee, are currently serving as focal points for greater urban development in that region under the growth center program.[85] Inasmuch as both rural and urban settlements and their accompanying economic and social activities are well developed and prospering in most of Western Europe, there is relatively little use there of the growth-center mechanism. Sweden, Finland, and Norway, however, are exceptions to this broad generalization; each of these countries has sizable land areas which are still essentially frontier in nature. In Sweden, for example, three towns have been classified as growth centers—Oxelösund, Märsta, and Stenungsund—each of which will be developed to a population of 30,000 to 40,000.[86] In Finland, too, Heikki von Hertzen, the charismatic "father" of Tapiola, has formulated a plan for seven communities of 50,000 to 200,000 inhabitants each—some completely new and others expansions of existing towns—in keeping with national economic development goals and the concept of a better distribution of urban population.[87]

THE RELEVANCE OF EUROPE'S PLANNING POLICIES AND PROGRAMS FOR THE UNITED STATES

Despite the fact that the United States has had the kind of urban problems which have barely touched Europe—a much more rapid rate of urbanization at an early stage in development, the technological pressures associated with affluence, and discrimination against racial minorities—the relevance of Europe's planning policies and programs for the United States becomes apparent when one recognizes that these two geographic areas share important characteristics, problems, and goals. First and foremost, there are common human requirements for space, light, clean air, safety, mobility, tranquility, and social unity which transcend even major differences in historical background and culture, and which must dictate the structure of every urban community if its residents are to function efficiently and happily. Second, besides sharing many cultural and political traditions, Europe and the United States are in a roughly comparable stage of urbanization. Third, both must cope with similar problems resulting from the increasing concentration of population in metropolitan areas. A related problem shared by Europe and the United States is how to deal with rising land prices in order to assure that such increases result in the allocation of land to its best use in an economic sense and that social priorities supersede economic priorities whenever the public welfare is at stake.

We will go on in Chapter 5 to describe how pre–Civil War community development in the United States reflected the best of European urban planning tradition and how this pattern broke down during the late nineteenth century under the pressures of immigration and industrialization. Not until the 1960s was there a revival of concern for the quality of urban life in America and, once again, a tendency to emulate more socially enlightened European urban planning policies and programs, as best exemplified, perhaps, by the new-towns movement.

Chart 4.1   Organization of Physical Planning in the Netherlands

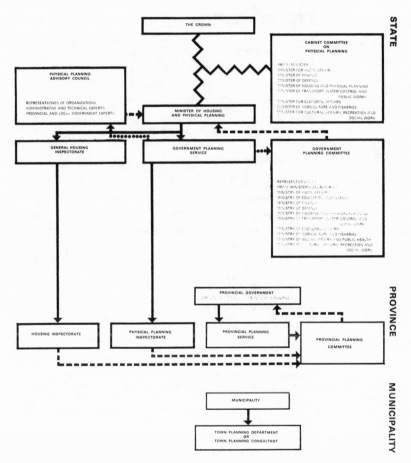

Source: R. Idenburg, *Spotlight on the Future* (The Hague: Government Publishing Office, 1971), p. 48.

Chart 4.2   The Statutory Procedure for a Municipal Development Plan

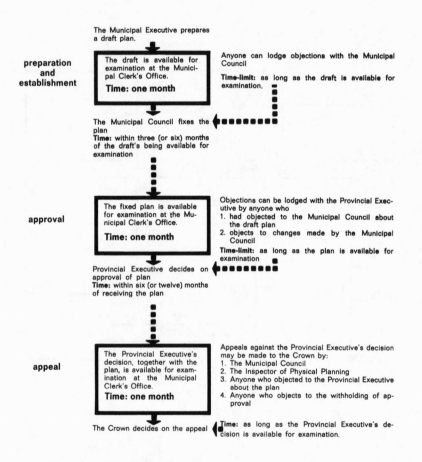

preparation
and
establishment

The Municipal Executive prepares a draft plan.

The draft is available for examination at the Municipal Clerk's Office.
Time: one month

Anyone can lodge objections with the Municipal Council

Time-limit: as long as the draft is available for examination.

The Municipal Council fixes the plan
Time: within three (or six) months of the draft's being available for examination

approval

The fixed plan is available for examination at the Municipal Clerk's Office.
Time: one month

Objections can be lodged with the Provincial Executive by anyone who
1. had objected to the Municipal Council about the draft plan
2. objects to changes made by the Municipal Council

Time-limit: as long as the plan is available for examination

Provincial Executive decides on approval of plan
Time: within six (or twelve) months of receiving the plan

appeal

The Provincial Executive's decision, together with the plan, is available for examination at the Municipal Clerk's Office.
Time: one month

Appeals against the Provincial Executive's decision may be made to the Crown by:
1. The Municipal Council
2. The Inspector of Physical Planning
3. Anyone who objected to the Provincial Executive about the plan
4. Anyone who objects to the withholding of approval

The Crown decides on the appeal

Time: as long as the Provincial Executive's decision is available for examination.

Source: R. Idenburg, p. 70.

Chart 4.3   Agglomeratie Amsterdam

Source: Reprinted by permission of the Public Works' Department, Amsterdam.

Chart 4.4 Suburban Residential Development by City District, Center Development, and Transit System Extensions in the Western and Southern Stockholm Suburbs.

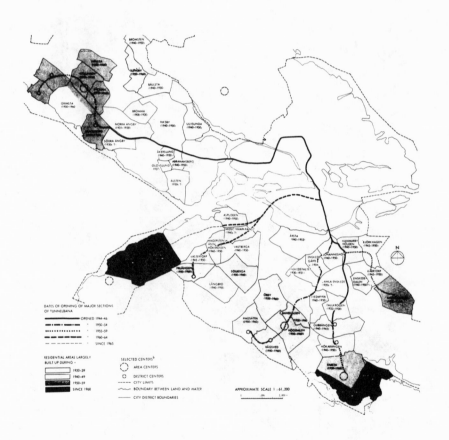

Source: David Pass, *Vallingby and Farsta—From Idea to Reality: The New Community Development Process in Stockholm.* By permission of the MIT Press.

Chart 4.5   Farsta (site plan)

Site plan: Scale 1:12,000. 1. Farsta Centre, 2. parking, 3. underground railway station, 4. higher secondary school, 5. secondary school, 6. primary school,
7. day nursery, 8. sport hall and open-air bath, 9. large sports ground, 10. riding school, 11. Farsta natural reserve, 12. substation for heating by atomic
power, 13. boiler room, 14. offices and laboratories for Royal Tele-Communi-
cations Service, 15. industrial area, 16. harbor for small boats.

Source: David Pass, by permission of the MIT Press.

Chart 4.6   Model for Stockholm's Post–World War II Suburban Communities

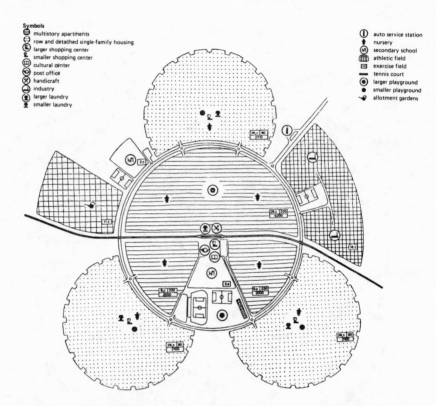

Symbols

- multistory apartments
- row and detached single-family housing
- larger shopping center
- smaller shopping center
- cultural center
- post office
- handicraft
- industry
- larger laundry
- smaller laundry

- auto service station
- nursery
- secondary school
- athletic field
- exercise field
- tennis court
- larger playground
- smaller playground
- allotment gardens

Development took place along the transit line, with a community center at the station. Multistory housing was constructed immediately adjacent to the Center, single family housing farther away. The Center provided facilities for social activities in a community hall, and there were premises for cultural activities for the community. However, in contrast to the English model, there was no local self-government. (Adapted from: Stockholms stads stadsplanekontor, *Generalplan för Stockholm 1952*, p. 123.)

Source: David Pass, by permission of the MIT Press.

Chart 4.7 Farsta Community Center

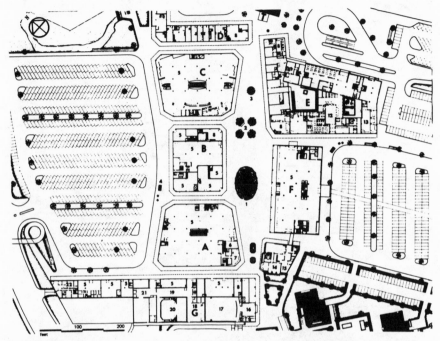

A Tempo department store
B Shops, library, and offices
C Kvickly department store
D Shops, offices, and church
E Shops, post office, pharmacy, medical and dental consulta-
   tion rooms, mothers' welfare center, public dental service
   and social welfare service
F NK department store
G Cinema, community hall, youth center, shops, offices,
   police station, car repair workshop, and premises for small
   industries
L Restaurant

1. pond,   2. fountain,   3. planted tree,   4 parcel delivery
office,   5 sales,   6. confectionery,   7. storage,   8. bank,
9. cafeteria,   10. news and ticket office,   11. pharmacy,
12. post office,   13. liquor store,   14. restaurant,
15. restaurant kitchen,   16. cinema,   17. cinema foyer,
18. assembly hall,   19. vestibule,   20. theater,
21. youth center,   22. police station.

Source: David Pass, by permission of the MIT Press.

135

Chart 4.8 Tapiola
(site plan)

136

Source: Tapiola Information Center, Tapiola, Finland.

Chart 4.9   New Towns of Britain

Source: Ministry of Housing and Local Government

138

Chart 4.10   Cumbernauld, Scotland (site plan)   Source: Cumbernauld Development Corporation

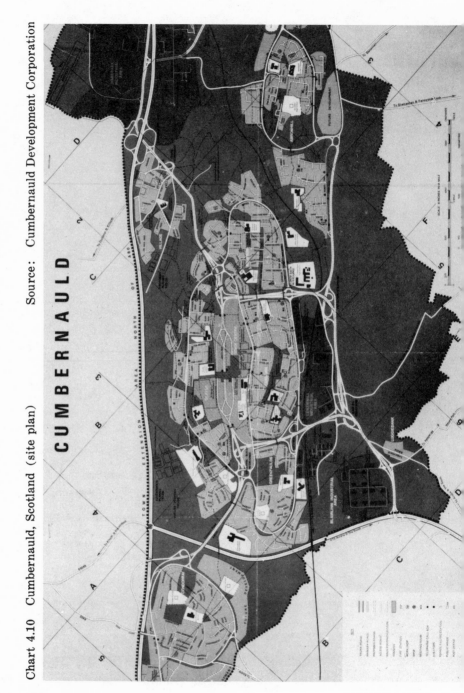

Chart 4.11   Town Centre Planned Layout (Cumbernauld, Scotland)

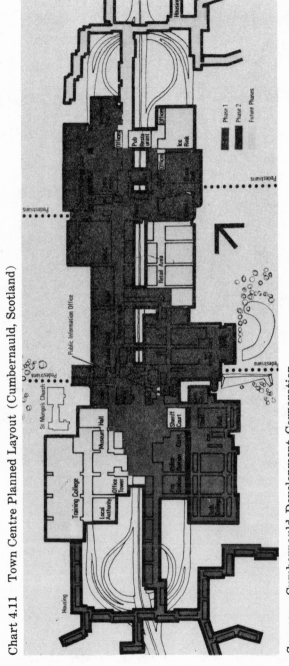

Source: Cumbernauld Development Corporation

Chart 4.12   Crawley Road Map

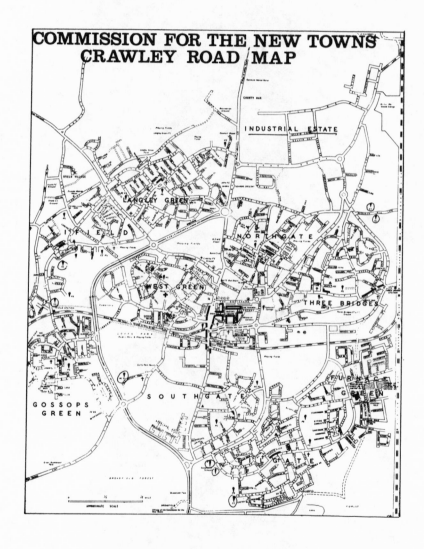

Source: Commission for the New Towns, Crawley, England, 1970.

Chart 4.13   The Greater London Council's Rent Rebate Scheme

The Council's rent rebate scheme, introduced in September 1968, was modified for the third time in March 1971 to allow payment of more generous rebates. Basically the system operates by (a) establishing the income of husband and wife (allowing for certain deductions), (b) determining how much of this income is necessary for essentials, excluding rent, (c) calculating what income then remains so as to see what part of it can be afforded as rent, bearing in mind that a small minimum rent is always payable and that all adults—not only tenant and wife—should contribute towards the rent and (d) comparing what can be afforded with the normal rent to see if a rebate is to be granted.

Looking at these four stages in greater detail:

(a) *Reckonable income* — Comprises the gross weekly income of husband and wife from all sources, including pensions, income from investments and education grants payable to the tenant. Family allowances and maternity benefit are excluded along with the first £2 of the wife's earnings and the first £2 of any disability pension. Any contributions made by other members of the household are ignored (but see also (c) below).

(b) *Amount necessary for essentials* — Known as the 'basic family income requirement', this is fixed at £7.50 a week for a single person, £12 for a married couple or a widow or widower with dependent children. £1 is allowed for each dependent child.

(c) *Amount that can be afforded as rent* — From what is left, if any, after the amount needed for essentials is taken from the family income, it is assumed one fifth of the first £5 and one quarter of the remainder can be paid in rent. To this must be added the minimum rent payable in all cases (50p to 87p a week according to size, age and type of dwelling). The rent that can be afforded must also allow for an assumed contribution from other adults and an addition is made of 50p per week for anyone aged 19 to 20 and £1 for anyone 21 and over. The total under (c) is known as the tenant's 'rent paying capacity'.

(d) *Amount payable as rent* — What the tenant can afford as rent (the rent paying capacity) is then compared with the actual rent of the dwelling. If it is higher, the full rent is paid; if it is lower by at least 10p, the tenant pays only the rent paying capacity and receives a rebate equal to the difference between this and the fixed rent of the dwelling.

As with other local authorities, rebates are only granted if application is made by the tenant. Certain categories of dwelling (e.g. higher rented accommodation) are excluded from the scheme as also are tenants receiving supplementary Social Security benefits, taking full account of the rent payable under the tenancy.

Example 1. Family consisting of husband, wife, and 3 children, living in a flat with a normal rent of £4 per week.

(a) Assume husband earns £15 per week, excluding Family Allowances.

	£ p
Basic allowance for husband and wife	12.00
Basic allowance on 3 children	
3 at £1	3.00
	£15.00

Actual income also equals £15
Therefore he pays only the *basic minimum net rent*—87p and gets a rebate of £3.13.
This rent will not be increased unless his financial position improves.

(b) If the husband earned £22 a week, his rent paying capacity would be as follows:

	£ p
On first £15 as above	0.87
On next £5 (one-fifth)	1.00
On balance of £2 (one-quarter)	0.50
Total rent paying capacity	£2.37

Rebate £1.63

Example 2. Widow, with 3 children.
Earnings £15 per week. Family allowances ignored.

	£ p
Basic allowance for widow	12.00
Basic allowance 3 children	3.00
	15.00
Earnings £15, less £2 as a "wife" at work	13.00

This is less than the basic allowance so she pays only the basic minimum rent, say 75p to 87p, although the actual rent is £3.50 net

Example 3. Family consists of husband, wife, and 2 children.

Husband earns £22, wife earns £10.

	£ p
Basic allowance, husband, wife, and 2 children	14.00
Rent paying capacity	
On basic allowance as above (£14)	0.87

Take earnings of £32, allow £2 for wife earning and £14 for basic allowance, leaves £16.

	£ p
On first £5 (one fifth)	1.00
On remaining £11 (one quarter)	2.75
Rent paying capacity	4.62
Actual net rent (new flat built 1969)	5.50

Rebate 88p.

Source: The Greater London Council, London, England, 1972.

Chart 4.14   Crawley Town Centre

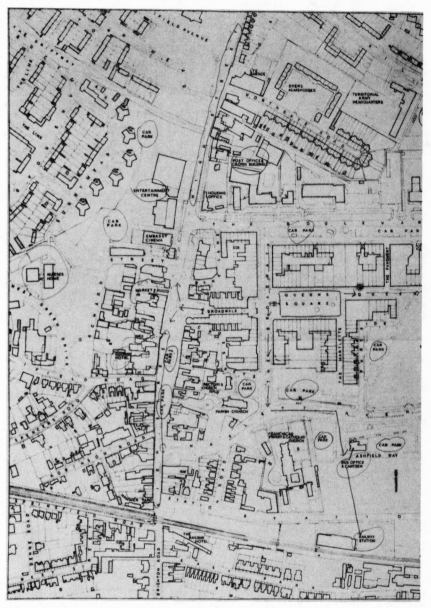

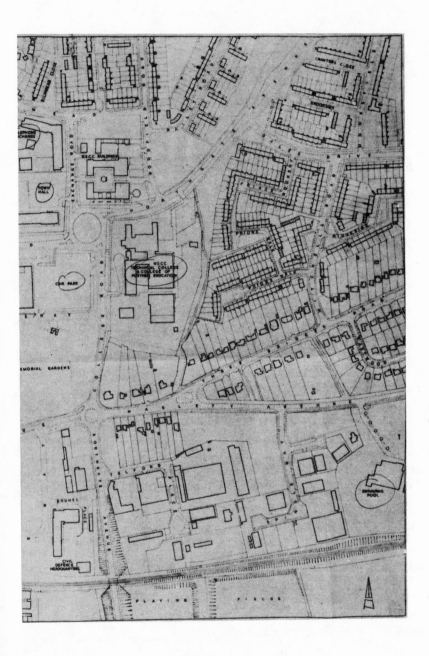

Source: Commission for the New Towns, Crawley, England, 1969.

Chapter 5

Urban Planning Policies and Programs: The American Experience

Some of the most inspiring town planning in the history of America occurred in the colonial period, in great part due to the tremendous spirit of creativity of the pioneers as they settled a new nation. The new communities built by our forefathers reflected their determination to prevent the overcrowded conditions that prevailed in the European cities from which they had come, and introduce such features of Renaissance urban planning as public gardens, plazas, and squares which not only enhance the appearance of a city but facilitate social interaction and the enjoyment of nature. The intensity of their determination must have been very great indeed, considering that the new communities which they established were completely surrounded by open space and forests. However, the first urban planning legislation in America was imposed upon the colonists in 1573 by King Philip II of Spain, whose Laws of the Indies specified in detail the criteria for selecting the location and for designing the layout of such new communities as St. Augustine and Pensacola, Florida; San Antonio, Texas; and Los Angeles and San Diego, California.

144

In the New England area, significant new community development did not occur until settlement of the Massachusetts Bay Colony around 1630. Once it began, however, a gridiron pattern was followed in most instances, the central square constituting the community center which typically contained a church representing the principal denomination in the town, a meeting house, and other public facilities. The best example of this plan was New Haven, Connecticut, established in 1638, which could boast that the central square of its nine constituent blocks was the largest village green in New England.[1] From the standpoint of controlled growth, the new communities in New England were in an extremely favorable position because many of their landowners also had properties in the surrounding countryside, and as they were committed to the idea of preserving a greenbelt around urban settlements, the character of these properties as farmland or woodland was retained. Another powerful incentive, of course, was the colonists' need to grow their own food and provide for their fuel (wood from the trees) from these properties. As a result, not until recent years did many of America's earliest new towns in New England expand beyond their original boundaries. Whenever population exceeded the optimum level for the town's prescribed limit, the surplus people simply moved elsewhere and established other communities. Surplus population from the fishing-farming village of Ipswich, Massachusetts, for example, moved to Marietta, Ohio, a community established by the Ohio Company of Associates under the leadership of the creative town planner, General Rufus Putnam.[2] Contemporary planning officials who contend that new towns are an unrealistic and untested solution to relieving the congestion and attendant problems of America's cities would do well to recall that this approach is not new. Indeed, it is as old as our nation, dating back to colonial times.

The first new-town legislation originating in the United States was passed in Virginia and Maryland between 1662 and 1706, designating twenty fifteen-acre sites in the former colony and fifty-seven hundred-acre sites in the latter for the development of new communities, some of which formed the nucleus of present cities in these two states. Few of the new towns resulting from this legislation possessed a unique design, however, the most notable exceptions being Annapolis, Maryland, and Williamsburg, Virginia, both laid out with a diagonal street plan by Francis Nicholson (who became Lieutenant Governor of Virginia in 1695 and Governor of Maryland in 1699). Nicholson's plans for the two towns reflected his familiarity with and admiration for the plans of Sir Christopher Wren and John Evelyn for the reconstruction of London following the Great Fire of 1666.[3] William Penn's plan for Philadelphia executed in 1683, however, was by far the most impressive and effective of all American seventeenth-century urban-development schemes. Although the plan utilized the conventional gridiron pattern (see Chart 5.1), its creation of the first inner-city park in the United States and its broad scope, including the conversion of about 10,000 acres of land outside the city into agricultural villages and the development of a road system to link them with Philadelphia, made it spectacular for the times. During the early part of the eighteenth century, Savannah was the most notable new community developed (1733). General James Oglethorpe's plan for Savannah was certainly not distinctive for its gridiron pattern (see Chart 5.1), but it was notable for its provision of gardens specifically designated for research in agronomy, botany, and horticulture.

The most significant urban planning decision during the eighteenth century, however, was that of George Washington, around 1791. He decided to establish the seat of the federal government in Washington, fulfilling his requirement that the city selected proffer a route to the west, for he envisioned a canal linking the Potomac River with the Ohio River—the gateway to the frontier.[4] Pierre L'Enfant, the young architect who planned the city, combined his European experience with the aristocratic tastes of our Founding Fathers, eschewing any distinctively American features. Instead of following the gridiron plan of Savannah or Philadelphia, he laid out Washington's streets in irregular rectangles and superimposed upon them a diagonal system of avenues which made possible many open spaces in squares, circles, and triangles. While L'Enfant's design had an impact on two other cities (Buffalo, New York, established in 1804, and Indianapolis, Indiana, in 1821), the conventional gridiron or checkerboard pattern remained the popular one throughout the nineteenth century, as indicated by the plans for the cities of Denver, Dallas, Seattle, and San Francisco.

The gridiron system permeated the planning of American cities for more than a century, mainly because it facilitated the dividing and subdividing of land into lots by developers.[5]

THE PRE-CIVIL WAR INDUSTRIAL
AND RELIGIOUS COMMUNITIES

The initial impact of industrialization upon America in the early nineteenth century was felt in the New England area, where the labor force in the mills consisted largely of single females; the War of 1812 and the burgeoning frontier made heavy demands upon the male population. Realizing, however, that no self-respecting father would permit his young daughter to venture into factory life unless certain protective measures were taken, Francis Cabot Lowell provided boardinghouses with chaperones for the female loom operators employed by his textile mill in the Massachusetts company town which he built in 1822 and named after himself.[6] Subsequently, his company town was repeated with variations throughout New England, notably in Waltham and Chicopee Falls, Massachusetts, and in Manchester, New Hampshire. The urban-industrial labor force of that period was guaranteed humane employment conditions and high wages because of the existence of the frontier, for the availability of cheap land in the west made it possible for discontented laborers to readily escape oppressive working situations. Thus the quality of life in the pre-Civil War company towns far excelled that which prevailed later when a labor surplus and historical influences altered the entire character and structure of company towns.

The most successful new town developers during the nineteenth century were the Mormons who constructed several relatively large, viable communities in spite of the fact that they were subjected to constant persecution for their strong sense of commitment to their leaders and to their religious beliefs. In 1840, for example, they built the city of Nauvoo, Illinois, which embodied the criteria for a Mormon community set down by their leader, Joseph Smith, anticipating by over fifty years Ebenezer Howard's ideal garden city concept: delimited city size; zoning to prevent undesirable land uses; wide streets; density and aesthetic controls.[7] Under the leadership of Brigham Young the Mormons were also responsible for the creation of the last major planned city in the United

States prior to the Civil War—Salt Lake City, Utah. Construction began in 1849 based on plans for the "City of Zion," the utopian community concept which contained many innovative features embodied by twentieth-century American and European new towns and which was transmitted by Joseph Smith to the Elders of the Mormon Church in 1833. Salt Lake City was also the last to be built of the new communities sponsored by various religious groups over a one-hundred-year period beginning with the Moravians' establishment of Bethlehem, Pennsylvania, in 1741.[8]

The three-century history of American community planning and building from the colonial period to the Civil War was a reflection of the nation's youth and the pioneering spirit of its settlers. In the slightly more than a century since the Civil War, however, that three-hundred-year-old tradition of creative community planning and controlled urban growth has been almost completely obliterated. Even Washington, D.C. has been allowed to expand beyond the limits of L'Enfant's plan and to become integrated into the sprawling six-hundred-mile-long megalopolis extending from Boston, Massachusetts, to Fairfax County, Virginia. Following this trend set by the nation's capital, urban communities throughout the United States have been growing largely by unplanned agglomeration. While efforts to emulate the planning philosophy of the pre–Civil War period have recurred from time to time up to the present, they have been isolated projects undertaken by diverse groups with varied motivations rather than constituting a nationwide integrated and systematic effort to build a better urban America.

THE POST–CIVIL WAR PERIOD
THROUGH THE
POST–WORLD WAR II PERIOD

PRIVATELY FINANCED COMMUNITIES

One significant category of new communities built between 1865 and 1950 was the company towns designed by various private industries to accommodate their workers. In most instances, the factory owners responsible for these towns were directed by the same basic motive that prompted southern plantation owners who provided housing for their slaves before the Civil War, namely, the desire to control every facet of the lives of their labor force. There was such an oversupply of industrial labor in the United States during the late nineteenth and early twentieth centuries due to heavy immigration from abroad that anyone who complained about his working and housing conditions could be easily replaced, and there was no protective labor legislation to which he had recourse.

Company Towns

Pullman, Illinois, was a notable exception to the totally exploitative situation prevailing in company towns at the time. Built between 1881 and 1885 by George Pullman, owner of a factory producing railroad sleeping-cars, it constitutes a valuable reference point in American planning because it was the first company town conceived and built under the direction of professional designers rather than a company engineer.[9]

> Pullman featured cultural, educational and athletic facilities ... and numerous playing fields. Housing quality exceeded general contemporary standards, consisting largely of two- or three-story row structures of red or yellow brick, although a number of single-family detached dwellings were built for higher paid workers. All dwelling units were rented at a price which included construction and maintenance costs.[10]

Despite its positive physical attributes, however, Pullman continued the nineteenth-century tradition of company towns in the sense that it lacked any provision for resident participation in policy making. The management's policy of unilaterally instilling middle-class values in the residents and fining or cajoling them into following the Pullman guidelines for a "better" life intruded into their personal lives. In addition, the residents were discouraged by the management's policy whereby rents were fixed to yield a 6 percent return on the company's investment. The final blow to the harmony of the community was the famous Pullman strike of 1894.[11]

In Gary, Indiana, constructed in 1905 by the United States Steel Corporation at a cost of $80 million for a population of 200,000, the situation was just the reverse of that in Pullman. While the company did not attempt to dominate the community's social and political life, the town's physical appearance was far from ideal.

> The single attraction of the site was its location midway between the iron ore of Minnesota and the coal of Pennsyl-

> vania and West Virginia, and squarely in the center of
> a rapidly expanding market for steel products. In all other
> aspects the land seemed ill-suited for its purpose. Swamps
> and sloughs alternated with great stretches of deep sand
> heaped along the lake shore. . . . There was little ground
> cover and [there were] practically no trees except along
> the streams. Three railroad lines cut across the site which
> was further broken by the Calumet River.[12]

Moreover, Gary was designed according to the unimaginative grid pattern

> in rather unsystematic fashion . . . United States Steel
> created a new industrial metropolis on the Indiana dunes,
> but failed sadly in its attempts to produce a community
> pattern noticeably different or better than elsewhere. In
> this largest of all the company towns in America, the
> greatest opportunity was thus irrevocably lost.[13]

Some arrangement for joint corporation and governmental develment might have avoided this unfortunate result. Under the conditions that prevailed at the time the town came into existence, however, such a joint venture would have been impossible. Local government functions were traditionally limited and did not include large-scale building development. Moreover, business viewed govermental activities with considerable distaste and would hardly have welcomed government influence in determining company town policy.

But the inadequate social and physical planning represented by the company towns of Pullman and Gary, however, should not be blamed entirely on their founders. The culprits, if they must be charged, could have been indirectly the Chicago World's Fair of 1893 and the philosophy which preceded and inspired it:

> First, industrial leaders came away impressed by the
> idea of large-scale planning as a technique for better
> ordering the communities in which their plants might
> be located. Second, the formal, axial disposition of the
> fair buildings came to be regarded by many industrialists
> as the desirable plan according to which company towns
> might be shaped.[14]

Western mining towns as a whole were the worst of the company towns in the post–Civil War period. Candidly replying to a query about the difficulties involved in organizing miners living in company towns, one union official declared:

> These company-owned towns were barricaded, either by wood or wire with a guard at every entrance and egress, and unless the miner and his family were identified they had no entrance or egress to the operation. Persons not connected with the company ... were not permitted in these company towns without permission of the super-intendent of the camp. This, of course, made it especially difficult in trying to organize miners who lived in com-pany-owned towns, since union organizers were prohibited from entering any company camp and the only contacts with the miners would be when the miners were permitted off the property, which was usually on Sundays when they went to the towns nearest the camps, but this was not very often.[15]

Coal companies have received more unfavorable publicity in connection with their company towns than any other industry. The 1914 massacre at Ludlow, Colorado, deplorable sanitary conditions found in coal camps by federal commissions in 1923 and 1947, pub-licity given by unions to management's refusal to negotiate on housing and other social problems, and the fact that most coal camps were located in areas which were at best difficult to make attractive have all contributed to the poor public image of company-owned towns in the coal fields. An exception to the generally nega-tive reputation of the western mining towns was Anaconda, Mon-tana, which was the pride and joy of Marcus Daly, who discovered the famed Anaconda copper lode in 1881. The city was well planned from the beginning, with the objective of making it a permanent community of home owners. Houses were built for sale to workers, merchants purchased lots in the predetermined business area, and Daly spent over $500,000 in an unsuccessful effort to make his town the capital of Montana. Anaconda's town of Anaconda, there-fore, developed in a more orderly fashion than the usual company town, but only with continual company interest and support.[16]

Hershey, Pennsylvania, initiated a new breed of company towns in the early twentieth century. In 1893, Milton Hershey, a candy manufacturer, visited the Chicago World's Fair and pur-chased some German chocolate-manufacturing equipment exhibited there. At this time he also visited Pullman, Illinois, where he developed the idea of combining his proposed chocolate plant with a new town for its employees. Subsequently, in 1903, he purchased a site between Harrisburg and Reading and succeeded in convincing the Pennsylvania Railroad to erect a new station and the federal government to establish a new post office there. Hershey built his new plant north of the railroad, locating a park and some recreational fields nearby. Later, he added a stadium, a coliseum, a zoo, and other cultural and recreational facilities. Business and residential portions of the community lie south of the tracks. The town square facing the plant fronts on the most important commercial and civic buildings. While the founder's paternalistic policies continue to the present day, they have not elicited the troubles that once beset Pullman. The town remains small and the country atmosphere is marred only by the chocolate-scented smoke which, when the wind blows from the north, pervades the town as a reminder of its reason for existence.[17]

Kohler, Wisconsin, another exemplary company town, was founded in 1913 by a manufacturer of plumbing fixtures. It was planned first by Werner Hegemann and Elbert Peets and later by the Olmsted firm. The plan finally adopted has no central focal point, although most of the public buildings are located in the northeast quadrant near the factory. Here the street system is rectangular, but west of Ravine Park, which divides the town, the streets follow freer lines. The Kohler Company constructed all the houses in its town but, unlike Pullman, made them available for purchase and at favorable terms. Kohler was also incorporated as a village from the beginning, giving the residents full control over their governmental affairs.[18]

Kingsport, Tennessee, also built in 1913, and for the Kingsport Development Corporation by John Nolen, Sr., the most prominent city planner in the United States at that time, was an unusual company town in the sense that it was designed as a multi-industry rather than a single-industry community. Moreover, it was fortunate in securing the first major branch plant of the Eastman Kodak Company, as well as a major publisher, a large tannery and leather working company, a cement plant, and several other sizable industries early in its history. Even during the Depression, Kingsport was able to retain these successful industries and, therefore, to maintain full employment when many other company towns went out of existence with the industries which had sponsored them. Kingsport is still a thriving multi-industry community in eastern Tennessee, although much of its original planned excellence has been destroyed by weak enforcement of inadequate zoning laws.[19]

The Garden City Movement

The first American advocate of the garden city was Clarence Stein who, upon visiting England shortly after World War I and becoming a disciple of Ebenezer Howard, decided to build a garden city with the succesful real estate developer Alexander M. Bing. Prior to undertaking the project, however, a brain trust was formed which pooled the talent and experience of such planning notables as Stein himself, Henry Wright, and Lewis Mumford, who used to gather on weekends during the 1920s at Stein's Hudson Guild Farm at Netcong, New Jersey, to discuss ways of improving the American city and countryside.[20] Sunnyside, New York, their first project, was intended as a dress rehearsal for the development of the garden city of Radburn, New Jersey. Emphasizing economy in planning and building, they built Sunnyside over a four-year period (1924 to 1928) on a seventy-seven-acre plot, constructing 1,200 dwelling units to house 25,000 people.[21]

The City Housing Corporation, a limited-dividend company which Mr. Bing had organized for the purpose of building an American garden city, had profited when in the autumn of 1928 it had finished its building of Sunnyside. This was not only because of good management, low-cost land close to rapid transit, economical planning, and orderly large-scale building; it was also the result of fortuitous circumstances among which was the colossal postwar demand for homes. Sunnyside houses were sold and apartments rented as soon as they were completed. In addition, there was the rapid rise of land values; for example, 671,000 square feet of land purchased by the corporation but not used increased in value from 50¢ to $1.62 per square foot between 1924 and 1928. Lewis Mumford, who lived in Sunnyside for eleven years, had this to say about the aesthetic appeal of the garden city:

> It has been framed to the human scale and its gardens and courts have improved year by year as the residents' gardening skills have improved and as the plane trees and poplars have continued to grow.... So, though our means

were modest, we contrived to live in an environment where space, sunlight, order and color—those essential ingredients for either life or art—were constantly present, silently molding all of us.[22]

After Sunnyside proved to be a success both artistically and economically, Stein and Bing turned their attention in 1928 to the development of Radburn, New Jersey, which was to accommodate 25,000 residents on a 1,000-acre site sixteen miles from New York City (see site plan, Chart 5.2). Because of Radburn's proximity to a developed area, however, it was not possible to circumscribe the community with a greenbelt; the only green areas reserved were a narrow parkway on the northern boundary of the town, a recreation field along the Saddle River on the east side, and the "parks" in the center of the superblocks.[23] Consequently, Radburn failed to conform to one of the primary ingredients of Ebenezer Howard's garden-city paradigm—the greenbelt.

Two major influences besides Howard in the development of Radburn were Frederick Law Olmsted and Clarence Perry. Olmsted's contribution, similar to what he had done in New York City's Central Park, was executed in Radburn by Alexander Bing's City Housing Corporation, and consisted of a network of paths, sunken roads, bridges, underpasses, and green spaces which attractively separated pedestrian, equestrian, and vehicular traffic. Clarence Perry, associate director of the Department of Recreation at the Russell Sage Foundation from 1913 to 1937, hypothesized that "the total community should be planned as a series of separate neighborhoods linked together by a common community center and by pedestrian thoroughfares separated from those for traffic. Such a settlement of completely integrated neighborhoods would produce many social benefits."[24]

Radburn's layout, then, rather than a grid, consisted of three huge superblocks thirty to fifty acres in size within which single-family dwellings, primarily of mock Tudor or New England design, were grouped about cul-de-sacs in such a way that kitchens and garages faced the "lanes," while living rooms faced on the large common open space in the center of each superblock. Moreover, each means of circulation in Radburn was designed for a single purpose: main highways for through traffic; the lanes mentioned above for parking garages, delivery, and other services; and walkways, separated from vehicular thoroughfares by underpasses. There was one elementary school for each superblock, a centralized junior-senior high school, and, in addition, a commercial area. Provision was also made for an industrial sector at the southwest edge of the superblocks which was close to a railroad line and a major highway. Built with private financing and without government subsidy or loans, Radburn was opened for occupancy during May 1929.[25]

Despite its beautiful residential layout and the idealism of its founders, the new town struggled through the Depression years and managed to attract only four hundred families prior to World War II. The factors explaining this situation were basically economic. First, because Radburn's housing was relatively expensive, only middle- or upper-class families could afford to live in the town, a fact which is true even today. Second, Radburn did not offer any incentives for prospective employers to locate in the community, and even if it had, industry would not have responded because the railroad line adjacent to the town's proposed industrial sector was not a main route. Moreover, because of Radburn's inadequate transportation links with other New Jersey cities and New York City, few people with jobs in these areas were interested in moving to the new town. Thus, Radburn has never become an economically and socially balanced community. Yet, it has proved to be highly successful experiment in two important respects. First, in terms of design, its principal features—cul-de-sac streets, the separation of vehicular and pedestrian traffic, superblock neighborhoods, and planned open space—have become classic elements in new community planning both in Europe and in the United States. Second, the social life and community involvement fostered by Radburn's citizens' association have been major factors inducing many persons reared in the community to remain there or eventually to return to establish and raise their own families.

The Radburn Citizens' Association, formed within two months after the first family moved into the town, has certain major purposes: to discuss questions of community interest; to formulate and express community opinion; and to cooperate in creating a community life. The upper floors of the Plaza Building, which accommodates all of Radburn's stores, are used as Radburn's Community Center, housing the offices of the Radburn Citizens' Association, the Radburn Library, and several recreation rooms. One of these rooms with a stage and raised floor is used for theatrical presentations, and another with an adjoining kitchen has served a wide variety of social functions.[26]

But planners have also profited from Radburn's mistakes, the primary one being that the founders lacked a regional perspective. In other words, Stein and Bing did not realize in 1928 the importance of working with neighboring governmental units to obtain essential background information on the areas surrounding the site, to secure vitally needed financial assistance and cooperation in such matters as building codes and zoning regulations, and to coordinate the planning of public utility and transportation facilities. As Stein remarked later in his account of Radburn, "A private corporation has only a gambling chance to carry through to completion the building of a city.... There must be a certain amount of government cooperation."[27] At the same time, in order to maintain its unique identity and to determine its own destiny regarding the type and quality of public amenities and the limits of population growth, a creatively planned community must be politically independent rather than dependent upon some envious neighboring community. Radburn's residents discovered the validity of this fact when, in 1935, their proposal for a new high school was decisively voted down by their "neighbors" in Fairlawn, the borough in which Radburn is encapsulated. And, eventually, due to its lack of a protective greenbelt, Radburn was "swallowed up" by this burgeoning community.

The privately financed "garden cities" of the immediate post–World War II period, like those of the prewar period, failed to achieve self-sufficiency. For example, Park Forest, Illinois, constructed in 1947 by American Community Builders as a satellite of Chicago, fell victim to financial pressures and the developer's planning mistakes. Schools and commercial facilities were not constructed until three years after initial occupancy; attempts to attract any of the proposed industrial facilities failed, and property taxes were insufficient to cover operating costs. Moreover, the limitations of a developer-oriented local government, along with the multiplicity of overlapping jurisdictions in the area, complicated the resolution of the community's public service and financial problems. A related sources of difficulty was the developer's reluctance to

share planning responsibility with local and county officials.[28]
Similarly, the Levit brothers constructed Levittowns on Long Island in 1947, in Pennsylvania in 1951, and in New Jersey in 1958,
but mainly for financial reasons they failed to introduce any new
land use ideas or even to emulate Radburn's garden city principles.
The major drawback to the success of the first two Levittowns was
the necessity for the developers to negotiate separately with several
local governments, causing changes in plans and stoppage of activities in building and administering the new communities. Thus
there were serious omissions and inadequacies in satisfying resident needs. In the case of Levittown, New Jersey, the developers'
major difficulty was their attempt to dominate local politics and
administration in the rural township where their community site
was located.[29] The only logical conclusion which can be drawn
from these experiments in private new town construction in the
United States is that as long as land development is primarily a
profit-motivated venture unguided by any regional objectives, balanced community development will be extremely difficult, if not
impossible, to achieve.

FEDERALLY SPONSORED COMMUNITIES

World War I Projects

The first involvement of the federal government in new
community building after the Civil War did not come until World
War I when a severe housing crisis threatened to inhibit the war
effort. In 1918 Congress appropriated a total of $175 million—$75
million going to the Emergency Fleet Corporation, an agency of the
Shipping Board, and $100 million to the Bureau of Industrial Hous-
ing and Transportation created in February of that year by the Department of Labor—for the construction of housing near munitions
plants. During the late summer of 1918, Congress authorized the
Bureau of Industrial Housing and Transportation to work with the
United States Housing Corporation, which had been established by
a presidential order on July 8, in the construction of additional
wartime housing.[30]

It was decided that unmarried workers would be housed in
temporary dormitories provided with individual sleeping rooms
and common recreation rooms, but it was thought necessary to

build houses of durable construction for married couples and their families. Previous experience with temporary housing in Chicago, San Francisco, and Galveston had shown that after an emergency was over, temporary dwellings had been vacated or had rapidly deteriorated into slum housing. Moreover, in the northern part of the country structures had to be built sufficiently strong and weatherproofed to provide protection against harsh climatic conditions. Finally, it was reasoned that the small savings which would be realized by erecting temporary houses would be more than recovered from the sale of permanent ones.[31] Consequently, the three federal housing agencies decided to construct permanent houses in those communities where a demand for additional housing after the war was anticipated, and temporary units elsewhere. Next, minimum housing standards were drawn up, relating to such matters as ventilation, sanitation, yards, and room sizes, most of which were an improvement on current practice. Architects then drew up more or less uniform house plans in the hope of reducing costs through standardization and large-scale production.

From the best overall estimates, it may be concluded that 46,000 workers were housed by direct government construction and 30,000 by private builders under contract to one of the three federal agencies involved in the emergency wartime housing program.[32] The projects in which this housing was constructed generally reflected advanced techniques in land planning, for the dwellings were not built as isolated units but as parts of a community. The usual rectangular block was abandoned where advisable and streets were made to follow the contours of the land. An attempt was also made to achieve harmony without uniformity through the thoughtful siting and spacing of houses and apartment buildings, as well as through variety in the treatment of basic structural types. The structures themselves possessed a quality and durability previously unknown in the low-income housing market. Indeed, it seemed to many people at the time that they were not only too good but too costly considering the purpose for which they had been built. Following World War I, when the Wilson Administration refused to continue the federal government's involvement in the housing field, the well-planned and efficiently operated wartime communities were auctioned off.

New Deal Projects

Even while the nation was courting prosperity during the twenties, early symptoms of the Great Depression were already becoming apparent. Eventually, bread lines, foreclosures, job-hunting queues, and bank failures made evident the total economic breakdown of the country. The dreams of the planners for "garden cities of tomorrow" were shattered by the crash of 1929, and as the Depression settled in, private money was held as tightly by the philanthropist as by the misanthrope. Once again people turned to the federal government for material relief and psychological assurances. In 1935 President Franklin Delano Roosevelt responded with an executive order creating the Resettlement Administration to build new communities and appointed Rexford Guy Tugwell director of the program.[33] Subsequently, architects, engineers, and planners gathered in Washington to design homes and communities for families with an annual income of less than $1,250. These technicians were given the utmost freedom to experiment, their only guidelines being the purposes of the Resettlement Administration: (1) to give useful work to men receiving unemployment relief; (2) to demonstrate the practicality of planning and operating towns according to garden city principles, including that of economic self-sufficiency; and (3) to provide low-rent housing in physically and socially healthful surroundings for low-income families. With the garden city concept and Radburn as their chief influences, the planners suggested the construction of twenty-five greenbelt towns throughout the United States, but only three were eventually funded and completed: Greenhills, Ohio; Greendale, Wisconsin; and Greenbelt, Maryland.[34]

Greenbelt, Maryland, by far the best known of the three communities, rose on 3,370 acres of sparsely settled farm and woodland in Prince Georges County, thirteen miles from downtown Washington, D.C. Most of its first 2,831 occupants were low-income government workers picked by a special committee which made certain that those chosen were in proportion to the nation's prevailing religious groups. Thus, 7 percent of Greenbelt's first families were Jewish, 30 percent were Catholic, and 63 percent were Protestant. Besides occupying housing priced well below its economic cost

(rents ranged from $21.75 to $45.85 a month), Greenbeltians bene-
fited from a library, a recreation center, a 25-acre lake, and a cooperatively run shopping center. The sickle-shaped, carefully landscaped town was laced by 18 miles each of paved roads and pedestrian walks so arranged that neither school children nor shopping
housewives were ever exposed to the perils of crossing a major vehicular thoroughfare.

Partly because of their midwestern location, the other two
greenbelt towns—Greendale, Wisconsin, and Greenhills, Ohio—
have attracted less attention than the Maryland experiment. The
site for Greendale, Wisconsin, which lies only three miles southwest
of the Milwaukee city limits, contained 3,140 acres, while that for
Greenhills, Ohio, five miles north of Cincinnati's city limits, contained 5,900 acres.[35] Though all three greenbelt towns were laid
out by disciples of Clarence Stein and were built simultaneously,
neither Greendale nor Greenhills carried out Radburn's separation
of auto and pedestrian traffic as completely as Greenbelt, Maryland.

Unfortunately, soon after construction of the greenbelt
towns had begun, Resettlement Administrator Tugwell, a strong
proponent of garden cities, resigned, and in December 1936 President Roosevelt assigned responsibility for the three communities
to the Agriculture Department which, in turn, designated responsibility for their supervision to a constituent agency, the Farm Security Administration. In February 1942, Roosevelt shifted responsibility for the greenbelt towns to the National Housing Agency
which later became the National Public Housing Authority and,
still later, the Public Housing Administration. Finally, in 1949,
Congress voted to sell the greenbelt towns to private companies,
with preferential purchase rights to nonprofit and limited-dividend
groups of veterans or tenants.[36]

At this time, residents of Greenbelt, Maryland, attempted to
retain control of their community by organizing a housing cooperative, but they were eventually forced to sell out to commercial developers because of their inability to secure sufficient capital and
competent management to maintain the project. Following World
War II, several freeways were built through Greenbelt, facilitating
commuting to and from jobs in Washington, D.C., but obliterating
the community's physical integrity. In Greenhills, Ohio, the federal
government sold most of the single-family homes to their occupants

and 750 acres of its undeveloped land to the Greenhills Home Owners' Corporation which demonstrated its nonaltruistic motivation
several years later when it became a profit-making organization.
A poorly financed civic group, the Cincinnati Development Corporation, purchased the remainder of Greenhills' undeveloped land, but
eventually it sold all 3,400 acres to Warner Kanter, a commercial
developer, who subsequently converted the tract into a community
known today as Forest Park. The town's greenbelt area was divided between the county park system and the Army Corps of Engineers for flood-control purposes. Greendale, Wisconsin, is the
only one of the three greenbelt communities which has retained its
original character as a garden city to the present day, thanks to the
idealistically oriented Milwaukee Community Development Corporation which purchased the town as a unit from the federal government in 1953.[37]

Unfortunately, like most of the company towns discussed earlier in this chapter, the New Deal greenbelt towns failed to become
exemplary models for their successors, the new towns, because none
of them, even Greendale, Wisconsin, ever developed completely as
designed by its planners, especially in terms of economic self-
sufficiency and the preservation of a protective greenbelt. Their
major claim to fame, therefore, lies in the intensity of the federal
government's role in regard to various facets of their development,
including financing, land acquisition, planning, construction, selec-
tion of tenants, management, and large-scale maintenance. Indeed,
the greenbelt towns were an invention of the federal government;
there was no coordination with state and local governments, and
this fostered a spirit of noncooperation after the war.

To architects and planners, however, the federal greenbelt
towns offered an unparalleled opportunity to test new concepts on
a broad scale and in diverse settings. In the words of Paul K. Con-
kin, professor of American intellectual history at the University of
Wisconsin: "They rank high among New Deal accomplishments;
in the field of public works they are hardly excelled, even by the
Tennessee Valley Authority, in imagination, in breaking with precedents, and in broad social objectives. They represented ... the
most daring, original, and ambitious experiments in public housing
in the history of the United States."[38] Despite their success from
the viewpoint of these professionals, the greenbelt towns were bit-

terly opposed by most laymen, to whom the notion of a planned community seemed more akin to socialism than to the American tradition of free enterprise. Perhaps it is not surprising, therefore, that no plans were drafted for new towns in the United States for more than thirty years after the New Deal greenbelt towns were begun.

Another New Deal project carried out under the supervision of the Resettlement Administration simultaneously with the construction of the greenbelt towns was the relocation of families from the depressed rural areas of Kentucky, Tennessee, Arkansas, and Oklahoma into cooperatively managed villages. One of these, Yuba City, California, became a successful permanent community. Due to the government's limited investment in the project, however, most of the relocation sites resembled refugee camps. There were also two federally sponsored new communities built in connection with power and reclamation projects during the Depression. The first was Boulder City, Nevada, built in 1932 near the site of the newly constructed Boulder Dam (later Hoover Dam), but undoubtedly one of the most exemplary new communities ever initiated by the federal government was Norris, Tennessee, built by the Tennessee Valley Authority between 1933 and 1935 on a site four miles from the Norris Dam project.

The idea of a new town in the Tennessee Valley originated with the then newly elected President Roosevelt, who was familiar with the work of the New York State Commission on Housing and Regional Planning under the leadership of Clarence Stein, as well as with that of the New York Regional Planning Committee under Frederic A. Delano, the president's uncle, and Charles D. Norton. Perceiving regional planning as an opportunity to solve both farm and city problems, President Roosevelt proposed that the nation plan for a redistribution of the American population away from the larger cities and toward smaller country communities by encouraging industrial location in rural areas, which were becoming feasible sites for such economic activity with the availability of electric power and improvements in transportation and communications. Looking for an opportunity to work out the elements of this program on a small scale before it was attempted nationally, the president proposed to the designated chairman of the TVA Board, A. E. Morgan, that TVA build a model rural industrial community near the site of the Norris Dam project. Financing of the community was to come from the $1.4 million which had been included in the dam project for the temporary housing of workers on the project.

At the first meeting of the TVA Board on June 16, 1933, Earle S. Draper was employed as director of TVA's Division of Land Planning and Housing, his first assignment being to prepare a specific Norris new-town proposal for consideration by the TVA Board. Draper submitted his recommendations on August 2, 1933, and three days later, the TVA Board authorized acquisition of the new-town site. The man hired by the TVA Board several months later, in November 1933, to head up the staff which would plan the new town in detail was Tracy B. Augur, one of that close circle of friends—the Regional Planning Association of America—who shared a broad interest in town and regional planning, including new-town development. The influence of this group and the English new-town movement is clearly evident in Augur's concept of Norris. Norris was to be a permanent community with an immediate size of 350 family units—capable of being expanded to 1,000 or 1,500 units—which would function as a satellite to Knoxville but would have some small, light industries and offices. The first 150 houses would be used to demonstrate electric heating and facilities, and the community as a whole would have streets, utilities, and other services equal to those of a larger town. Finally, there was to be unified control of the whole development in the interest of the community. The overall result was to be a town of modest homes set in a community which would respect the natural features of the landscape and provide an interesting and livable environment.

In late October 1934, Augur submitted a completed land-use plan for the town of Norris, which contained a total of about 4,200 acres, with less than 1,000 acres designated initially for homes and related community structures and facilities. The Augur plan, indicating areas for immediate development as well as those to be used to bring the town to its ultimate planned size for 3,000 to 4,000 people, had three focal points: the town center contained the community school, the shopping area, and the "Commons"; the Shop Area, designed for woodworking and ceramic shops, and the town maintenance yard was seen as the town's future industrial area; and the Construction Camp was later to be converted into an office and community facility area. The protective greenbelt on the south and west sides of the town was to be used as the location for the freeway which would divert traffic around the community, and, on the north side, for a town forest, park, and protected watershed.

Employment on the Norris Dam project peaked at about 2,500 workers in 1935; by mid-1936, employment had fallen to 700 people. However, while employment at the dam site declined, TVA received more applications for Norris homes than it could accommodate. The TVA Division of Forestry and several hydraulic and ceramic laboratories were now located in Norris and the employees of these operations, plus the dam operators and managers and operators of the Norris community programs, gave a small but substantial employment base to the town. By March 1936, 160 of the 350 houses in Norris were already occupied by TVA employees of these operations, and another twenty houses were rented to TVA employees working in Knoxville. Later that spring, the TVA Board adopted a policy permitting 25 percent of the houses in Norris to be rented to non-TVA people, and, by the fall of 1936, twenty-one non-TVA families lived in the town. Because the school and other community services required continuing federal financial support, Congress finally demanded that Norris be put on a self-sustaining basis, and the TVA agreed that Norris could be considered a successful town only if it could be integrated with a system of local government commonly employed in the Tennessee Valley. Consequently, the town was sold as a unit at public auction on June 15, 1948, to Henry D. Epstein, head of a Philadelphia investment group. Existing tenants were given a year's occupancy right and preference in the purchase of single-family homes. The first step was thereby taken in the transformation of Norris from a temporary to a permanent community, and the success of that transition may be gauged by how well the community has performed three tasks essential to new town development: the maintenance of the town's original physical plan; the establishment of a viable economic base; and the organization of a government capable of providing and maintaining a high level of community amenities and services.

With the decision to dispose of the town, TVA encouraged Norris residents to establish committees to study the problems associated with transition to private ownership. Tennessee planning legislation permits the organization of a formal planning commission in unincorporated communities upon petition and approval of the Tennessee State Planning Commission. Such a community planning agency was established on May 17, 1948, its area of jurisdiction, with a few minor exceptions, being the corporate area of the city of Norris. In a little over six months, the Norris Community Planning Commission prepared a major street plan, subdivision regulations, a public lands plan, and a zoning resolution which was adopted by the Anderson County Court on January 3, 1949. On June 14, 1949, the first meeting was held of the city councilmen elected under the special Norris incorporation act passed by the Tennessee General Assembly on April 5, 1949, which provided for a municipal boundary coterminous with the Norris Community Planning Region. Thus, the citizens of Norris secured the legal basis required to preserve the character of their town as one of the best planned communities in the United States.

The Epstein investment group, which purchased Norris in June 1948, contributed little to the town. In 1953, after selling all the town's single-family homes, the group sold its remaining real estate holdings to the Norris Corporation, a local corporation formed by Norris residents, for $280,000. The new corporation immediately sold the town's shopping center, its five apartment buildings, the warehouse, and the community building, which was purchased by the city for its offices and for general public use. These disposals reduced the major corporation holdings to about 800 acres divided into two tracts of roughly equal size, one located north and the other east of town. According to Augur's original plan, the north tract could be served by existing utilities and was suited to residential use, while the east tract required a new utility system and was considered best adapted to small farms. Nevertheless, the Norris Corporation decided to make its major developmental effort on the east tract, a decision which brought the first new spurt of building since the town was originally established in 1935. By 1959, some 235 building permits had been issued for 86 new dwellings, 4 commercial buildings, and 129 additions to existing structures.

In 1972, the citizen-owned Norris Corporation decided to sell its landholdings to an "outside" development group organized under the name of the New Norris Corporation, which subsequently employed an architectural and engineering firm to prepare a plan for the 366-acre tract north of the developed portion of the original town, a tract Augur had designated as suitable for residential use. After a year of discussion, the corporation and the planning commission agreed upon a plan which was highly consistent with Augur's original town plan, maintaining the same open pattern. Assuming that the land is successfully developed and marketed, the population of the town should approach the originally planned size of 3,000 to 4,000 within the next fifteen years.

With the sale of the town and incorporation as a Tennessee municipality in June 1949, Norris began immediately to put together a public service package for the community. The Norris School was already operated by Anderson County, but the city continued to provide support for improved instruction. The Clinton Power Commission took over electric service, but the city of Norris acquired and operated the water and sewer systems. The city also set up a volunteer fire department, a police department, a garbage and trash collection system, a recreation program, and a system for street repairs. Finally, it reestablished the old Community Planning Commission as the Municipal Planning Commission and adopted a zoning ordinance as well as a system for tax and license administration. Establishment of a viable economic base for Norris, however, has been a persistent problem. Although TVA remains the largest employer, its employees represent a decreasing portion of the town's residents. The Atomic Energy Commission and related private operations at nearby Oak Ridge are also major employers, but in recent years there has been a steady increase in the number of resident retirees so that now they constitute about 25 percent of the household heads.

Norris demonstrates that a major advantage of a new town is that it provides from the start a good living environment in which to build. From the early days to the present, the town residents have recognized the environmental values in the town plan and have adopted development policies to support these values. And if the New Norris Corporation carries out an aggressive developmental and marketing program for its planned residential extension of the town, Norris will attract additional residents which will help provide a broader base for better and more efficient community services. But the success of Norris as a planned town will continue to be gauged by how well it maintains itself as a pleasant and desirable place to live. The completion of the I-75 highway link to

Knoxville is perhaps the single most important factor influencing what may happen in Norris during the next decade. I-75 will provide the kind of access needed to make Norris a true satellite community to Knoxville, as originally envisioned by Augur. However, developmental pressure is already evident outside the corporate limits at the Norris-Clinton Interchange and to a lesser extent in the vicinity of Andersonville, a small community a few miles east of Norris. Faced with these trends, two policy alternatives were considered by the city: (1) holding to the existing corporate limits, retreating behind the greenbelt and seeking to protect the present environment; and (2) systematically extending water and sewer systems into the growing area between the interstate highway and Norris, cooperating with state and other local agencies in the establishment of desirable development and service standards. The second alternative was chosen, and to carry out this decision Norris is now joining with the city of Clinton and Anderson County in studies of ways to establish desirable standards.[39]

World War II Projects

The federal government's final major efforts in new community construction came toward the end of World War II and were motivated by the Atomic Energy Commission's urgent need for secrecy in testing the atomic bomb. Three towns were constructed around the chosen test sites established in widely separated and relatively isolated locations—Los Alamos, New Mexico; Oak Ridge, Tennessee; and Richland, Washington, for the Hanford Project.

The Hanford Project is often referred to as one of the engineering marvels of all time, for just twenty-seven months after the start of construction, Hanford plutonium was used as the explosive in the world's first nuclear detonation at Alamogordo, New Mexico. Today the project is still distinctive in the sense that it has the largest operating nuclear reactor producing electrical power in the United States, as the Hanford site has abundant cold water for reactor cooling.

Work on the Hanford camp began in March 1943, and within a few months it housed 51,000 employees of E. I. du Pont de Nemours and Company, the original contractor under the Corps of Engineers, Manhattan District. The first reactor was completed in September 1944, and was started up immediately thereafter, less than twenty-four months after the self-sustaining uranium fission process had been first demonstrated at the University of Chicago. By March 1945, three reactors and three chemical separation facilities had been completed. Richland, a town of about 250 people, was then acquired by the federal government and over 4,000 new homes were constructed there, together with utilities, stores, schools, and other municipal facilities. In September 1946, the General Electric Company became the operating contractor of the Hanford Project, replacing E. I. du Pont de Nemours and Company, and shortly thereafter, in January 1947, the Atomic Energy Commission assumed responsibility for the Hanford Project, replacing the Corps of Engineers. From 1947 to 1955, five additional production reactors and two large chemical plants for fuels reprocessing, Purex and Redox, were constructed. During this period, the city of Richland was expanded to accommodate 23,800 residents.

Under the provisions of the AEC Community Act of 1955, the Atomic Energy Commission was empowered to sell the city of Richland to its residents and to make community assistance payments. Sale of the city began in 1957 and took about two years to complete, at which time, Richland was incorporated. Subsequently, the Atomic Energy Commission contributed community assistance payments totaling $3.6 million to the city of Richland, $1 million to Richland's Kadlec Hospital, and $16.5 million to the Richland schools, including $7.7 million for new construction and remodeling of the twenty-year-old school facilities. In 1956, construction was started on the expansion of existing laboratories into the Hanford Laboratories complex. Through the use of these laboratories, Hanford technical programs were developed in nuclear waste management and solidification, reactor materials, reactor physics, plutonium fuels preparation, environmental technology, and life sciences research. In 1959, construction began on the last Hanford reactor, N Reactor, which produces plutonium and steam as a by-product, and the reactor was in operation by the end of 1963. That same year, the Washington Public Power Supply System constructed the 800-megawatt Hanford electrical generating plant to utilize the by-product steam from N Reactor.

As part of its long-term planning program, the Atomic Energy Commission conducted in 1962 a study on means of assisting communities economically dependent upon Commission activities in the event of curtailment of those activities, and thereafter declared a policy of cooperation in industrial development efforts. The following year, leaders in the three communities surrounding the Hanford Project (Richland, Kennewick, and Pasco) formed the Tri-City Nuclear Industrial Council as a nonprofit group whose primary purpose would be to work with the AEC, other local organizations, congressional personnel, and government agencies in helping to attract private industry to the area. By the end of 1963, all nine Hanford reactors and their supporting fuels preparation, reprocessing, and waste management facilities were operating at full capacity; the entire Hanford Project employed 9,600 people. In January 1964, however, a decision was made to reduce production at the Hanford Project by 25 percent over a three-year period and to shut down three of the nine reactors. Over the next several years, five other production reactors were shut down, leaving N Reactor as the only operating reactor after January 1971. Fuels fabrication and reprocessing plants at the Hanford Project were also shut down in phase with the reactor shutdowns.

When the decision was made in 1964 to shut down three reactors at the Hanford Project, the Atomic Energy Commission and the General Electric Company also agreed that the contract work involved with the operation of the Hanford Project should be transferred to several other contractors. By the end of 1965, the transition from a single contractor, the General Electric Company, to multiple-contractor operation had been completed and a new era had begun. The selected contractors were as follows: (1) Atlantic Richfield Hanford Company, a subsidiary of the Atlantic Richfield Corporation; (2) Battelle Memorial Institute—Pacific Northwest Division; and (3) Douglas United Nuclear, Inc., jointly owned by McDonnell Douglas Corporation and United Nuclear Corporation. In establishing multiple-contractor operations at Hanford, the AEC included in each request for proposal a requirement that the successful proposer would contractually commit itself to financial investment in the economic development of the surrounding communities.

To date, the selected operating contractors have expended approximately $50 million in implementing their various economic diversification activities, which employ about 1,000 persons. Atlantic Richfield Hanford Company has invested more than $10 million in a number of projects, including the following: (1) the 150-room

Hanford House Hotel, a resort and convention center built at a cost of more than $3 million; (2) a cattle feedlot capable of feeding 100,000 head of cattle annually and constructed at a cost of about $1 million; (3) the largest beef packing plant in the northwest, built at a cost of about $5 million; and (4) a risk capital investment firm, Tri-City Equities Corporation, organized with a capitalization of $1 million to assist manufacturing industry to locate and develop in the Tri-Cities area. Battelle Memorial Institute promised to make a substantial investment in new facilities to support private contract research as a means of aiding economic diversification and growth in the Tri-Cities area, and during its first decade of service in the Pacific Northwest, Battelle invested more than $56 million in implementing its mission. The major result is an integrated laboratory-office complex in north Richland which comprises six buildings: the Physical Sciences Laboratory, the Engineering Development Laboratory, the Mathematics Building, the Research Operations Building, a 300-seat auditorium, and the Life Sciences Laboratory, the latest addition which provides 100,000 square feet of space for environmentally controlled studies in biology and aquatic ecology. Investments made at Hanford by Douglas United Nuclear and its parent organizations are as follows: (1) a $150,000 allocation for the Small Business Investment Corporation; (2) $500,000 for the construction of the Joint Center for Graduate Study, which is operated by the University of Washington, Oregon State University, and Washington State University; (3) $4 million for the construction of the Donald W. Douglas Laboratories, whose major emphases are nuclear and biomedical engineering, radiation effects and nuclear safety dosimetry and shielding, and computer software; and (4) a $7-million joint venture with Sandvik AB of Sweden to construct the United Nuclear Corporation, a plant specializing in zirconium and stainless steel tubing fabrication for nuclear fuels.

Recent Hanford achievements include: (1) establishment of the Hanford Engineering Development Laboratory to support the Liquid Metal Fast Breeder Reactor Program; (2) the expansion of multiprogram activities into diverse energy fields; (3) research and planning of ultimate disposal methods for commercial nuclear wastes; and (4) the start of a Hanford Energy Center with Washington Public Power Supply System's construction of an 1135-

megawatt nuclear power reactor at the Hanford Project and with applications filed to construct two additional nuclear power plants on the site. More specifically, current Hanford programs include plutonium production, liquid metal fast breeder reactor development, nuclear waste management research, biomedical and environmental research, controlled thermonuclear research, solar and geothermal research, and fossil energy research. It is expected that in the future Hanford will continue to contribute to the nation's energy development programs, not only through nuclear science but in all areas of the broad charter contained in the new Energy Research and Development Administration. This expectation reflects continued use of Hanford's physical assets, its technical expertise, and local popular acceptance of Hanford's nuclear operations which so far has not posed a problem.

Indeed, the population of the Tri-Cities area surrounding the Hanford Project has grown from about 6,000 in the early forties to well over 80,000 people today, and the development of recreational, educational, cultural, and employment facilities has paralleled this growth. The three communities—Richland, Kennewick, and Pasco—are located on the Columbia River where it is joined by the Snake and Yakima Rivers, and the lake behind McNary Dam provides opportunities for boating, fishing, and swimming. Five miles of shoreline between Kennewick and Richland have been developed into the 600-acre Columbia Park, with camping, picnicking, golf, boat launching, archery, tennis courts, and water ski ramps. There are more than 7,500 boat owners in the Tri-Cities area so that a family boat is almost as common as a second car. Nowhere is the pride of Tri-Cities families better reflected, however, than in their insistence on high educational standards in the primary and secondary schools. During the past three years, over $11 million has been spent in capital improvements on Tri-Cities schools including the new $6.3 million Hanford educational park which has a high school, a junior high, and a grade school, all in one complex. Moreover, cooperation between the five high schools in the three cities makes possible vocational classes on an interdistrict basis which include such offerings as data processing, nurses-aide training, television production, horse management, auto mechanics, and carpentry. In addition, special education programs are offered for slow learners, the mentally retarded, the blind, the deaf, and the physically handicapped. Columbia Basin Community College in Pasco, whose academic transfer program is designed to provide a fully accredited education for the first two years of college, has an enrollment of over 5,000, including approximately 2,000 full-time day students and some 3,000 part-time evening students. Graduate programs in several disciplines are offered through the Center for Graduate Study in Richland.

The Tri-Cities area offers cultural advantages unmatched by many cities several times its size. The Players, now in their second quarter-century of continuous operation, own their own little theater with more than six-hundred member families; the Richland Light Opera Company provides two productions each year, including some of the most demanding of Broadway musicals; and the Mid-Columbia Symphony is one of only three orchestras in the state of Washington to employ a full-time musical director and conductor. An active Arts Council assists in coordinating and promoting the efforts of nearly thirty arts groups. The Tri-Cities area is also growth-oriented in an economic sense. A combination of agriculture, food processing, manufacturing, and nuclear industry and research provides a strong industrial base, the 600-square-mile Hanford Nuclear Project alone employing over 6,000 people.[40]

THE RISE OF METROPOLIS
AND THE BIRTH OF THE NEW-TOWNS MOVEMENT
AFTER WORLD WAR II

Since World War II, a new kind of urban community has been gradually emerging in the United States: metropolis, the sprawling city bearing little resemblance to utopian community ideals, to European new towns and satellite cities, or to the pre–Civil War American tradition of building new communities. One major source of encouragement regarding America's urban future, however, is the new-towns movement which began about ten years ago with the private developments of Columbia, Maryland, and Reston, Virginia, and which has been gaining momentum since passage of the Housing Acts of 1968 and 1970 providing federal government financial assistance to both private and public new town sponsors.

During the 1970s, many "new towns" have been and will be constructed across the United States, transforming the physical environment and the social milieu of millions of urban Americans.

Many of them, however, will not conform to Gurney Breckenfeld's definition of the term:

> A new town must not only contain homes and apartments for people in varied age and income brackets; it must also have shops, recreational, educational, and cultural facilities, plus an employment center with offices and factories. As a rule of thumb, no town with fewer than 30,000 projected population or 6,000 acres will be big enough to accommodate the necessary range of activities. Ordinarily the town lies in the path of metropolitan development at the exurban edge of a major city. . . . [Finally,] a new town should in time become a self-governing political unit.[41]

According to one recent estimate, California already has about sixty self-styled "new towns"; Arizona, Texas, and Florida together have "given birth to" at least thirty; and the regions around Washington, D.C., and Chicago have about fifteen and five, respectively. Many of these differ only slightly from conventional subdivisions; other are special-use communities (notably, the retirement cities of California and Florida); and some are vacation home developments, such as New Seabury, Emil Hanslin's prizewinning community on Cape Cod, and the Sea Ranch, a lovely 5,000-acre project on the rugged California coast north of San Francisco.[42] Most contemporary "new towns," however, have at least incorporated the landscaping features of Ebenezer Howard's garden city concept so that they include parks, playgrounds, artificial lakes, fountains, sculptures, flowers, shrubs, and open spaces to a much greater degree than conventional communities; a few have even succeeded in becoming partially economically self-sufficient and in securing racially and socioeconomically balanced populations. The latter achievement, of course, may be due more to forced compliance with the regulations of the Civil Rights Act of 1968, (the Federal Fair Housing Act which banned discrimination in the sale or rental of 80 percent of the nation's housing units) than to the humanitarian values of the new town sponsors.

NEW TOWN DEVELOPMENTS
FINANCED WITHOUT FEDERAL ASSISTANCE

All surveys conclude that California leads the nation in terms of the number of privately financed new towns. Some of these communities have been developed by large landholding families, which means that their sponsors were able to avoid troublesome and protracted land aggregation problems and the tremendous financial burden of purchasing land at inflated prices and interest rates. Two examples of California new towns currently being developed under such circumstances are Irvine Ranch, which occupies 93,000 acres of land in Orange County south of Los Angeles and whose target population is 80,000 inhabitants, and Valencia, which is being developed by the Newhall Land and Farming Company on the Newhall family's 44,000-acre ranch in the mountains north of the San Fernando Valley for a projected population of 120,000 (see list of principal new towns privately developed in the United States, Chart 5.3).[43]

The Metropolitan Fund of Detroit, a nonprofit research corporation working with a $100,000 grant from the governor of Michigan which he had received from the U.S. Department of Housing and Urban Development, has proposed the construction of a "paired new town" in the Detroit metropolitan area, one portion of which would be built on one of nine inner-city sites ranging in size from 635 to 2,000 acres, while the other portion would be built on one of ten suburban sites ranging in size from 3,600 to 8,000 acres (see Chart 5.4).[44] It was proposed that the inner-city portion of the "paired new town" would accommodate 25,000 residents and that the suburban site would house 75,000 residents. Although the two portions of the new town would be 20 to 40 miles apart, they would be paired economically in terms of having the same development corporation whose greater costs in building the inner-city portion would be compensated for by the lesser costs involved in the suburban portion of the project.

Also proposed was political pairing—one government unit for both portions of the new town, but operating on a neighborhood level within each portion—as well as educational pairing—one school system for both portions, with high school students having the option of attending the high school outside the portion in which they reside. The only distinction between the two high schools would be in curriculum specialization so that the students' choice would be based solely on academic considerations. Rapid transit lines between the inner city and suburban portions of this "paired new town" would facilitate not only the transfer of high school students but also the shifting of residential location by present inner city and suburban residents. The Metropolitan Fund's research team contends that many inner-city residents would prefer to live in a suburban location if they could easily commute to the inner city for work and other purposes and that many suburban residents would prefer to live in the inner city if they would not incur such disadvantages as inferior schools and higher crime rates. Consequently, the Metropolitan Fund's proposal for Detroit's "paired new town" also called for high-quality housing and residential amenities in both the inner city and suburban portions, with lower-income families receiving housing subsidies in order to ensure a socioeconomically heterogeneous population in each location. While the research team acknowledged that either private industry or a government agency could build their proposed new town, they strongly urged the formation of a state development corporation, such as New York State's Urban Development Corporation, to undertake the project, which they estimated would cost $1 billion and take twenty years to complete.[45] Dr. Hubert Locke, the project's director and an associate at Wayne State University's Urban Studies Center, thinks the plan is worth this investment in money and time:

> We're trying to develop a new life-style to overcome social problems. This entire region will stand or fall together. Today there are people living in a sea of social and economic decay while affluence blooms around them. If the present situation continues, the city will be dead in ten years, and the suburbs will go in the eleventh.[46]

Large corporations are rapidly becoming another source of private activity in the new-towns movement. Lake Havasu City, being developed on a 16,250-acre site in Arizona by the McCulloch Oil Corporation, has a projected population of 100,000 (see Chart 5.3), but because of its isolated location and lack of a heterogeneous industrial base, slow growth is expected. To offset these disadvantages, the developers purchased London Bridge in 1968 and reassembled it in Lake Havasu City to stimulate tourist trade.[47] Another new town in Arizona, Litchfield Park, is being developed outside Phoenix on 12,300 acres of one time cotton land owned by the Goodyear Tire and Rubber Company for a future population of 75,000 (see Chart 5.3). While presently drawing on Phoenix for home buyers, public services, cultural events, and employment opportunities, Litchfield Park will eventually become more autonomous, its commercial and industrial areas providing enough jobs for 50 percent of its working population. Moreover, every home in Litchfield will be within walking distance of an elementary school so that school buses will never be needed, and stores, recreational areas, and jobs will be made similarly accessible to residential areas.[48]

The Westinghouse Electric Corporation is so pleased with the success of the new town, Coral Springs, developed by its Florida real estate subsidiary, Coral Ridge Properties, that it has already purchased land for a second new town near Naples, Florida. Another new-town developer is the First National City Bank, which has invested through its Trust Department in the Rancho San Diego project east of San Diego, California. Still other corporations have co-financed new-town developments, two conspicuous examples being the Sears Roebuck–Marshall Field–Aetna Insurance New Century Town north of Chicago, and the sponsorship of three new towns in the Hartford, Connecticut, metropolitan area by the Greater Hartford Corporation, a consortium of thirty private enterprises.[49] In brief, a tremendous variety of American corporations, both singly and in combination, have found new-town development an enticing type of investment.

New towns in-town have also captured the interest and financial backing of corporations, as exemplified by the four-corporation sponsorship of Philadelphia's 50-acre Franklin Town; IC Industries' 83-acre new town in-town for 50,000 Chicagoans extending east from the Loop to Lake Michigan; the Ford Motor Company's 2,360-acre town of Fairlane built on a portion of the Henry Ford I estate in Dearborn; Ralston Purina's proposed 140-acre new town beside its St. Louis headquarters; and U.S. Gypsum's two-tiered (one for pedestrians and one for vehicles) new town being planned for a fringe area of Boston.[50]

Generally speaking, corporations purchase land for their prospective new towns and then hire architects and site planners to determine land use patterns and building types, densities, and arrangements for the towns. The site planners, in particular, must comply with, or secure exemptions from, the zoning codes of the local government in whose jurisdiction the new town will be located and upon whom the completed new town will depend for public utility services. Because of the substantial front-end financial investment involved in new town construction, rapid returns are essential, and the adequacy of these returns is measured directly by the rate at which the land purchased for the new town can be absorbed into the development marketplace. Two factors are critical in this regard: markets that are large in relation to the size of the projected new town and the prospect of significant penetration into these markets. Experience indicates that market penetrations in the 5 to 10 percent range are possible but ambitious. To achieve this, strongly competitive, attractively designed, and effectively merchandized housing that offers a high value and a unique environment must be created. This is why new towns in-town and suburban new towns seem to offer the most consistently viable settings, for it is in and near major metropolitan areas that the two tests of a major market and significant penetration can be met most effectively.

The economic significance of new towns goes beyond marketing factors, however. Two other important goals are, first, to provide a diversity of jobs within the community, thereby offering an ample range of employment opportunities to residents with a minimum work-to-home journey and, second, to provide a range of housing choices, at appropriate price and rent levels, large enough to accommodate all those who work within the community. The relationship between workers/residents and the marketing of residential and commercial sites is mutually reinforcing. Key employers provide jobs initially, thereby generating housing demand from their employees. The workers and residents will in turn require services, thus generating support for more employees who will need housing in or near the new town. This cycle is basic to all types of new town development. Not all residents of new towns work in them, however; nor do all who work in new towns live in them. This pattern is to be expected because of the range of housing choices available and because some who choose to live in a new town may not be able to find jobs there. But for one group—low-income families—the choice is severely constricted. Not less than 20 percent of the population, and in some areas as high as 25 to 30 percent, has been excluded from the range of housing choices, even where these choices have included such federally assisted housing as that built under the Section 235 and 236 programs.[51]

To meet the financial strains of early-stage development, even the best intentioned new-town developers will decide to build high-revenue-producing housing first. Once the first wave of high-middle- and middle-middle-income families has been served, resistance to low-middle- and low-income housing heightens. And so most new towns have ended up catering to a clientele not much different from that of the customary suburban developments and have had a negligible impact on the problems of providing decent low-priced housing and easier access to new jobs for lower-income families. This is generally true, despite some low-cost, even public, housing tucked away behind or alongside industrial parks or a few scattered subsidized units physically undistinguishable from the moderate-cost unsubsidized units.[52]

AMERICA'S MOST FAMOUS NEW TOWNS:
RESTON, VIRGINIA, AND COLUMBIA, MARYLAND

That Reston, Virginia, and Columbia, Maryland, are not only the best known but the most frequently emulated American new towns is not surprising, since they launched the new-towns movement in the United States. Yet neither Reston nor Columbia conforms as well as the British new towns to the strict definition of new towns, for while both have some employment opportunities, the majority of their gainfully employed residents commute to jobs in Washington and Baltimore, and it is extremely unlikely that either will ever become a politically independent entity.

However, Reston is the American new town most influenced by Ebenezer Howard's garden city—not surprising in view of the fact that the developer's father, Robert E. Simon, Sr., helped finance the Howard-inspired community of Radburn, New Jersey. The younger Simon, who formed the name Reston from his initials, perceives an ideal community as follows:

> It must provide a wide range of recreational and cultural activities ... and a housing mix that encourages a heterogeneous community, reflecting the diversity of the core city.... The focal point for all planning must be the needs of the individual. People must be able to live and work in the same community.... Beauty, both natural and structural, is a necessity of the good life.[53]

Reston, Virginia

In 1961, Robert E. Simon, Jr., found a 7,400-acre woodland eighteen miles northwest of Washington, D.C., which he purchased from its single owner at a cost of $13 million, paying $800,000 in cash and mortgaging the remaining $12.2 million.[54] Subsequently, Simon engaged two New York architects, Julian Whittlesey and William J. Conklin, to design a master plan for his proposed community of Reston, which he conceptualized as having a heterogeneous population of at least 75,000 by the year 1981. The plan which the architects finally evolved divided the town into five village centers, each accommodating 15,000 to 20,000 residents, a variety of housing types (from apartments and town houses to single-family detached dwellings), and a full range of community facilities (shops, schools, churches, and recreation/social centers). But it was necessary for Simon to persuade Fairfax County officials to prepare a new section for their zoning ordinance which would apply exclusively to "planned residential communities," because the existing law did not permit Reston's mixture of residential and commercial land uses or its clustering of houses surrounded by large open spaces. Indeed, one of the most remarkable aspects of Reston's plan was its allocation of almost 50 percent of the site to public uses including open spaces and recreational areas such as an artificial lake, a soccer and football field, two eighteen-hole championship golf courses, two riding stables, four basketball courts, thirteen baseball diamonds, and numerous swimming pools, tennis courts, playgrounds, and hiking trails.[55]

The shoreline of Reston's thirty-acre Lake Anne was chosen by the planners as the site of the town's first village center which they named after the lake and designated as the major focal point for the entire community's commercial and social activity. Restonians can come to their town center by boat if they wish, but many people prefer to drive (there is a parking lot behind the center), and still more prefer to use the winding walkways by which any resident can reach the center within ten minutes. Washington Plaza which fronts on Lake Anne is famous for its "contemporary Gothic" architecture and features a pedestrian piazza; several fountains; a wooden "sun-boat" sculpture by the Uruguayan artist

Gonzalo Fonseca; a three-story brick apartment building with stores; a library; a restaurant and a community meeting hall on the ground floor; and the fifteen-story, sixty-unit Heron House apartment building at the very edge of Lake Anne. This is Reston's mark of identification and symbolizes its urban tradition. Near the entrance to Lake Anne Village Center is a nine-story, 138-unit apartment building for senior citizens built by a nonprofit corporation, Fellowship Square Foundation, Inc., with funding obtained under Title 202 of the National Housing Act of 1968.

Despite Reston's beautiful natural setting and master plan, however, within two years following the opening of Reston's village center in December 1965, only six hundred homes had been bought and Reston's population had reached a mere 2,700. What were the principal causes of Reston's plight? First, the thirty-six-mile round trip between Reston and Washington, D.C., discouraged many buyers with jobs in the capital city, and at the time there was neither an entrance nor an exit at Reston leading to or from the four-lane expressway which splits the new town and connects Dulles Airport with downtown Washington. Second, Reston was plagued with financial problems. While its $23,000 town houses in Lake Anne Village Center were quickly sold, an entire cluster of avant-garde town houses worth $35,000 to $47,000 proved to be so unpopular that the Reston Development Corporation was finally forced to rent most of them.[56] Moreover, many of Reston's prospective home buyers experienced difficulty securing mortgages. The "tight-money" economy of 1966 affected the entire nation, but it was especially harmful to new communities like Reston which urgently needed to sell lots and homes. One builder in Reston was actually forced into bankruptcy because of this situation. Then there was the unwise decision of the Reston Development Corporation to expedite full occupancy of the fifteen-story lake-front apartment tower by renting efficiencies for $140 a month and two-bedroom units for $290, but it was soon discovered that the revenue derived from this rent pattern covered only maintenance expenses and interest on the mortgage, and not the principal.[57]

The Reston Development Corporation's third source of difficulty which caused expensive delays in construction was the constant inquiries from officials of the federal and local governments about insignificant details. The Federal Housing Administration,

RADBURN, NEW JERSEY
Opened for occupancy in 1929; created by Clarence Stein.

Radburn:　Common green space shared by residents of several homes

Radburn:　Town hall

Radburn: Homes sharing common open space, a concept for which
the Radburn Plan is famous internationally

Radburn: Protective pedestrian underpass

Radburn: One of many cul-de-sacs typical of Radburn

LEVITTOWN, PENNSYLVANIA
One of three towns created by Levitt Brothers: Levittown, Long Island, New York, 1947; Levittown, Pennsylvania, 1951; and Levittown, New Jersey, 1958.

Levittown: Pedestrian mall, town center

Levittown: Violetwood shopping center

Levittown: Town center

Levittown: Typical two-story home, early 1950s

Levittown: Ranch-style home

Levittown: Typical one-story home, early 1950s

GREENBELT, MARYLAND
Project developed under the auspices of the United States
Resettlement Administration in 1935. One of three greenbelt
communities built during the Depression by the federal government.

Greenbelt: City Hall

Greenbelt: Lake and wooded recreational area

Greenbelt: Typical row housing (3 examples)

RESTON, VIRGINIA
Created by Robert E. Simon, Jr.; opened for occupancy in 1965.

Reston: Lake Anne Village Center with fifteen-story heron house
(apartment building) on the left

Reston: Town center

Reston: Two-story home

Reston: Garden apartments

Reston: Town houses along a canal

Reston: Split-level home

Reston: Protective pedestrian underpass with mosaic designs on walls

Reston: Garden apartments along a canal

Reston: Plant facility in the Issac Newton sector

Reston: Pedestrian walkway

Reston: Wooded pathway

Reston: Industrial sector

Reston: Bridge over a canal

COLUMBIA, MARYLAND
Project begun by James W. Rouse in 1963.

Columbia: Woodward and Lothrop department store, a major
shopping facility facing front entrance of town center

Columbia: Rear view of town center

Columbia: Town houses

Columbia: Oakland Mills shopping center

Columbia: Wooded area and open space

Columbia: Howard Community College

Columbia: Pedestrian overpass

Columbia: Volvo plant in industrial area

for example, challenged everything from Reston's clustered building pattern to the form of its home owners' association charter. (Offsetting these negative experiences with FHA were two positive responses in 1966 from the U.S. Department of Housing and Urban Development—a $200,000 grant to the Reston Community Programs Foundation for the construction of two hundred low-income housing units and a medal to Simon for his achievements as an urban pioneer.) Fairfax County officials also gave the Reston Development Corporation troubles, the nature of which Simon described in an interview with Gurney Breckenfeld, an editor of *Fortune* magazine and former editor of *Architectural Forum*: "We tried to get help from the county board of supervisors at saving the trees.... The supervisors did agree to let Reston slash a smaller swath through its beautifully wooded rolling hills than the county had normally required for streets. But the official in charge of streets and drainage interpreted that decision as meaning that we'd have to justify each tree we wanted to save.... He cost Reston an enormous amount of money."[58]

In the final analysis, however, it must be recognized that Reston was headed for financial problems several years before construction began. Simon had been so enthusiastic about building his dream town in 1962 that he failed to even estimate the cost, much less to secure a loan, starting the project with his own $1.8-million capital. Simon claims, however, that he made an oral agreement with the Washington Gas Light Company for a low-interest $6-million loan in exchange for making Reston an all-gas (for heating, cooling, and refrigeration) community, but that a year or so later when he needed the money, the utility company denied that they had made such a deal and refused to advance the loan. Fortunately, however, Simon was able to persuade the Gulf Oil Corporation in 1964 to lend him $15 million, in return for which Gulf received first mortgages on all undeveloped Reston land, options to buy 40 percent of the stock of the development corporation, Reston, Incorporated, and all of the town's forty gasoline station sites.[59]

By 1967, however, Reston's financial condition was such that Gulf Oil decided to take control of the town in order to protect its $15-million investment, creating a new development organization— Gulf-Reston Incorporated—and replacing Simon as president with Robert H. Ryan, former vice-president of a Boston development firm, Cabot, Cabot, and Forbes. Simon subsequently served as a consultant to Reston's new development corporation, but when he objected to Ryan's plans to build more conventional-looking detached homes and fewer town houses and to compromise on the ideal of mixing low- and high-income housing, he was promptly fired. Nevertheless, when Simon left Reston, his initial $1.8-million investment in the town, and a 20-percent share of the stock in the development corporation, he was still optimistic that someday the town would become a profitable venture.[60]

Upon taking over Reston in 1967, Gulf wrote off $7 million of its original $15-million investment and then invested another $35 million to stimulate development by offering 90 percent mortgages to anyone who would buy a home in Reston. But, in spite of this inducement, only 9,000 persons resided in Reston by mid-1970—four and a half years after the town was opened for occupancy. Industrial growth was also slow; by mid-1970 there were thirty-three firms in Reston, but they employed only 2,100 residents. Dissatisfied with Ryan's performance, Gulf-Reston replaced him as president with William H. Magness, a former general manager of Gulf's Iranian operation, and made Ryan a "consultant" as had been done with his predecessor Simon. In 1968 the Reston Community Association had inaugurated express commuter bus service between the new town and Washington in an effort to attract more residents; currently operated by Gulf-Reston, Inc., fifty buses make the round trip daily. While this service has always proved to be both popular and profitable, it is almost certain that Gulf-Reston's chief opportunity for making a substantial profit from Reston is rising land values, for even as early as 1967, six years after Simon had bought the town site for $2,000 an acre, he sold one industrial site for $40,000 an acre, and a residential site for the elderly was appraised at $70,000.[61]

The year 1971 marked a significant change in Reston's financial situation. For the first time in its ten-year history, a positive cash flow was established and a margin of profit was experienced in the operating budget, proving that a new town can be a profitable venture. Moreover, on February 10, 1971, a major milestone was reached with the formal opening of the western access ramps to the Dulles Expressway at the Reston Avenue overpass, which made it possible to reach Dulles International Airport from Reston in seven or eight minutes, and produced a profoundly positive impact upon Reston's industrial sales. Soon after, on March 14, 1971, ground was broken for the $10-million Sheraton Inn (300 rooms) and International Conference Center. The latter (opened in 1972) includes the most extensive conference and seminar space in northern Virginia, a 205,000-square-foot high-rise office tower, a 700-seat twin cinema, shops and stores, and an urban mall with a fountain. By July 1971, Reston's residential property sales had eclipsed the entire 1970 volume, and by the year's end the town's population had reached 16,000. The year 1971 was also an award year for Reston. On May 24, William Houseman, editor and publisher of the *Environment Monthly*, presented to William Magness, president of Gulf-Reston, Inc., and to Vernon Walker, director of the Reston Nature Center, one of twenty-four awards given to U.S. corporations which had made "environmental excellence a basic condition in the pursuit of corporate goals."[62]

By January 1976, Reston had more than tripled its mid-1970 population with 28,000 residents, and three more village centers— Hunters Woods, Tall Oaks, and South Lakes—had been added to the original Lake Anne Village Center, leaving only one more to be completed. Moreover, about one-third of the projected 25,000 residential units were constructed and occupied, including 3,662 apartment units, 945 garden apartment and town house condominiums, 3,354 town houses, and 179 single-family detached homes. Rents ranged between $120 and $180 per month in subsidized dwelling units (constituting 15 percent of all housing in Reston) and between $255 and $500 per month in unsubsidized units. Dwelling units for sale are priced from $26,250 to $200,000, the average price ($60,000) being about the same as that for Fairfax County in which Reston is located. However, while minorities constitute about 13 percent of Reston's population, they constitute only 5 percent of Fairfax County's population.[63]

Although only 20 percent of Reston's gainfully employed residents currently work at one of the town's 7,400 jobs, the ultimate goal is one job per household or 25,000 jobs. The core facility within the 1,300-acre Reston Center for Industry and Government is Isaac Newton Square which contains the national headquarters of the U.S. Geological Survey, a $50-million facility employing approximately 2,800 persons. Other facilities located in Reston's Center for

Industry and Government, along with over one hundred others, are the American Newspaper Publishers Association which represents 90 percent of the U.S. daily newspaper circulation and which moved from Manhattan to Reston in 1972; the American Press Institute, which moved to Reston from the Columbia University campus in 1974; and the Council for Exceptional Children which also moved its headquarters to Reston in 1974.

Higher education and cultural opportunities are accessible to Restonians. Northern Virginia Community College, which grants associate degrees, and George Mason College, a four-year branch of the University of Virginia, are both located nearby in Fairfax County, and the Virginia Polytechnic Institute and State University offers graduate-level courses in Reston itself. At VPI's New Communities Study Center in Reston, some of the leading figures in the American new communities movement share their experiences with planning and development officials, builders, academicians, and other professionals. Finally, Filene Center at Wolf Trap Farm Park located just a few miles from Reston off the Dulles Expressway brings the best in popular and classical arts to the Washington metropolitan area during the summer months.[64]

Reston as a constituent of Fairfax County enjoys the benefits of the urban county executive form of government which has a working structure similar to that of a large municipal government. The Virginia statutes creating this government have protected Reston from competition by providing that no unincorporated community in Fairfax County could become incorporated as a town or city after 1966. Fairfax County renders some services to Reston through its various departments and others through special districts and authorities. In addition, Reston has its own Town Council composed of the village council presidents and citizen members of the Reston Homeowners Association board of directors whose president chairs the Town Council. The purpose of the village and town councils is to keep the Reston Homeowners Association functioning according to the wishes and needs of the residents by establishing Association policies and by assisting the Association's professional staff to carry out these policies at the village and town levels. The Homeowners Association not only maintains all of the town's recreational facilities, but operates the boat and canoe rental service at Washington Plaza and exercises an architectural review function whereby no structure may be erected or externally altered in Reston until the Homeowners Architectural Review Board approves the site and building plans. Every town house owner in Reston belongs to a cluster association as well as to the Homeowners Association. The cluster associations are responsible for maintaining and improving their commonly owned land, just as the individual town house owners are responsible for maintaining their own homes and grounds. Services provided by the cluster associations, either through contracts with commercial agencies or through the members themselves, include the upkeep of landscaped areas, the care of playgrounds and parks, sidewalk repair, snow removal from private streets, and the installation and maintenance of outdoor lighting facilities. Still another important service rendered by a private non-profit organization in Reston (the Common Ground Foundation) is the community bus which operates on set schedules eight hours daily Monday through Saturday. Not only is the purchase of the system's minibuses financed by donations, but they are driven by volunteers operating on two-hour shifts and are serviced free of charge at the local Gulf service stations.[65]

Columbia, Maryland

The American new town from which urban planners can learn the most is Columbia, Maryland. In 1957, a mortgage banker named James W. Rouse founded Community Research and Development, Inc., and proceeded to search the east coast for a site large enough to build a new town which would have a heterogeneous population of 100,000 by 1985. The site selected was located about midway between Baltimore and Washington, D.C., in Howard County, Maryland, and had not yet been touched by surburban development. Then, early in 1963, after initially purchasing some land on his own, Rouse was able to persuade Connecticut General Life Insurance Company, Teachers Insurance and Annuity Association, and the Chase Manhattan Bank to back his new town project with $50 million of long-term financing, a figure subsequently raised to $85 million with additional loans from Manufacturers Hanover Bank and The Morgan Guaranty Trust Company. Less than a year later, Rouse purchased some 14,000 acres of land from 140 separate owners within the Howard County site, accomplishing the entire task through third parties in order to conceal the purpose for which the land would be used so that it would not be sold at inflated prices.[66]

Next, Rouse set out to plan a community that would be, as he put it, "truly in scale with people." From October 1963 to November 1964, therefore, he held biweekly meetings with educators, psychologists, sociologists, and experts in the areas of communications, health care, and recreation—specialists community builders almost never consult—which were similar to the work groups which preceded the construction of Radburn in 1928. As a result of these meetings, Columbia's developers established four key goals at the outset:

1. To build a new town for the Washington-Baltimore region that would contain all the elements which might normally be located in a community of approximately 100,000 persons.
2. To respect the terrain, tree and plant life, soil conditions, bodies of water, and other natural features in developing the new town.
3. To emphasize the needs of the residents of the community in cultural, economic, political, recreational, and social terms.
4. To comply with the requirements of the marketplace in planning and programming the community's development.[67]

Construction was begun at Columbia in 1966 and the town was opened for occupancy in 1967. Since that time seven of the eight villages planned for the town have been completed. Each of the villages—Wilde Lake, Harper's Choice, Oakland Mills, Long Reach, Owen Brown, Hickory Ridge, and King's Contrivance—has a population of 10,000 to 15,000 people divided among three neighborhoods. As of January 1976, Columbia's population had reached 40,000, 18 percent of which was nonwhite, and approximately 12,000 of the planned 28,000 dwelling units had been constructed—4,600 single-family detached homes, 3,800 apartments, 2,800 town houses, and 600 condominiums, each of these types of dwelling units being represented in each village. Rents ranged between $100 and $296 per month in subsidized units which constitute 7.5 percent of the total, and between $165 and $470 per month in unsubsidized units. Dwelling units for sale were priced from $9,990 to over $100,000.[68]

Each of Columbia's neighborhoods contains such essential facilities as day care centers, kindergartens and elementary schools, community meeting rooms and recreational areas, and small stores selling provisions for daily use. The village centers serving several neighborhoods include junior and senior high schools, churches, medical facilities, and more extensive retail and service areas, as well as more elaborate recreational facilities. Finally, the entire town is served by a "downtown" area which includes the enclosed Columbia Mall containing large branches of Washington's Woodward and Lothrop Department Store and Baltimore's Hecht Company, in addition to over one hundred specialty and service shops (eventually there will be over two hundred); four office buildings; an exhibition hall; Columbia Hospital; Howard Community College (there are also branches of three Baltimore colleges and universities in Columbia: Loyola, Johns Hopkins, and Towson State); the Cross Keys Inn (with 150 rooms, a restaurant, and cocktail lounge); two cinemas; the 10,000-seat Merriweather Post Pavilion of Music; the Garland Dinner Theater; Symphony Woods (a forty-acre permanent downtown park); and the thirty-two-acre Lake Kittamaqundi where fishing goes on most of the year, where sailboats, rowboats, paddleboats, and canoes may be rented during the summer, and where ice skating takes place during the winter.[69]

In the foreground of Columbia's "downtown" area is the town's symbol, a bronze sculpture popularly known as The People Tree. An area adjacent to the major road passing through Columbia has been reserved specifically for large-scale industry. This industrial area is separated from the rest of the town by extensive parklike open spaces similar to those surrounding the "downtown" area and each of the residential villages. In addition, small parks and recreational areas are located within each of the seven completed villages, emphasizing the fact that 25 percent of the total land area in Columbia has been permanently allocated to open space.[70]

There is a complete system of specialized roadways in Columbia, ranging from major thoroughfares connecting the town with surrounding communities to service roads between villages and within neighborhoods. Of particular significance from the standpoint of Columbia's regional connections are U.S. Route 29 passing through the town and Interstate Route 95 lying adjacent to it, both of which link Washington, D.C., with Baltimore. Daily the Columbia Association operates thirteen commuter buses to Washington, D.C., two to Baltimore, one to the Social Security Administration, and one to the National Institutes of Health. In addition, Trailways buses make several stops daily in the community. Columbia's internal public-transportation system, ColumBUS, operates on a regularly scheduled run, taking the town residents between the village centers, the mall, and the Columbia Hospital clinic, but there are many pathways for walking and biking which reduce dependence upon motorized transportation and which are all protected against traffic at major intersections by underpasses or overpasses.[71]

In order to conform to the strict definition of a new town, but also to strengthen the demand for Columbia's housing and to insure the community's fiscal viability both now and in the future, Columbia's management has put special emphasis upon the development of the town's economy. While only 25 percent of Columbia's gainfully employed residents worked at one of the town's 20,000 jobs as of January 1976, the goal is to provide 60,000 to 65,000 jobs for 50 percent of Columbia's employed population when the town is completed in 1985. The firms currently located in Columbia represent many kinds of business and industry including distributing, light manufacturing, and research and development. Among them are the Bendix Field Engineering Corporation, Hittman Associates, Inc., the Japan Food Corporation, Concorde Fibers, Inc., Merck, Sharp and Dohme Pharmaceuticals, ITT Electro-Physics Labs, Inc., NCR Regional Systems Center, RCA Service Center, Great Northern Paper Company, Toyota Distributors, Inc., and the General Electric manufacturing and distribution complex which is expected to employ 10,000 people by 1980.[72]

Columbia is an unincorporated town governed by Howard County, Maryland. The county's charter form of government, established in 1968, provides Columbia with such services as education, fire and police protection, sanitation, sewerage, and water. Columbia residents, both property owners and renters, have a voice in community affairs through their respective village associations. Finally, all Columbia property owners—residential, commercial, and industrial—support the Columbia Association, a private, nonprofit corporation formed to build, operate, and maintain a wide range of community facilities, such as parks, playgrounds, swimming pools, golf courses, meeting rooms, nursery schools, and those related to the public transportation system, and to develop a vari-

ety of programs beneficial to the well-being of the people living and
working in Columbia.[73]

Unlike any other American new town to date, Columbia has
developed exactly as planned and is our nation's closest approxima-
tion to the world's best examples of the new town, those in Britain,
thereby proving that city building in the United States can become
an art as well as a business and can once again provide for "the
good life" as it did during the early years of our history. No less an
authority than former Secretary of Housing and Urban Development George Romney agrees:

> Columbia is a prototype of what the great monuments of
> this century must be if our century is to deserve a monu-
> ment: a place for man to live; a decent, happy place where
> one can stand in the sun and breathe clean air; a place
> for children to run and play and learn—indeed, a place
> where people of all ages can become lifelong learners; a
> place where black, brown, white, yellow, and red people
> from all economic and ethnic segments of our society can
> live together in peace and harmony.[74]

NEW-TOWN DEVELOPMENT
FINANCED BY THE FEDERAL GOVERNMENT

The financial problems which confronted Rouse in Columbia
and especially Simon in launching Reston are dramatic evidence of
how difficult or even impossible it would be for private enterprise
alone to undertake the nationwide new towns program recommended
in 1968 by the National Committee on Urban Growth Policy. It
takes a tremendous amount of "seed money"—at least $60 million—
just to assemble and improve the land and to install public facilities
for a moderately sized site, and once these basics have been accom-
plished, millions more are required to construct dwelling units and
commercial facilities for which the demand may be far less than
anticipated. Thus, the risks are great and the profit-making days,
if any, are a long way off.

When new-town legislation was first proposed to Congress in
1964 and a second time in 1965, the big-city mayors opposed it for
fear that it would divert government grants from existing urban
programs. And when weak federal legislation on behalf of new
towns was finally passed in 1966, it drew only lukewarm approval

from the mayors.[75] Then, during the fall of 1968, following the long hot summer of ghetto rioting in 1967, the National Committee on Urban Growth Policy, a prestigious bipartisan group of senators, congressmen, governors, mayors, and other officials sponsored jointly by the National Association of Counties, the National League of Cities, the United States Conference of Mayors, and Urban America, Incorporated, made a study of new towns in Europe, especially in Britain and Scandinavia, and concluded that such new communities were an essential element of a national strategy to shape future urban growth in the United States. Moreover, they recommended that one hundred new towns for 100,000 inhabitants each and ten new towns for 1 million inhabitants each be built in the United States within the next thirty years or by the year 2000.[76] It was against this background that Congress passed the Housing and Urban Development Act of 1968.

Under this act, the Department of Housing and Urban Development (HUD) recognized four kinds of new-town developments as being eligible for government aid: self-sufficient or free-standing new towns located more than twenty miles from a large city; satellite communities located less than twenty miles from a large city; growth centers built as extensions of existing cities; and new towns in-town, that is, planned communities within large central cities, the last category being added to obtain the support of the nation's mayors. To qualify for HUD aid, all new-town developments had to meet several criteria: (1) combine open space with sufficient density for the creation of an urban life-style; (2) plan for a balanced development of commerce and industry along with residential and recreational facilities; (3) offer equal opportunity for all minority groups in employment and housing; and (4) provide a substantial number of low-cost housing units.[77]

Title IV of the Housing Act of 1968 authorized HUD to issue loan guarantees to private new-town developers, enabling them to borrow long-term private capital at considerably lower interest rates than would otherwise be possible. Loan guarantees under the 1968 act were limited, however, to a total of $250 million and to a maximum of $50 million for a single project. Title IV also authorized some supplemental grants to local governments for the acquisition of land for open space and for the installation of water and sewer lines in HUD-financed new towns.[78]

Congress renewed and expanded its commitment to new towns in the Housing and Urban Development Act of 1970, Title VII of that law increasing total loan guarantees from $250 million to $500 million and extending the guarantee program from private to public agencies. It thus enabled HUD to issue loan guarantees covering 100 percent of the cost of acquiring and developing land for public new town sponsors and about 85 percent of the cost for private developers. Moreover, under Title VII's loans and grants program, new town developers can borrow money from the government for a period of up to fifteen years to pay the interest on money borrowed from private sources without a federal loan guarantee. Under the same program, grants may be made to public and private new-town developers to cover the cost of essential services—education, health, and safety—during the first three years of their projects' existence. Finally, the 1970 Housing Act authorized HUD's Community Development Corporation to build its own new towns on the federal government's surplus land. New-town developments approved by HUD also have priority for assistance under thirteen other federal aid programs which encompass almost every conceivable kind of public facility, from waste treatment works and access roads to hospitals and neighborhood centers. Consequently, in addition to the millions of dollars in loan guarantees and direct loans and grants available under the Housing and Urban Development Act of 1970, hundreds of millions of dollars from other federal loan and grant programs can be funneled into the new-town program.[79]

Privately Initiated New-Town Developments

The privately initiated new town developments which HUD has decided to support financially represent a rich mixture of projects, some of which are being used to test various innovations (see list of HUD-approved new towns in the United States, Chart 5.5). Jonathan, Minnesota, for example, the recipient of HUD's first loan guarantee in February 1970, has formed a separate corporation for the construction of experimental low-cost housing in partnership with Olin Mathieson Chemical Corporation, Northern Natural Gas Company of Omaha, Burlington Industries, and the Stanford Research Institute. It is also investigating possible community applications for a two-way, wide-band television system. Another example is Cedar-Riverside, the first new town in-town to be

awarded a HUD loan guarantee (in June 1971), which is testing
the concept of building a new community within a major city—
Minneapolis—as a means of accommodating growth while improving the environment. Moreover, HUD is "pairing" Cedar-Riverside
with Jonathan twenty miles away; it is this federal government encouragement of the development of a new town with both an urban
and a rural component which makes this Minnesota project unique.[83]
The Cedar-Riverside–Jonathan "paired new town" constituted the
spearhead of a federal effort to foster planned self-supporting communities free of urban decay and sprawl. For this reason, it seems
appropriate to elaborate upon the details involved in the launching
of its two component projects.

Although the Jonathan and Cedar-Riverside projects are being
developed by two separate corporations, former Minnesota state
Senator Henry T. McKnight heads both of them. In the mid-1960s
McKnight quietly began buying land around a farm he owns near
the town of Chaska, which has approximately 4,000 residents.
Then, in August 1967 he announced his plan to build a community
for 50,000 residents on an 8,914-acre site which he decided to name
after Jonathan Carver, an early explorer of the area. During the
winter of 1967–1968, however, few people were buying homes in
Minnesota, and McKnight was forced to stop construction on Jonathan's town center. So he turned to the federal government, won
certification under the 1970 Housing Act, and in October 1970,
sold $8 million in guaranteed debentures for the development of the
Jonathan site, which was described as having "gently rolling land
. . . heavily wooded ravines . . . and broadleaf hardwoods which support wildlife ranging from . . . gophers, chipmunks, raccoons, squir-
rels, and rabbits to white-tailed deer." In return for the HUD loan
guarantee, the Jonathan Development Corporation agreed that 50
percent of the residences would be built for families of low and
moderate income.[81]

As Jonathan's developers surveyed its pastoral setting, they
visualized a community with half of its 50,000 residents living in
five villages and the other half around the town center which might
consist of one huge winter-proof building. They also saw the site
as the home of a significant number of poor and working-class families—white, black, and American Indian. Residents would be able
to walk to shopping facilities, to schools, and possibly even to work.

Three areas would be used for industrial development, and one village was expected to emerge as a sort of college town around a learning center which would provide education for students of all ages.[82]

While McKnight was developing Jonathan, the Cedar-Riverside project was evolving. One evening, Gloria Segal, a housewife and mother of four, drove to the University of Minnesota to attend a symphony concert and was unable to find a parking place. Subsequently, upon the advice of Keith R. Heller, a former assistant to the Dean of the Business School at the University of Minnesota, she purchased a parking lot in the vicinity of the university. Thereafter, Segal and Heller combined financial resources, formed a corporation, Cedar-Riverside Associates, and purchased a 100-acre site on which to construct an apartment building in the Cedar-Riverside area of Minneapolis. This area, once the home of European immigrants, had gradually deteriorated into a conglomeration of bars, experimental theaters, residences for the aged, and rundown houses occupied by students, poor families, vagrants, and assorted social dropouts. Then, in 1968, McKnight, Jonathan's developer, joined Cedar-Riverside Associates as chairman of the board, bringing other investors with him.[83]

When an urban renewal plan for Cedar-Riverside was approved by the city of Minneapolis, Cedar-Riverside Associates was designated as the redeveloper of the area, but no definite plan was devised for the character of that redevelopment. It was not until the University of Minnesota decided to build a major campus in Cedar-Riverside that the development corporation decided to convert the area into a new town in-town, providing the diversity of amenities generally associated with a relatively self-sufficient community. Cedar-Riverside Associates proposes to accommodate an eventual population of 31,250 in apartments priced from low to luxury levels, employing David Cooperman, a University of Minnesota sociologist, to portray verious life-styles of future residents as a guide in designing the apartments. Thus, for example, living units are being planned for the dedicated student who requires a lot of study space in his apartment and who does not socialize at home, for the middle-class families of faculty members and civil servants, and for doctors and other professionals who congregate near a university or hospital. Eleven buildings arranged around a plaza built atop a parking garage will constitute the town center, but commercial and community facilities will also be scattered throughout the residential area.[84]

The idea of "pairing" Cedar-Riverside with Jonathan suggests that the flow of ideas between the rural and urban components of the new town is as important as the exchange of people and the sharing of facilities. Jonathan's planners, for example, have already proposed the installation of a cable television system and a transportation network which would not only link Jonathan and Cedar-Riverside, but link both components with downtown Minneapolis.[85] While it is too early to assess the long-range success of the Jonathan-Cedar-Riverside projects, the basic assumption of their planners is that, despite the failures of the past, new-town developments are still worth the effort.

St. Charles Communities, twenty-five miles southeast of Washington, D.C., and Park Forest South, thirty miles from Chicago— two other new-town developments selected for HUD's financial backing (in June 1970)—are being used as sites for testing standards to guide the development of the fringes of major cities. At the same time, Park Forest South is experimenting with a mass transit system connecting its compact linear town center with Chicago's Loop, and St. Charles is developing housing for groups with moderate income.

A HUD objective in the central Ozark region is to attract more industry and employment to the area which has been steadily losing both population and jobs over the years. This was its rationale for granting a loan guarantee in December 1970 to the new town of Maumelle, Arkansas, located twelve miles northwest of Little Rock on the banks of the Arkansas River (which was recently opened to ocean-going vessels upon the completion of a $1.2-billion waterway and flood-control project connecting with the Mississippi River). By contrast, Flower Mound, Texas, received a HUD loan guarantee at the same time because it is situated in an area of inevitable growth between Dallas and Fort Worth just four miles away from an 18,000-acre regional airport—the largest in the world—which became operative in 1973. In Flower Mound HUD hopes to demonstrate the advantages of organizing growth around our nation's major airports, rather than allowing it to occur haphazardly as at present. Quite appropriately, Flower Mound is researching con-

struction methods which would alleviate the effects of noise pollution, while Maumelle is designing a system of educational parks as
alternatives to traditional elementary schools.[86]

In December 1971, six months after its acceptance of the Cedar-
Riverside project in Minneapolis, HUD granted a $12-million loan
guarantee to Robert Simon, Reston's founder, for the construction
of Riverton, HUD's first new town in the northeast, currently undergoing construction on a 2,437-acre site nine miles south of Rochester, New York. Designed for a population of 25,632, Riverton will
mix the 25 percent of its 8,010 dwelling units reserved for families
of low and middle income with higher priced housing in all residential areas. Moreover, Riverton's housing will be organized around
a major bikeway-walkway system connecting homes with a twenty-
five-acre public park and the town center, which fronts on a four-
acre lake adjacent to the residential areas and which will eventually
contain apartments, office towers, theaters, and restaurants.[87]

Another new community near Rochester (twelve miles east)
for which HUD guaranteed a $22-million loan in April 1972 is Gan-
anda, New York, developed by New Wayne Communities, Inc., a
New York state charter corporation organized by Rochester business and community leaders. Of special interest is the fact that the
New York state legislature created a special school district for this
new community which wil be empowered to lease multi-use facility
space on a long-term basis from the Gananda Community Association, making it unnecessary to float bonds to finance school buildings. Another unique feature of Gananda is the fact that it will be
developed around twelve family centers which will house educational, cultural, governmental, health, religious, and social facilities
and offer legal advice, consumer-protection information, and senior-
citizen activities among its many services. A full range of housing
opportunities (types and densities) will be available, and land use
within the community and the surrounding district will be controlled by a unique zoning ordinance requiring retention of an 800-
yard greenbelt around the town. At full development in twenty
years, Gananda will accommodate more than 55,808 people on its
5,847-acre site in 9,500 dwelling units, 49 percent of which will be
reserved for rental or sale to families with low and moderate income. Major industrial growth is also planned for Gananda; existing lines of the Penn Central Railroad will serve as the focus of

heavy industry, while research-oriented and light industry will be located on other sites compatible with neighboring land use.[88]

The Woodlands, being built twenty-eight miles north of Houston, Texas, by the Mitchell Energy and Development Corporation of Houston, is not only the largest new town (about 17,000 acres) so far to receive a HUD loan guarantee (in 1972), but it will be the first to receive the maximum guarantee: $50 million. Moreover, it will be both timely and unique—timely, because Greater Houston's population is expected to double to four million by 1992, and unique, because never before has a project of this size been so thoroughly master-planned for social and environmental suitability. Mitchell has already invested more than $1 million in planning the new town, utilizing the nation's leading new-town planners and designers over a two-year period to bring The Woodlands to development stage.

Design standards established by the planners of The Woodlands assure the best possible environment for self-determination, good health, cultural achievement, and, generally, for living "the good life." For example, residential areas covering 6,339 acres will provide for a mixture of ethnic and income groups in 49,160 dwelling units which are expected to house 150,000 people by 1992. Moreover, each neighborhood will contain an interfaith religious center, a health center, recreational and cultural centers, shopping centers, and a variety of schools up to the junior-high level. In addition, the developer has donated 400 acres of the site for construction of a 15,000-student branch of the University of Houston. About 2,000 acres of The Woodlands' site are designed for industrial development in order to provide employment opportunities for 40,000 persons. Finally, concern for the environment and ecology is demonstrated through its twenty-year development period. One of every four acres in the new town will be preserved as open space or developed as recreational areas, and land use, sewage-treatment systems, storm drainage, roadways, and paths will be designed to assure minimum air, ground, and water pollution. Moreover, great importance will be placed on the preservation of wildlife on the new town site; wildlife corridors covering 3,360 acres of open space will also serve as buffer zones between the various land uses in the new town, all of which will be designed for compatibility with the area's rural, wooded environment.[89]

In the second half of 1972, two more new towns were approved by HUD: Soul City, North Carolina, and Harbison, South Carolina. Soul City was the first new town to receive federal assistance in which the principal sponsor was a black-operated enterprise, the Soul City Company, a combination of about ten firms organized by Floyd B. McKissick, former director of CORE (the Congress of Racial Equality), to foster minority owned and controlled businesses. Soul City is a model of cooperation between private and public agencies in that the state of North Carolina matched the initial capital for the venture provided by the North Carolina National Bank of Raleigh, the Mechanics and Farmers National Bank of Durham, and the Chase Manhattan Bank of New York City.[90]

Located forty-five miles north of Raleigh and Durham, the 5,287-acre Soul City site is expected to house 44,000 residents in 13,326 dwelling units within the next thirty years. Residential development will include high-rise and mid-rise apartment buildings, garden apartments, and single-family detached homes grouped near commercial, educational (an educational park has been proposed as the site for all public educational facilities above the elementary level), and recreational facilities, all linked by bicycle and pedestrian pathways separated from the internal roads. During the first few years of development, however, major emphasis will be upon industrial rather than residential construction, all factories locating in the new town being required to pretreat all their wastes and to follow strict standards to protect the environment. The 1,771 acres designated for recreation and open space will include a 180-acre municipal park adjacent to the town center, five 33-acre community parks, a 160-acre eighteen-hole golf course, and 700 acres of permanent wilderness.[91]

Harbison, to be developed on a 1,734-acre site acquired by the United Presbyterian Church almost a century ago, is the first new town sponsored by a private nonprofit organization to receive a guarantee of federal assistance. Located within the Columbia, South Carolina, standard metropolitan area, Harbison is expected to accommodate 23,558 residents in 7,362 dwelling units within the next twenty years. Fourteen miles of pathways for pedestrians and bicyclists will tie residential areas to schools, parks, playgrounds, shopping areas, and other community facilities. The town center will contain major department stores and offices, secondary schools, a library, a center for the arts, and an arena for organized sports in the Dutch Fork area of which Harbison will be a part. A 226-acre industrial corridor will flank I-26, the north-south interstate highway which bisects the site and against whose noise residential areas will be shielded by earth mounds planted with trees and shrubs. Child care centers will be planned in conjunction with each of the four elementary schools in Harbison.[92]

The first new town to receive a guarantee of federal assistance in 1973 was Shenandoah, Georgia, which will be developed within the next twenty years on a 7,200-acre thirty-five miles south of Atlanta. Eventually, it is expected to accommodate 69,000 residents in 23,000 dwelling units, 27 percent of which will be allocated to families of low and moderate income. Shenandoah's housing will be clustered around eleven activity areas containing parks, playgrounds, shopping facilities, and day care centers. Seventy-five percent of the residential buildings will be multifamily structures, including town houses, garden apartments, and mid-rise apartment buildings. The 925-acre industrial center and the 445 acres planned for commercial development are expected to create 24,000 permanent jobs in Shenandoah. An eighteen-hole golf course and seven man-made lakes for fishing, swimming, and boating will constitute the major recreational facilities in the new town. Formerly cotton and corn fields which were abandoned during the 1930s, the Shenandoah site is now largely a woodland, and wherever possible trees will be retained during development, and building will be banned on steep slopes and in low areas subject to erosion or flooding. All industrial wastes will be pretreated to provide additional protection against ground and water pollution.[93]

In November 1973, the first federally approved new community in Ohio, Newfields, was launched with an $18-million loan guarantee from the Department of Housing and Urban Development. Located in the fastest-growing county in Ohio (Montgomery), Newfields is being developed by a subsidiary of the Donald L. Huber Development Corporation of Dayton, Ohio, on a 4,032-acre site seven miles northwest of downtown Dayton. The town, which is expected to accommodate 40,000 residents by the year 1993, is located within ten miles of Dayton's Cox Municipal Airport and will also be served by the Penn Central Railroad, I-70, I-675, and State Route 35. Newfield's master plan calls for a community composed of four villages situated around a major town center. The villages, to be separated by a network of streams, parks, and recreational areas, will be connected by pedestrian pathways. Special care is being taken to preserve the gently rolling site's streams, creeks, and woodlots, as well as its archaeological and historical characteristics. In compliance with federal new-communities policy, Newfields will provide a full range of housing, employment, medical, educational, recreational, and cultural opportunities for its residents. Just over 50 percent of the Newfields site will be allocated to 12,218 dwelling units; the remaining land will accommodate industrial, commercial, and office space, schools, community facilities, and recreational and open-space areas. The development process is expected to generate about 5,600 industrial and office jobs and, in addition, to create an adequate tax base for the provision of educational and other essential community services.[94]

New-Town Development
Initiated by Public Benefit Corporations

Since the 1970 Housing Act made HUD loan guarantees available to public as well as private new-town developers, municipal, state, and even regional government agencies have been applying for aid. Lucas County, Ohio, has the distinction of being the first local government to develop a new town, Spencer-Sharples, located ten miles west of Toledo. Moreover, four states—Maryland, Arizona, Tennessee, and Kentucky—have enacted new-community legislation, emulating New York's pioneer legislation of 1968, and three others—Massachusetts, Pennsylvania, and Ohio—have legislation pending. New-town activity on the regional level is evidenced by the Appalachian Regional Commission's efforts on behalf of loan guarantee applications for four new communities in Kentucky, Pennsylvania, and Ohio, as well as by its own plans for about a dozen more.[95]

As stated above, New York pioneered state-level new-community legislation, its primary vehicle being the New York State Urban Development Corporation (UDC) headed by Edward J. Logue, the ingenious rebuilder of New Haven and Boston who is respectfully acknowledged among professional planners as "Mr. Urban Renewal." UDC combines the energies of private enterprise with a variety of public programs to help renew New York State's cities and towns;

to plan and develop the orderly growth of new urban areas; to increase low- and moderate-price housing; and to alleviate unemployment, revitalize industry, and expand community facilities. In addition to condemnation powers, it has authority to override local
zoning restrictions and to issue up to $1 million in tax-exempt
bonds. Besides its commitment to construct 25,000 housing units
in thirteen central cities across New York State, UDC has planned
three new town developments in each of which middle-income, low-
income, and elderly families will be mixed in the ratio 70-20-10 respectively: a 147-acre new town in-town for 20,000 residents on
Welfare Island in the East River between Manhattan and Queens,
and two satellite communities—Lysander, in the Syracuse metropolitan area, for 18,000 residents, and Amherst, ten miles northeast
of Buffalo, for 25,000 inhabitants. While Logue has applied to
HUD for loan guarantees in excess of $125 million for these new
towns, UDC recently marketed $250 million in bonds to raise
money for their construction.[96]

Most of the public new-town development agencies which are
being organized in ever-increasing numbers will have financing
powers similar to those of UDC, making them independent of tax
revenues. For example, the Battery Park City Authority, another
independent New York State corporation, is currently developing
a ninety-one-acre new town in-town in lower Manhattan for which
it has sought Title VII aid, but it can float up to $300 million in
bonds to complete the project if its application is rejected.[97] It is
important to emphasize the fact that the bonds of public benefit
corporations do not involve any increase in state or local government debt; rather, users of the projects financed in this way pay
the bonded indebtedness over a period of years.

AMERICAN NEW TOWNS:
FROM OBSCURITY TO POPULARITY

New towns are rapidly becoming a fact of life in America.
Like most new ventures, however, they are capable of being exploited by hucksters who seek personal gain from any worthwhile program. Moreover, experiments aimed at a drastic transformation of new-town structures have produced several prototypes
of dubious merit, notably, the "floating communities" proposed by
the Triton Foundation, which were to be built in bodies of water

adjacent to existing urban centers, and the domed "Experimental City" proposed for rural Minnesota by Athelstan Spilhaus, who is currently at the Woodrow Wilson International Center for Scholars in Washington, D.C.

The Experimental City research project initiated in 1967 at the University of Minnesota received about $250,000 in funding from three federal government agencies—the departments of Commerce; Health, Education, and Welfare; and Housing and Urban Development—and about $80,000 from private industries in the Minneapolis–St. Paul metropolitan area. Following a year of extensive literature and experience surveys, and conferences and workshops by national experts representing many disciplines, laboratory evaluations of new concepts and systems were made, with experiments being conducted on small-scale models so that a choice could be made among the various alternatives. The model prepared by famed architect Buckminster Fuller, a member of the Experimental City Steering Committee, finally emerged as the ideal one.

Experimental City was to have a target population of 250,000 at a density of one hundred persons per acre on a 2,500 acre site, and it was to be separated by an insulating greenbelt from any existing urban center closer than one hundred miles in order to preserve its identity, cleanliness, and experimental freedom. Certain portions of the city were to be enclosed within domes that would be conditioned as to temperature, humidity, fumes, and light. These domes, two miles in diameter and made of glass, would have cost an estimated $80 million in 1968, but it was argued that they would eliminate the need for snow removal and make heating more efficient and less costly. Savings equivalent to the cost of their construction could be realized in a ten-year period, the proposal asserted. Land leasing rather than land ownership combined with innovative technology was proposed to free architects from stereotyped ground and building plans. It was suggested, for example, that space might be leased in a three-dimensional sense and that the forms architects could use in this type of setting might be enhanced by pedestrian thoroughfares. It was further suggested that both public and commercial buildings could be made extremely flexible with adjustable floors, walls, and ceiling heights; that it might be possible to have inflatable buildings which could be instantly deflated; and that housing units might be precast and even prefurnished in the manner of Expo 67's Habitat so that, like building blocks, they might be arranged and rearranged as desired.[98]

The Experimental City project never passed beyond the research and discussion phase, but Spilhaus's original plan was that subsequently a suitable nonprofit corporation would be formed to implement the next two phases of the project, contracting with a quasi-governmental, quasi-private corporation to build the city and to supervise its operating upon completion. Despite the somewhat bizarre and unrealistic concepts embodied in both the "floating community" and "Experimental City" proposals, however, it must be acknowledged that their designers realized the importance of new towns as vehicles for a better urban life.

Thus, while it would be fatuous to contend that new towns constitute a panacea for all urban problems, it would be a serious mistake to ignore their well-defined role in alleviating them: as Hoyt Gimlin has said, "There is a tendency to look for a single solution to all urban problems. For those who regard new towns as that solution, only disappointment is likely in the foreseeable future. But where the aims of the well-wishers are more modest, there is hope for partial fulfillment."[99]

What's Good About New Towns?

One feature of new towns which especially sets them apart from the modern metropolis is their humaneness; that is, their developers have clearly thought about people and their needs. Hence, for the convenience of women pushing shopping carts and baby carriages, and for the safety of children, the aged, and the disabled, there are ramps at steps and curbs, and bridges over, or tunnels under, vehicular thoroughfares; there are shelters at bus stations to protect people from the snow and rain and from the intense rays of the sun; there are supervised children's recreational facilities at shopping centers, allowing parents to conduct their business unencumbered; there are numerous day-care centers for children of working mothers; there are specially equipped dwelling units for the aged and the handicapped, as well as social and recreational programs designed for these people; and new-town centers are pedestrian domains where one can shop at leisure or sit down on benches to watch people, to read, to chat, to enjoy the decorative flowers, shrubs, fountains, and sculptures, or to have some refreshments purchased from a nearby kiosk or fruitstand. Although indoor groceries, restaurants, and snack shops are always busy, outdoor vendors are a familiar sight. Bringing merchandise to the people is an important part of retailing in new towns, enabling customers to feel, smell, hear, and sometimes taste, as well as see, what is offered for sale.

New towns eliminate such obsolete practices and conditions as commuting long distances to a job, driving to shopping centers, standard zoning, street parking, lack of open space, and crowded housing. They offer unusual opportunities for cooperation between public and private agencies; for municipal reorganization, some positive by-products of which might be the merging of governmental units and the pooling and sharing of their financial resources to solve common problems; and for a truly democratic living experience with a mixture of different ethnic, racial, and socioeconomic groups in every neighborhood (granted that this last opportunity may necessitate a responsible and sensitive relocation program offering such benefits as subsidized housing, job training, family counselling, and day-care centers). Columbia, Maryland, and Reston, Virginia, for example, have already proved that new towns can successfully integrate residents of all races and socioeconomic classes.

New Towns Versus Central Cities?

The glamor of the new-town approach, however, must not be allowed to eclipse the important objective of revitalizing our central cities, for even if we were to implement the recommendation by the National Urban Growth Policy Committee that one hundred new communities for 100,000 persons each and ten for one million persons each be developed within the next twenty-five years, we would thereby accommodate only 20 percent of the anticipated population growth in the United States by the end of this century.[100] The issue, then, is not *new towns versus old cities,* but rather, *new towns plus healthy old cities.* Indeed, new towns can be a useful tool in the revitalization of older cities. It has been noted, for example, that new industry is attracted to a region after a new town has been established, resulting in the economic diversification of the total metropolitan area and enhancing the attractiveness of that area for additional industrial development. While Baltimore, for example, will get no tax return from the General Electric plant in Columbia, the fact that the Baltimore metropolitan area now has a GE plant, along with its many other industries, will, in the long run, benefit the city of Baltimore. Moreover, as Columbia develops, construction money will be borrowed primarily from Baltimore banks, and insurance of all kinds—title, property, fire, and so on—will be purchased mainly from Baltimore insurance companies.

Perhaps the greatest contribution which new towns can make to central cities, however, is the opportunity to resolve their ghetto problems. According to Bernard Weissbourd, lecturer in architecture at the Chicago Circle Campus of the University of Illinois, and Herbert Channick, vice-president of Metropolitan Structures, a Chicago development firm which participated in Baltimore's Charles Center Urban Renewal Project, Detroit, for example, could, over a five-year period and based on the current national rate of 1,500,000 housing starts each year, build new towns outside the city for a population of 834,000. Of this 834,000 population, an estimated 76,000 (about 9 percent) could be blacks from Detroit's ghettos. Another 265,000 blacks could move from Detroit's ghettos into its better central-city neighborhoods and surrounding suburbs, at the same time that 265,000 whites could move from the latter areas to the new towns. The net result after five years, according to Weissbourd and Channick, would be a reduction of 56 percent (from 607,000 to 266,000) in Detroit's ghetto population, no population increase within the better central-city neighborhoods and suburbs, and a new town population 82 percent white and 18 percent black. Similar benefits would accrue to other metropolitan areas in the United States if this sequence of events were to take place (see Chart 21). Such proposed schemes are likely to remain hypothetical, however, unless our federal government formulates a national urban policy which would legislatively mandate such schemes in every large metropolitan area of the United States. This, of course, would require much greater citizen consensus than currently exists regarding the "rightness" of such a solution to the problem of racial and socioeconomic polarization in our large metropolitan areas, as well as a willingness to bear the heavy tax burden of subsidizing such an expensive undertaking.

In the final analysis, the success of both new towns and central cities will depend upon a high degree of cooperation and mutual assistance. Not only must new towns rely heavily upon existing cities for residents in the early stages of development, but even after attaining their target populations they will find central cities essential to the full life which their residents expect, for few new towns have large zoos and botanical gardens, sports arenas seating 100,000 persons, major universities and libraries, and the full spectrum of cultural activities. Moreover, only in the central city can be found the colorful life-styles, the historic buildings and monuments, and the hustle-bustle which stimulate the curiosity, the imagination, and the emotions of many people. At the same time, however, central cities will depend upon new towns for relocating their disadvantaged and surplus populations, for broadening their economic base, and for open space. Thus, we may conclude that new towns and central cities are not intrinsically incompatible, but, rather, that if there is cooperation between them the end product can be greater than the sum of its parts. Indeed, this is the basic premise upon which the national urban policy recommended for the United States in Chapter 6 is built.

Chart 5.1   Philadelphia and Savannah

PHILADELPHIA

William Penn commissioned the surveyor Thomas Holme
to lay out the city in 1682. A rigid gridiron plan was
adopted. Two major streets crossed in the center of the
town and formed a public square. A square block park was
placed in each of the four quadrants. The early dwellings
were single-family houses. In the middle of the eighteenth
century it became common practice to build dwellings on
the side lot lines resulting in continuous rows of buildings
which cut off access to the rear yards. Alleys were then cut
through the center of the blocks. These alleys have since
become streets.

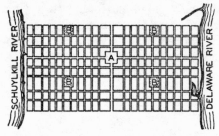

A City Square
B Park

SAVANNAH

Laid out in 1733 by Oglethorpe,
Savannah was a regular pattern
of rectangular streets with park
squares liberally spotted in alternate blocks. The plan is similar to Philadelphia with a more
generous allocation of open
spaces.

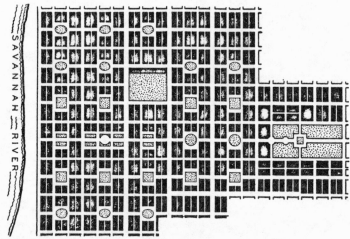

Source: Arthur B. Gallion and Simon Eisner, *Urban Patterns*, 3rd
edition, copyright © 1975 by Litton Educational Publishing, Inc. Reprinted by permission of Van Nostrand Reinhold Company.

Chart 5.2   Radburn, New Jersey

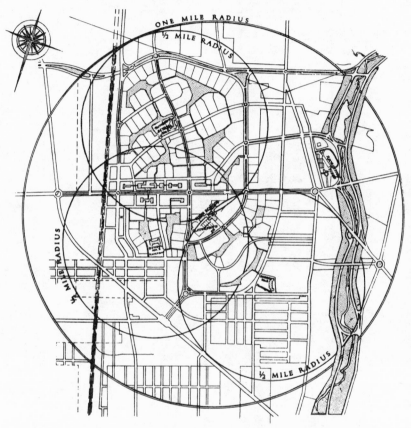

—*General plan showing neighborhoods.*

Source: Clarence Stein, *Toward New Towns for America*, copyright ©
1957 by Litton Educational Publishing, Inc. Reprinted by permission of
Van Nostrand Reinhold Company

Chart 5.3   Principal Non-HUD-Supported New Towns in the United States

Name	Location	Developer	Acres	Projected Population
Irvine Ranch	Orange County, Calif.	The Irvine Co.	93,000	80,000
California City	Riverside Co., Calif.	Kaiser-Aetna	90,000	60,000*
Valencia	Near Los Angeles	Newhall Land & Farming Co.	44,000	120,000
Columbia	Howard County, Md.	James W. Rouse	18,000	120,000
Lake Havasu City	Lake Havasu, Ariz.	McCulloch Properties	16,250	100,000
Clear Lake City	Near Houston	Humble Oil	15,000	125,000
Litchfield Park	Near Phoenix	Goodyear Tire & Rubber Co.	12,300	50-75,000
Westlake	Near Los Angeles	American-Hawaiian Steamship Co. and Prudential Insurance	12,000	70,000
El Dorado Hills	Near Sacramento	Alan H. Lindsey and Prudential Insurance	9,000	75,000
Laguna Niguel	Orange County, Calif.	Avco Community Developers	7,936	80,000
Reston	Fairfax County, Va.	Gulf-Reston Inc.	6,810	75,000
Rancho Bernardo	Near San Diego	Avco Community Developers	5,800	50,000

*By 1985.

208

Chart 5.4 Detroit's New-Town Plan

DETROIT'S NEW-TOWN PLAN

Metropolitan Fund's plan for "paired new-town" communities

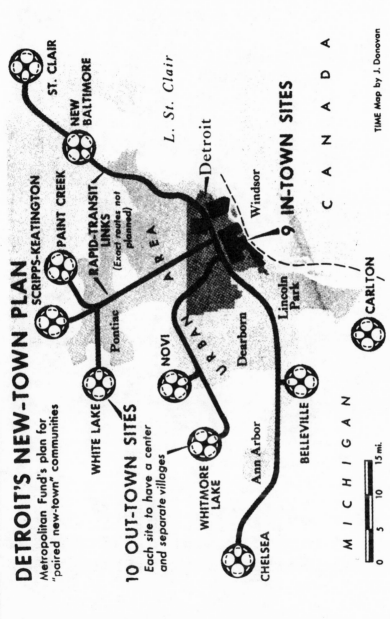

ST. CLAIR

NEW BALTIMORE

SCRIPPS-KEATINGTON

PAINT CREEK

RAPID-TRANSIT LINKS
(Exact routes not planned)

Pontiac

10 OUT-TOWN SITES

Each site to have a center and separate villages

WHITE LAKE

NOVI

WHITMORE LAKE

Ann Arbor

CHELSEA

BELLEVILLE

L. St. Clair

Detroit

Windsor

9 IN-TOWN SITES

Dearborn

Lincoln Park

CARLTON

U R B A N   A R E A

C A N A D A

M I C H I G A N

0   5   10   15 mi.

TIME Map by J. Donovan

Source: *Time*, The Weekly Newsmagazine; copyright Time, Inc., March 1, 1971.

Chart 5.5   Summary of New Towns Approved by HUD.

	Cedar/Riverside*	Flower Mound	Gananda	Harbison	Jonathan	Maumelle	Newfields	Park Forest South	Riverton	St. Charles	Shenandoah	Soul City	Woodlands
DEVELOPMENT													
Year Started	1971	1971	1972	1975	1970	1971	1973	1971	1972	1970	1974	1974	1972
Acres	100	6,156	5,847	1,734	8,914	5,221	4,032	8,163	2,437	7,600	7,200	5,287	16,937
Development Period	20	17	20	20	20	31	20	20	16	20	20	30	20
HUD Guarantee in Millions of Dollars	24	18	22	13	21	14	18	30		24	25	5	50
PROJECTIONS													
Population	31,250	64,141	55,808	23,558	50,000	33,131	40,000	110,000	25,632	79,145	69,000	44,000	150,000
Dwelling Units	13,039	18,326	9,500	7,362	15,504	10,863	12,218	38,214	8,010	27,730	23,000	13,326	49,160
Employment	4,609	16,454	12,890	7,071	14,143	22,937	5,643	28,633	11,180	14,890	24,000	8,200	40,000
Industrial (Acres)		427	250	226	1,989	838	405	1,012	400	492	925	928	2,000
Residential (Acres)	83	2,989	2,930	793	2,436	1,950	217	4,871	1,070	4,320	2,303	1,736	6,339
Commercial (Acres)	11	262	175	58	230	150	138	348	170	214	445	165	467
Public Use (Acres)	6	2,478	1,359	432	1,705	1,860	806	1,932	524	1,954	2,950	1,771	3,359
Single family (DU's)		7,812	12,241	1,892	7,751	7,595	4,502	10,135	4,647	14,800	17,250	2,412	27,325
Multi-family (DU's)	10,207	10,514	4,959	5,470	7,753	3,268	7,716	28,079	3,363	9,930	5,750	10,914	20,050
%Low & Moderate Income Units	43	20	49	21	50	23	25	15	25	80²	27	28	27
Reserve or Other (Acres)			1,593	225	1,834	423	512		120		672		4,774
ACTUALS (2/1/76)													
Population	-0-	-0-	-0-	-0-	2,300	40	105	5,250	945	600	-0-	-0-	600
DU's Occupied	-0-	75	-0-	-0-	692	14	30	1,500	270	200	-0-	-0-	171
Employment	700	-0-	-0-	63	1,500	46	186	2,200	50	200	18	-0-	1,300

¹ Cedar-Riverside—statistics only for Title VII portion of project (Title VII of the Housing and Urban Development Act of 1970).

² St. Charles—proposed plan change will reduce % to 25-30%.

³ Roosevelt Island—50,000 sq. ft. rentable commercial space on ground floors of residential bldgs.

Chart 5.6   Population Movements, 1970-1975: Detroit, Chicago, Washington, Philadelphia

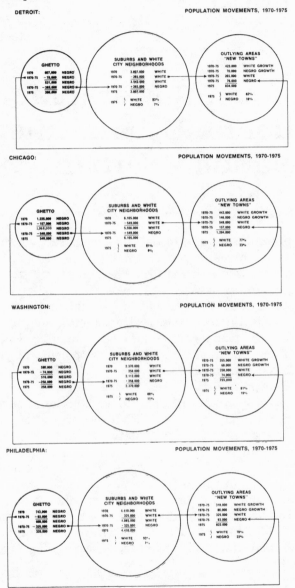

Source: *Center Magazine,* A publication of the Center for the Study of Democratic Institutions, Santa Barbara, California, September 1968.

Chapter 6

The Formula for a More Humane Urban America: A National Urban Policy and New Towns

At its present rate of growth, the population of the United States will have increased from 203 million in 1970 to 314 million by the end of the twentieth century. The fact of growth is not debatable, but where that growth will take place is of great concern. If present patterns continue, about 85 percent of the growth will be concentrated in the country's twelve largest regions,[1] and most of the crowding, as planners have long been warning, will occur in four areas of continuous metropolitan development referred to by urbanologists as megalopolises: Boston to Washington, D.C., Chicago to Pittsburgh, San Francisco to San Diego, and Jacksonville to Miami. Former Secretary of Commerce Maurice Stans envisaged "a nation jammed together in an 'anthill society'" unless the federal government in the near future formulates and implements an effective national urban policy."[2] The idea that there should be a national urban policy is relatively new; in fact, the first step by the federal government in this direction was the establishment of the Urban Affairs Council by former President Nixon on January 23, 1969, to "advise and assist" with respect to urban affairs and specifically "in the development of a national urban policy, having regard for both immediate and long-range concerns and for priorities among them."[3]

212

The historical causes of the present urban crisis are easy to discern. Indeed, not until fairly recently has city planning been considered a prime government responsibility, probably because it was not until 1920 that the proportion of our nation's population residing in urban areas surpassed the 50 percent level. No less a dignitary than President George Washington, for example, fired Pierre L'Enfant, the Frenchman who gave Washington, D.C., the finest city plan in our nation's history, because he felt that L'Enfant was not worth his pay—$5 per month.[4] Hence, most large cities in the United States have grown from untamed youth to decaying old age with a minimum of professional direction. Especially following the heavy immigration of the post–Civil War period, the internal structure of most American cities may be described as cramped and congested, with houses built wall to wall to save space and money and to afford greater protection against harsh weather conditions. Streets were narrow since they had to accommodate only pedestrians and an occasional horse and carriage. City populations huddled close to their waterfronts, for it was here that the majority of the gainfully employed worked—in industries dependent upon water power. Moreover, housing conditions were deplorable and sanitation standards were virtually nonexistent. It is not surprising, therefore, that serious fires and epidemics were recurrent phenomena.

Beginning in the late nineteenth century, the railroads, electric trolleys, and then automobiles, enabled an increasing number of families and industries to move away from the inner core to the periphery of the nation's large cities, but the ultimate result was not an improvement in the quality of urban life. Indeed, the outcome was the phenomenon recently labeled "urban sprawl"—an incoherent mass of urban development. Sprawl may occur with three types of physical development. It may result from very low-density development of a large area where single-family homes are built on lots of two to five acres or more, consuming large amounts of land that professional planners argue should be developed at higher-density ratios. A second form of urban sprawl results from more intensive development extending out from built-up areas along major highway routes, with the space between the strip development left underdeveloped. Public services are usually more expensive to provide under this condition, often referred to as "strip sprawl," than under conditions of low-density urban sprawl. Finally, sprawl may be characterized by leapfrog developments where relatively compact urbanization takes place surrounded by substantial amounts of undeveloped land. Such developments not only require the greatest initial capital expenditures for urban services, but they absorb open space urgently needed for recreational purposes. Furthermore, it spirals public service costs for sewer and water lines and school bus transportation and frequently destroys any possibility for an efficient and economical mass transit system. Marion Clawson has succinctly summarized the case against urban sprawl as follows: "(1) A sprawled or discontinuous urban development is more costly and less efficient than a compact one. . . . (2) Sprawl is unaesthetic and unattractive. (3) Sprawl is wasteful of land since the intervening land is not used for any specific purpose. (4) Land speculation is unproductive, absorbing capital, manpower, and entrepreneurial skills without commensurate public gains. . . . (5) It is an inequitable system which requires the new land-occupier to shoulder a heavy burden of capital charges for site costs which are, in large part, unnecessary and avoidable."[5]

Two special circumstances have aggravated the trend toward urban sprawl in the United States: first, the tremendous migration of southern blacks to northern cities during the first half of the twentieth century, and, second, the post–World War II population explosion (90 million babies were born between 1946 and 1968).[6] The already inadequate housing facilities and municipal services were overtaxed, producing rapid physical decay, psychological frustration, and social unrest in central cities. Motivated by these conditions as well as by racial prejudice, many middle- and upper-class whites fled to the suburbs, leaving the central cities to the elderly, the poor, and racial minorities, with the result that they have become literally human cesspools—that is, depositories for the disadvantaged, the helpless, the unwanted, and the problem-ridden segments of our society.

Factors contributing to our nation's urban crisis—belated government involvement in urban planning, the growing trend toward population concentration in a dozen or so megalopolises across the country, the ghettoization of minorities and the poor—are added to by the despoiling of the physical environment. Special emphasis was given to this problem by former President Nixon in his 1970 State of the Union message: "The great question of the seventies," he said, "is whether or not we shall make peace with nature and begin to make reparations for the damage we have done to our air, to our land, and to our water."[7] Many contemporary experts on urban affairs, including the author, are convinced that a nationwide government-subsidized new towns program would constitute one of the most effective responses to the problem of environmental pollution, as well as to the other problems underlying our urban crisis, and that this program should become an integral part of our national urban policy if and when one is formulated.

Daniel P. Moynihan, now a United States senator, formerly a professor of urban politics at Harvard University, and former urban affairs advisor to President Nixon as well as former United States delegate to the United Nations, has been an especially outspoken advocate of a national urban policy for our country. He has expressed his concerns in this matter as follows:

> [Our urban problems,] for the most part, represent the failure of urban arrangements to meet the expectations of the urban population in the areas of jobs, schools, housing, transportation, public health, administrative responsiveness, and political flexibility. [But] if all these [urban arrangements] are related one to the other and in combination do not seem to be working well, the question arises whether the society ought not attempt a more coherent response ... with something like a national urban policy. [In other words,] ought not the vast efforts to control the situation of the present be at least informed by some sense of goals for the future? ... However, in the evolution of a national urban policy, more is involved than merely the question of national goals and the provision of resources with which to attain them. Too many programs have produced too few results simply to accept a more or less straightforward extrapolation of past and present practices into an oversized but familiar future. The question of method has become as salient as that of goals. As yet, [however,] the federal government, [and, for that matter,] state and local governments, have not found an effective incentive system—comparable to profit in private enterprise, prestige in intellectual activity, rank in military organization—whereby to shape the forces at work in urban areas in such a way that urban

goals—whatever they may be—are in fact attained. . . .
[Hence,] we must seek not just policy, but policy allied to
a vigorous strategy for obtaining results from it. [And,]
finally, the federal establishment must develop a much
heightened sensitivity to its "hidden" urban policies.
There is hardly a department or agency of the national
government whose programs do not in some way have important consequences for the life of cities and those who
live in them, [but] frequently . . . the political appointees
and career executives concerned do not see themselves as
involved with, much less responsible for, the urban consequences of their programs and policies. They are, in
their minds, simply building highways, guaranteeing
mortgages, advancing agriculture, or whatever. No one
has made clear to them that they are simultaneously re-
distributing employment opportunities, segregating neighborhoods or desegregating them, depopulating the countryside and filling up the slums, and so forth. . . . Already
this institutional naiveté has become cause for suspicion;
in the future it simply must not be tolerated. Indeed, in
the future, a primary mark of competence in a federal
official should be the ability to see the interconnections
between programs immediately at hand and the urban
problems that pervade the larger society.[8]

BASIC PRINCIPLES OF A NATIONAL URBAN POLICY
FOR THE UNITED STATES

In the author's opinion, the following four principles are the
most basic ingredients of any national urban policy which might
be proposed for the United States:

1. GREATER GOVERNMENT CONCERN FOR THE
LIVING CONDITIONS OF ALL URBAN AMERICANS

The most basic principle of a national urban policy for the
United States should be that all individuals and families, regardless of their ethnic, racial, and socioeconomic backgrounds, have
an annual income sufficient to maintain a decent standard of living
and an opportunity for spatial and social mobility. While the desire
of certain social minority groups for residential segregation must
be respected, the ideal which should be propagated is residential integration throughout every urban community.

If we still regard America as the land of opportunity and desire low-income families to move into the economic mainstream rather than slip into welfare status, we must ensure that they come into contact with more prosperous families. Financial fears in suburban areas over prospective new patterns of housing should not be regarded as justification for restrictive land-use regulations aimed at maintaining islands of advantage amid the seas of social change, for these regulations are among the powerful forces at work polarizing our society. Local zoning laws are already under attack in some state legislatures as well as in the courts for going far beyond a legitimate concern for public health and safety. It is entirely possible to distribute housing for lower-income families in various parts of a metropolitan area in such a way that they will enjoy the benefits of fresh air, safe streets, good schools, and access to the increasing number of suburban jobs without changing the "character" of any existing community. It is not sufficiently understood that by following a pattern of "fair sharing," that is, each suburban community providing its fair share of housing for low-income families, not a single suburb will have its basic nature changed. The statistics of suburban growth and central-city decline in the 1970 Census make that clear.[9] On the other hand, as long as the problems of change are imposed selectively upon certain neighborhoods or particular ethnic and social groups, militant opposition becomes inevitable. This piece-meal approach also leads to rigid political positions that make it all but impossible to implement constructive public policy.

America's two most famous new towns serve as models of the successful integration of various racial, religious, and socioeconomic classes in highly desirable residential settings. As indicated in the sections in Chapter 5 on Reston and Columbia, 13 to 18 percent of the housing in these two towns has been reserved for people with below-average incomes. Moreover, there would be a greater number of families with low incomes in both towns if the federal government had acted more expeditiously on applications for housing subsidies; so far it has given little more than lip service to the idea of socially and economically balanced new communities. To prevent its three hundred subsidized dwelling units from being tagged as low-income housing, Columbia has built them on five different sites, and they are as handsomely designed as any others in the town so that they cannot be distinguished from the rest. This subsidized housing was sponsored by the Columbia Interfaith Housing Corporation which grew out of the town's cooperative ministry, a group which also sponsors an Interfaith Center in Lake Wilde Village Center where Catholics, Jews, and all Protestants hold religious services and seminars. Reston has put its 198 moderate-income families together into one apartment house complex called Cedar Ridge. Ten of the Cedar Ridge apartments are rented to families on welfare which fact is not known to the other residents. None of the families have come from the Washington or Baltimore ghettos, nor are all of them black. Rather, they are young teachers, factory workers, and store clerks, many of whom work in the new town and all of whom previously lived in the surrounding rural county.

The people who have moved into Reston and Columbia because they saw in them a new urban frontier are proud of their racial and economic mix. In Reston, a vocal group of early settlers has organized a group called Black Focus which continually urges the developer to make greater efforts to open the town to black people, to show black faces in their promotion pictures, and to hire black salesmen, and these urgings have had some effect. In Columbia, liberals boast that people who supported George Wallace for president of the United States live contentedly on the same street with blacks and members of various ethnic groups who were attracted to Columbia by its promise of racial and ethnic harmony. And this pioneering spirit seems to be contagious, for a 1969 University of Michigan poll found that 56 percent of the respondents in Columbia wanted people of different racial backgrounds living in their neighborhoods. However, Columbia and Reston tend to substantiate the contention frequently made by sociologists that most whites of all income groups do not object to racial integration as long as they are sure that the white group remains in the majority. That is surely "racist" thinking, but there is hope that planned communities can help overcome this racism by homeopathically, as it were, taking this prejudice into account, for a new town, more so than an impersonal city or suburb, is capable of resolving its problems in a spirit of community.[10]

In contrast to the creative, socially oriented planning described above, most urban planning in the United States has been corrective and physically oriented. Government agencies have made occasional entries into the difficult area of creative social planning (e.g., the greenbelt communities built by the federal government during the Depression) but not nearly so frequently as comparable agencies in Western Europe's most economically advanced nations.

There are several major explanations for the preoccupation with corrective physical planning in the United States. First, not only has the rapid and uncontrolled growth of American cities resulted in multitudinous physical and social problems, but their scope and complexity are tremendous due to the great size of our urban populations and because of the interrelationships among the problems. In brief, local government agencies, faced with many enormous and complicated problems, take the practical approach—heal the city's most serious wounds as well as possible before planning for its future. Second, the funds available for this therapeutic approach to the city's problems are often inadequate, so that a Band-Aid is about all that can be afforded. Under such circumstances, it is obvious that creative planning is a luxury in which local government agencies cannot indulge. Third, since most government officials are political animals, they tend to emphasize those projects which are most visible and appealing to the masses—improved streets, more frequent garbage and trash collection, and better fire and police protection. This predilection of America's urban masses for corrective physical planning reflects the persistence of their rural, tradition-oriented heritage, in contradistinction to the characteristic urban emphasis upon novel and often impractical concepts and ideas. As a result, creative social planning, historically the province of philosophers, political idealists, architects, educators, and social scientists, is not yet the explicit responsibility of any state government agency in the United States, with the notable exception of the New York State Urban Development Corporation, which will be discussed under the third principle of the national urban policy here proposed for the United States—greater state government responsibility for urban planning.

2. THE REORGANIZATION OF LOCAL GOVERNMENTS
    FOR GREATER EFFECTIVENESS
    IN RESPONDING TO URBAN PROBLEMS

The relatively ineffective response to urban problems by local governments in the United States is due at least partially to their fragmented structure. Most metropolitan area residents are served

by at least four separate local governments—a county, a municipality or township, a school district, and one or more special districts. In 1970 the 243 metropolitan areas in the United States were
served by more than 20,000 local governments, or an average of 90
local governments each. But this average covered great variations—
from fewer than 10 local governments in each of twenty metropolitan areas to such extremes as 1,113 local governments in Chicago,
871 in Philadelphia, 704 in Pittsburgh, and 551 in New York.[11]
The abuses resulting from such a multiplicity of governments are
many: discriminatory zoning which keeps low-income families out
of suburban areas by stipulating lot sizes beyond their economic
means; the prohibition of planned unit developments which could
accommodate more people in less space at substantial savings in
housing costs; and disallowing blue-collar industries which hire
largely unskilled and semiskilled labor. Still another abuse is excessive strip zoning for commercial purposes along main thoroughfares which produces more revenue for the municipal or county
government than if the land were left undeveloped. Not only are
many of these commercial developments gaudy and ugly, but because of the many curb cuts required they cause serious interrup-
tions in the flow of traffic. What is suggested, then, is to replace
the present multiplicity of local governments in our metropolitan
areas with a set of comprehensive units, each responsible for providing all local public services for its own defined territory and
each serving a population of at least 50,000 persons. In the process,
many unnecessary overlapping layers of local government, especially very small units and special districts, would be weeded out.

The key to the success of reorganizing metropolitan government is held by the state legislatures, for the lack of objectivity and
perspective on the part of local government in regard to this matter
is one reason why urban areas are already in such trouble. Within
the typical city planning structure, three separate groups operate
with varying degrees of cooperation: (1) the municipal executives—
the mayor, the city manager, and the city council or commission;
(2) the planning department—a group of professionals who are
full-time employees of the municipal government; and (3) the
planning commission—a group of unpaid laymen appointed by the
mayor or city council/commission with legal powers to participate
in the planning process. While the mayor or city manager and his

council constitute the legally recognized ultimate authority for city planning, and while the planning department has the responsibility for developing a master plan and for proposing planning projects, the planning commission can either accept or reject the plan and proposals, thereby determining what is presented to the ultimate planning authority for implementation. In reality, therefore, neither the elected officials nor the professional planners play the decisive role in planning.

Planning commissions are vestiges of a period when professional urban planning was nonexistent in the United States and when most citizens were ignorant of its importance. It was therefore necessary for a few community leaders to organize from time to time to demand that their city governments undertake certain urgently needed projects. Today, however, their role has become somewhat obsolete because the conditions which made their existence necessary no longer prevail. Moreover, since most members of the planning commission are businessmen, they lack the training and experience required to appreciate the true nature and scope of urban planning, tending to focus on the more obvious physical aspects of the process. Under these circumstances the personnel of the city planning department are likely to consider their work an exercise in futility. Sometimes, however, a single charismatic mayor, city councilman/commissioner, or planning director can surmount the power of the planning commission to bring about some truly creative urban development. In New York City, for example, city planning was stimulated largely by the former Mayor LaGuardia and the many-titled commissioner, Robert Moses. Similar individual catalysts have worked in other cities such as Philadelphia, Los Angeles, Milwaukee, Cincinnati, and Pittsburgh, but these are notable exceptions.

The ironic fact is that we know a lot more than we put to use in the battle to improve the quality of urban life. Workable, proven ideas are available in a thousand places. What we do not have in sufficient quality or quantity is the commitment to put these ideas to work in combination over a continuous period in an arena large enough to enlist the resources needed to make the ideas pay off. There are at least a hundred cities in the United States which have had studies made of trends in their local economies and other basic life-support systems, and another hundred cities could easily be found which have attempted to establish goals. But one would be hard-pressed to find a city which has tried to spell out in clear operational terms just what life could be like if it achieved its objectives and reversed undesirable trends or reinforced desirable ones. In other words, we expend our energies on diagnosis and prescription and never get around to describing how the results would look, feel, and act. We seem to have lost our way in the large cities as we simply try to cope with crisis after crisis and barely manage to survive. The result is "policy sprawl"—policy that grows in bits and pieces without any overall vision to follow—and the end product, just as in the case of urban sprawl, is that urbanites experience less and less of a sense of community and identification with their local governments.

3. GREATER STATE AND FEDERAL GOVERNMENT RESPONSIBILITY FOR URBAN PLANNING

In general, state governments have not been responsive financially to the problems of their constituent cities whose governments they have created, nor have they encouraged a more comprehensive regional approach to the solution of these problems, and the federal government has reinforced these tendencies by establishing a direct relationship with cities for the administration of most urban assistance programs. Moreover, many states as well as cities are walking a financial tightrope and some have even declared bankruptcy. The lack of money to solve urban problems explains why so many central-city residents have given up hope of saving the city and have either moved to the suburbs or, unable to move, have taken to civil disturbances, rioting, burning, and looting as an expression of their frustration and hostility. Strangely enough, in our "enlightened" society, it usually take such drastic measures to awaken the federal government to the fact that it must help the cities solve their problems. Inasmuch as federal income increases 1.5 percent for each 1 percent increase in the gross national product, while that of local governments increases only 0.5 to 0.75 percent, federal aid to cities (whether through revenue sharing or through categorical and credit assistance) should be doubled to constitute about one-third of local government revenues.[12] Finally, the dispersal of funds from federal and state treasuries to cities must be streamlined and expedited. At present, approximately 85 percent of every tax dollar leaves the cities for state and federal coffers, and while some of this revenue is returned to the cities, the burden of extricating these funds from state and federal agencies through an intricate set of procedures rests with the cities.

Another fact highly relevant to this discussion is that Hawaii is the only state which has a policy regarding the vitally important matter of land use. Every other state has adopted permissive legislation allowing local governments to use land within their borders purely on the basis of local concerns and without regard to the needs of the region or state. It is no accident that the new towns movement has been far more vigorous in Europe where the focus of public policy-making is national and where government administration is more centralized. For example, the master plan for land use in metropolitan Stockholm is not just a public relations package or an intellectual exercise. It is politically tenable because the power to make the plan and carry it out rests in the same place—in the national government. By contrast, the planning commission in most American cities is comparatively powerless in relation to the myriad agencies responsible for carrying out—or, often as not, thwarting—its recommendations. This is not to suggest that the answer to all of our urban problems in the United States is greater and more highly centralized government power to resolve them. The experience of the New York State Urban Development Corporation (UDC) illustrates the limitations of such a theory. UDC was established by the governor and state legislature of New York in 1968 as an independent public-benefit corporation designed to bring a comprehensive approach to the problems of urban deterioration, economic stagnation, unemployment, shortage of housing, and lack of civic facilities. The corporation can plan and carry out projects to supply housing for families of low, moderate, and middle income; to redevelop blighted areas through land use improvement projects; to assist industrial and commercial development in some circumstances; to provide needed educational, cultural, community, and other civic facilities; and, through a combination of these activities, to develop new communities. Moreover, UDC is authorized to issue its own bonds to finance such projects. The powers conferred upon UDC by the state of New York make it a versatile agency, but *only* as long as it operates *within* the parameters of broad public consent which imposes some major constraints or limitations on UDC's activities. For example, UDC is already viewed apprehensively by many people because of its statutory powers to override local zoning regulations and building codes. The political challenge confronting such agencies in the United States, therefore, is, on the one hand, to demonstrate their capacity to deliver the services and programs so desperately needed and, on the other hand, to invite and encourage participation in policy making and planning by the communities which these services and programs are designed to benefit. Traditional urban planning institutions have tended not to deliver or to deliver at the expense of community input, and often "community control" has been substituted for participatory democracy. The latter situation characteristically involves several rounds of confrontation which usually results in a great deal of rhetoric but in little or no concrete accomplishment. Hence, our urgent need is to work out a government apparatus which can combine sensitive communication with effective action in meeting the physical and social needs of our cities.

4. GREATER FEDERAL GOVERNMENT CONCERN
   FOR URBAN ECOLOGY AND AESTHETICS

The federal government, by its own example as well as by various positive and negative inducements directed toward the private sector of the society, must demonstrate a genuine concern for the quality of the urban environment. Four principles should govern this concern. First, the urban environment must be conceived in terms of the best that can be made available through manageable effort, at costs that can be computed and compared to other costs, and at performance levels that can be described and measured. A second principle involves scope; model cities, urban renewal projects, highway development, and many other commendable programs, for example, have simply not had sufficient scope and impact to make a significant difference in the quality of urban life. It would be much better if housing, transportation, and employment objectives were included within a single plan—a level of integration which is rarely found in urban redevelopment programs. A third principle dictates that the urban environment must incorporate an ever widening number of choices and differences in order to generate that critical mass of life activity that constitutes a growing community. The fourth principle is that there must be a

visible benefit for every cost and a visible return on every investment if the new environment is to be maintained by those who live
in it. A corollary of this principle is that the social and aesthetic
components of the urban environment should not be in any sense
contrary to expectations for economic growth, stability, and profitability. For example, it must no longer be economically profitable
for private industry to waste and despoil our natural resources. Not
only must penalties for violations be consistently rather than spo-
radically or preferentially imposed, but financial incentives or rewards should be offered by the federal government for those industries initiating pollution control programs and/or advancing pol-
lution-control technology. In sum, then, urban environments that
are meant to create new choices and opportunities, to provide jus-
tice and responsibility, and to supply a return to all who have a
stake in them, must be planned in a comprehensive and integrated
manner. This means that the interrelationships between all the basic life-support systems must be discovered, analyzed, and dealt
with at the level where they intersect in the lives of people.

The creative use of design in planning public and private buildings as well as total urban environments must also become an explicit concern of the federal government, because the major factor
which distinguishes a humane community from "just a place to live
and work" is an aesthetic arrangement of people, nature, and facilities in a cohesive unit which is both functional and psychologically
satisfying. The federal government has set a poor example in regard to the design of projects it has sponsored during the twentieth
century, notably in the area of public housing. It should now take
the lead, as have the governments of other countries which have
produced great cities (Greece-Athens, Holland-Amsterdam, France-
Paris), and encourage and rule into being a beautiful urban America with every means available. These would include rewards of
prizes or money to developers and contractors for innovative or
creative work; financial support for the work of building by cities
and states; and comprehensive rulings and laws regarding the form
to be taken.

Once the federal government and large private corporations
have demonstrated genuine concern for urban aesthetics in their
respective building and community-development projects, they
should disseminate this concern through at least three mechanisms:

1. Both the federal government and private corporations should encourage and subsidize local programs which not only are aimed at inculcating in youth a greater consciousness of, and sensitivity to, the quality of the urban physical environment, but give the young an opportunity to develop or participate in local projects designed to enhance that environment.

2. The federal government and private corporations should both encourage and subsidize local programs for individuals and groups such as mayors, city managers, city councilmen, planning departments and commissions, zoning and building commission officials, and businessmen which would impress upon them the importance of exercising the responsibility and power which they possess for the creation of a more stimulating urban environment.

3. Just as federal government aid for all urban improvement programs requires compliance with the regulations of the equal opportunity act, so should this aid be made contingent upon cities making innovations in the design of their physical environments an integral part of their comprehensive planning. The implementation of this creative kind of building would be greatly enhanced by the federal government's establishing a National Design Center which could serve as a consulting and coordinating agency to stimulate the imaginations of, and to promote the exchange of ideas among, planners, architects, builders, interior designers, landscape engineers, and all the other professionals who help to determine the shape and appearance of the cityscape.

The Basic Principles of Creative Urban Design

Historically, effective city planning and building have always been motivated by ideological objectives. Thus, the Greeks built their cities as settings for the Panathenaic processions; the Romans, to reflect the wealth and power of their vast colonial empire; the popes of the Middle Ages, to symbolize the glory of the church; the kings of the Renaissance period, to reflect the grandeur and opulence of their monarchical regimes; the early colonists in America, to express their new freedom and hope in the future; and the utopians and socialists of the early industrial era, to reform capitalist abuses.

During the past century or so in the United States the planning of our cities has been left largely to chance and the profit-making instincts of real estate speculators and mortgage bankers. But recently a reaction has set in demanding that social objectives guide urban planning, a trend which may be attributed in large part to the civil disturbances of the 1960s. As a first step, this approach requires that research be conducted into the needs and desires of the people living in cities. Too frequently, however, research becomes an end in itself, the planners filling several volumes which simply gather dust on the shelves of their offices. Failure to accommodate the needs reflected in the findings within a given space and time may be due to inadequate funds, apathy, or fear of the political consequences of disturbing the status quo. Hence, whatever planning is done results in few if any significant changes in the urban environment until perhaps another crisis evokes some drastic efforts to compensate for the relative inactivity of the past.

The modern planner is seldom a designer; he is concerned largely with densities, traffic patterns, and the accommodation of basic facilities and open spaces within a given area, rather than with such details or refinements as form and shape, light and shade, texture and color, vistas and enclosures, or with such amenities as fountains, sculptures, public benches, and light fixtures which bring a plan of life and evoke a genuinely human response. Finally execution of the planner's plan is turned over to private contractors whose sole concerns are making a profit from the project and, of course, complying with the local building codes. While these are both understandable objectives, the resulting aggregation of buildings rarely constitutes a socially responsible or a response-evoking place for people to live, as Eliel Saarinen expressed it so graphically:

> Were a great number of the most beautiful and famous buildings in architectural history all re-erected to form a single street, this street should be the most beautiful in the world, were beauty merely a matter of beautiful buildings. But such would most certainly not be the case, for the street would appear a heterogeneous medley of unrelated edifices. The effect would be similar to that produced if a number of the most eminent musicians all played the finest music at the same time—but each a different...melody. There would be no music, but much noise.[13]

How, then, can we design good cities? Modern urban planners

invariably look to Europe's past to understand what made its cities so attractive, civilized, human, and livable. Camillo Sitte explained the rationale for this approach as follows: "Having long since lost any natural sensitivity and instinct for building a good place to live, we must rediscover past principles of urban design."[14] With this understanding, urban planners are gradually developing a set of creative design principles relevant to our times. One of these is the separation of different means and destinations of movement, not only protecting pedestrians from automobile accidents but facilitating the flow of vehicular traffic, the latter by providing separate thoroughfares for slow-moving local traffic and fast-moving through traffic. Transportation planners now realize the practicality of this principle, but still lacking is cooperation between them and urban planners to integrate the city's transportation network with the pattern of buildings and open spaces.

The principle of human scale is another important element of creative urban design borrowed from Europe which has finally convinced us that most American cities are too large to make walking to work and to community facilities feasible and to facilitate intimate social interaction. Out of this stems the increasing acceptance of the new towns movement. Its American proponents recommend the establishment of over one hundred self-sufficient new communities of limited size in the open country and yet relatively close to metropolitan centers, as well as the construction of new towns in-town which would divide large cities into organic communities and neighborhoods.

An important third principle of creative urban design applicable to both new towns in the country and new towns in-town is the dispersion of amenities in such a way that all residents have about equal access to them. Thus, as German architect Hans Scharoun has suggested, "cultural institutions, large offices, stores, and parks should be woven like ribbons through the city to make them more available to everyone, much in the medieval town-planning tradition."[15] We should respond to this tradition not out of mere sentimentality but because of its humanism, and if we begin to master our technology in the service of this humanism, the chances are good that the present urban crisis will be the start of a new era of beautiful cities.

THE ELEMENTS OF URBAN BEAUTY

The major elements of urban beauty include the cityscape; such moderate-scale urban features as highway and street patterns, parking facilities, and public squares or plazas; and, finally, numerous smaller details, such as fountains, sculptures, trees, flowers, and "street furniture," each category to be discussed more fully below.

THE CITYSCAPE

The cityscape or general visual impression created by a city is a product of how urban space encloses buildings and vice versa, a subtle relationship to which many planners are insensitive. An attractive cityscape need not be entirely dependent upon original terrain. If it were, there would be no challenge in urban design, and most cities could never become beautiful, because there are relatively few land areas in the world where nature has provided a perfect setting for an urban community. Many of the world's most exciting cityscapes are almost entirely products of human ingenuity, such as those exemplified in the skillful modification of the terrain in Boston and Brasilia, or in the creative arrangement of buildings and space in Washington, D.C., and Paris, and in the assiduous control of waterways in Pittsburgh and Amsterdam.

It cannot be denied, however, that it is difficult for even the least skillful urban planners to ruin a magnificent natural landscape. San Francisco's unique natural beauty, for example, has not yet been seriously jeopardized by the city's conventional gridiron street pattern, by the ugly Bay and Richmond bridges, or by the real estate exploitation of the Twin Peaks. Nevertheless, San Francisco's ardent conservationists must be constantly vigilant to prohibit real estate developers from desecrating the Marin Hills as they did the Twin Peaks, to prevent Bay Area communities from attempting to increase their tax bases by landfill operations which would reduce the size of the Bay, and to regulate the pollution of the Bay waters by municipal as well as by private industries. Other cities of the west coast, such as Los Angeles, San Diego, and Seattle, have not been as fortunate as San Francisco, however; the hillsides of the first two cities have been bulldozed so frequently that there are constant threats of landslides, and Seattle has surrendered its beautiful waterfront to the highway builders just as Manhattan has done little by little in New York. Between the two coasts, the great cities of the Middle West, with the exception of Chicago, have demonstrated a similar disregard for the aesthetic and recreational value of their vast lake and river resources by blatantly polluting them.

The solution to such cases of defiling and misusing nature is not so much one of more zoning and antipollution legislation as it is of better enforcement of that which already exists—a job which will not be done conscientiously unless the American public in much larger numbers than at present demands it. Even then, this approach is a negative one. A much more sophisticated and positive approach is to emphasize the use of modern technology to make certain attractive features of the natural environment aesthetic assets to urban communities. Boston, for example, created two sizable lakes by damming the Charles River and a tidal stream, the Mystic, thereby substantially increasing recreational resources. Similarly, the canyon produced by Strawberry Creek which runs east and west through the Berkeley Hills on the University of California campus (at elevations ranging between 500 feet and 1,600 feet above sea level) has been converted into an 800-acre multi-purpose recreational and nature-study area which includes a clubhouse, an athletic field, two swimming pools, two tennis courts, a botanical garden, a poultry research laboratory, and the California Memorial Stadium which seats 80,000 people. The southern slope of the canyon has been densely planted with trees by the University of California's School of Forestry, while the northern slope features the university's Lawrence Radiation Laboratories constructed by the Atomic Energy Commission.

Another way of influencing the cityscape besides abusing, conserving, or even creating nature is by constructing new buildings. Residents of New York City's Park Avenue, for example, were seriously disturbed when Lever Brothers interjected its towering modern edifice among the street's elegant traditional buildings of uniform height, disrupting a pattern which had prevailed for decades. Eventually, however, several other tasteful skyscrapers, such as those of Joseph E. Seagram and Sons, Pepsi-Cola, and Union Carbide, joined Lever House on Park Avenue, with the result that the cityscape in this area changed but was as attractive as before and undoubtedly more consistent with the modern-day functions of Manhattan. But then the gigantic Pan-Am Building was constructed atop the Grand Central Terminal at one end of Park Avenue, producing a negative effect due to its bulky proportions, lack of architectural distinctiveness, and its abrupt termination of the street. So far, lower Manhattan has been somewhat more fortunate than Park Avenue with respect to the aesthetic effect of new buildings. The Chase Manhattan Bank, for example, slipped smoothly into the existing pattern of buildings because its scale and general character were consistent with the ensemble. But even such an ideal complex is not permanently immune to disfigurement. If many more equally high buildings were erected on the periphery of the present grouping, resulting in its being widened and visually flattened, a very unpleasant cityscape might result. The same negative effect can be produced by one extraordinarily high building, as exemplified by the initial impact of the Prudential Tower on the Boston skyline, and the potential effect if similar high-rise buildings were erected on San Francisco's famous hills, notably Nob Hill and Russian Hill.

Although one new high-rise apartment building has recently been built on Nob Hill at the corner of California and Jones Streets and another has been proposed for the corner of Sacramento Street and Sproule Lane, a group of residents calling itself the Nob Hill Neighbors has been organized to prevent the second development. In addition, it is fighting to have the legal maximum building height on the peak of Nob Hill reduced from 320 feet to 105 feet and that for the several surrounding blocks reduced from 240 feet to 40 feet. Another group of residents from Russian Hill—the shoulder of Nob Hill on High Street between Lombard and Chestnut Streets—was successful in blocking a Kansas City developer from building twin high-rise towers with 300 apartment units, as well as a local developer from constructing twenty-four luxury condominiums, in that area. This group is also determined to preserve as many trees as possible on Russian Hill.

It would be possible, of course, to prevent the cityscape from being an entirely accidental matter if zones for various building heights were established for an entire city in such a way as to produce the desired skyline, leaving most building specifications other than height to the discretion of contractors and their architects. Cities could exercise still stricter control by demanding that any request for the issuance of a building permit include studies of the cityscape both before and after the introduction of the new building; that the study be published and subjected to public criticism; and, finally, that it be approved by some public agency with the requisite powers. Such a procedure would prevent some of the worst abuses of the architectural cityscape.

In view of the increasing corporate concern about image, one might assume that buildings occupied by large corporations would be innovative, pleasing, and in scale. However, inasmuch as many corporations do not invest their capital in, nor direct the construction of, the buildings they occupy, the "corporate image" factor may be of limited effectiveness in terms of insuring an aesthetic cityscape. Frequently, entrepreneur-builders with no aesthetic inclinations and with little public image to risk construct large buildings entirely as speculative rental space, naming the building for the largest or longest-term tenant.

The architectural quality of most American government buildings, however, is much lower than that of most private corporation structures. A number of factors explain this situation. First, with respect to government office buildings there has been political resistance to housing civil servants in luxurious quarters and, in the case of public housing, a corresponding reluctance to "pamper" the subsidized poor. Second, there is the fact of uncultivated public taste with respect to aesthetic matters, a situation which several mass circulation magazines and professional journals have made a concerted effort to correct. Only a few newspapers in the United States employ professional architectural critics, and television programs devoted to the cultivation of aesthetic taste are sponsored almost exclusively by university-owned or public broadcasting stations. Third, distinctive architecture can never be achieved without utilizing the services of first-rate designers, but such experts usually reside in a few large cities here or abroad, and popular pressure on local politicians to "employ local talent" and "keep expenses down" is often difficult or impossible to resist.

In light of the uninspiring architectural quality of most government buildings, the following corrective measures are suggested. American cities might adopt a practice which is fairly common in

Europe of taxing local residents a certain percentage of the cost of erecting public buildings to provide for art, landscaping, fountains, and other aesthetic embellishments of these structures. Moreover, courses designed to cultivate public artistic taste should be required at every level of public education, and television networks should sponsor regular programs at prime time dealing with urban problems and with the successful efforts of certain cities to cope with them as examples for others to emulate. Finally, local planning and building commissions should not consist primarily of businessmen or of representative groups of lay citizens, but of persons with at least some training and/or practical experience in architecture, urban planning, or construction. All these measures will fail to produce more beautiful American cities, however, unless local governments either change their tax structure or receive more federal aid to improve their financial status and unless architects of exceptional talent are "imported," even at a premium price, to supervise the services of local professionals. This has been the approach of great cities throughout history, and it will continue to be so. The federal government can act as a catalyst by encouraging contemporary cities to employ these approaches and perhaps by offering a significant monetary prize annually or biannually to the city which has contributed most to urban aesthetics.

HIGHWAY AND STREET PATTERNS

In our automotive age, highway and street patterns constitute one of the most important features of the cityscape; indeed, in the inner city more space is allocated for this purpose than for any other single land use if one includes such auxiliary facilities as parking lots and garages. The percentage of space so allocated ranges from slightly less than 50 percent in older cities to 75 percent in Los Angeles, the average being about 66 percent. Like buildings, highways and streets can either be aesthetic assets or liabilities and, unfortunately, there is much more evidence of their having a negative than a positive effect. Where the effect is positive, as in a few isolated instances, highways traverse cities as attractively designed overpasses, thereby introducing excitingly innovative architectural forms to the urban environment, providing new, more stimulating views of the cityscape, and preserving the integrity of neighborhoods instead of ruthlessly dividing them. More-

over, some of the most exemplary highways and streets are sufficiently broad to permit attractive landscaping on both sides of
thoroughfares, not only enhancing the aesthetic quality of these facilities but buffering the adjoining neighborhoods against vehicular noises.

As in the case of public buildings, one of the major reasons for
the generally negative impact of highways and streets on the cityscape is the traditional attitude among politicians of getting as
much as possible for the least money. Moreover, the engineers responsible for the actual construction of these roads are usually not
design oriented, and the people residing in the neighborhoods
through which the freeways pass are not sufficiently articulate or
politically powerful to protest effectively against the resulting defacement of their physical environment. Considering the tremendous cost of building and maintaining the ugly highways and streets
we already have in this nation, only an enlightened federal program providing substantial grants to cities and states specifically
for the purpose of creating more aesthetic roadways will assure
any change.

PARKING FACILITIES

Every truly beautiful city must effectively regulate the flow
of motor vehicles through its roadway system and provide adequate
parking facilities in the downtown area. A still more desirable goal
would be the restriction of automobiles entirely from this sector,
linking it with outlying residential areas by an inexpensive and efficient rapid-transit system. At present, entirely too much surface
land area in American cities is being used for on-street parking
(which also interferes with traffic flow) as well as for parking
lots, which are, to say the least, one of the most unaesthetic features of the modern cityscape. Much to be preferred are architec-
turally attractive above-ground ramp garages, which are increasing in number and underground facilities such as those at Grand
Circus Park in Detroit, Mellon Square in Pittsburgh, and Union
Square in San Francisco.

PUBLIC SQUARES OR PLAZAS

Everyone admires the great open squares of such European cities as Rome, Venice, and Paris, and of such South American cities
as Buenos Aires, Quito, and Lima, but many of these squares are

of more aesthetic than practical value because their dimensions are too small to accommodate today's large urban populations. There is no reason, however, why this popular feature of some of the world's greatest cities should not become an integral part of American urban structure, but on a different scale. Large cities could, in fact, accommodate many public squares or plazas, each one, perhaps, having both a vehicular and a pedestrian level which would be joined by artistically designed thoroughfares to the vehicular and pedestrian levels of every other plaza or square within the city. The best prototypes of urban squares or plazas in the United States so far are largely the contributions of private individuals and corporations, such as the Seagram Building and Plaza, Rockefeller Center, and the Chubb Building and Galleria in Manhattan; the Mellon Bank Square and Alcoa's Allegheny Center in Pittsburgh; Henry Ford's Renaissance Center in Detroit; the First National Bank and Plaza in Chicago; the United Bank Center and Prudential Plaza in Denver; Alcoa's Golden Gateway Center in San Francisco; and Century City Plaza in Los Angeles. Several outstanding ones may also be attributed to the efforts of powerful mayors or committees (Penn Center in Philadelphia, through mayors Joseph Clark and Richardson Dilworth, and Charles Center in Baltimore, through the Committee of Downtown, Inc. in cooperation with the Urban Renewal and Housing Agency.) Other projects such as these could be brought into being by greater government support in the form of more flexible interpretation of antiquated zoning codes, more liberal tax deductions for those parties financing civic improvements, and the ceding of public land on a long-term lease basis (or at least in the form of an agreement to maintain, repair, landscape, and decorate the squares and plazas which are built).

"STREET FURNITURE" AND OTHER DETAILS

Most of our central cities need more trees, flowers, fountains, and sculpture such as adorn London, Paris, Rome, Vienna, Copenhagen, and Stockholm. The light fixtures, the trash containers, the mailboxes, the street signs, and the public benches in most of our cities could be redesigned in the interest of both form and utility. Even sidewalks could be made more attractive by the use of colors and various patterns such as one may observe in Rio de Janeiro and in Stockholm's satellites.

The United States certainly has both the financial means and the technical know-how to produce beautiful cities *if it really wants them,* but this implies an upsurge of popular concern for the urban environment far beyond present proportions. Such concern, however, is never self-generating; it must be elicited by the example of courageous and "foolish" men of public and private affairs who dare to "stick their necks out"—who are not embarrassed to be known as promoters of urban joy.

New Towns and Urban Growth Problems

Most of our cities have grown and continue to grow according to the whims of private developers. Farms are sold and houses are raised instead of wheat, corn, or potatoes; forests are cut, valleys are filled, and streams are buried in storm sewers; as traffic increases, new roads are built and old ones are widened, with countless service stations and food establishments cropping up along the way; and eventually an expressway is cut through the landscape, its cloverleaves encouraging the construction nearby of shopping centers, office buildings, and high-rise apartments. By this irrational process known as urban sprawl, noncommunities are born— formless places with no order or beauty and with no visible respect for people or the land, the product of thousands of small, separate decisions made with little or no thought of their relationship to one another or of their collective impact. Sprawl is not only ugly, oppressive, and monotonous, but also inhuman, for it creates areas out of scale with people—too big for them to feel a part of, responsible for, and important in. But we accept the deficits of noncommunity—the proliferation of facilities; the frantic, segmented living; the loneliness amidst thousands of people and bustling activity; the rising statistics in regard to delinquency, neurosis, alcoholism, drug addiction, and divorce; the destruction of nature and the unimaginative man-made replacements—as if they were a preordained set of circumstances beyond our capacity to control or change. The question is why there exists so much confusion and pessimism about building the kinds of communities in which people can live full, satisfying lives in a nation with such tremendous capacity for organization and production. Instead, our nation's urban growth should be viewed as an opportunity, challenging us to correct the past and to build new towns which are infused with nature and which stimulate man's sense of beauty—places which are in scale with people and which encourage and strengthen real community life by promoting concern, friendship, and brotherhood. This is the purpose of our civilization—indeed, the ultimate ideal toward which every truly great civilization should strive: to produce more creative, more productive, more inspired, more loving people.

It is fortunate, therefore, that an increasing number of individuals, big businesses, and government officials are beginning to realize that city building and rebuilding constitute our most promising new frontier. First, we must hastily direct our energies toward building new and complete communities on the existing open land outside our central cities, so much of which has already been wasted on random residential and commercial developments. Then we must demolish the slum cores of these central cities and replace them with new towns in-town. The most appropriate place to build new towns is near metropolitan areas where the nation's greatest population gains and major economic growth are occurring, and ideally they should become part of the metropolitan regional fabric—its physical layout, its transportation network, its cultural, economic, and social systems. In such a rational regional organization of facilities and activities, new towns would complement existing central cities by providing them with additional residential alternatives, a broader occupational base, and accessible amenities such as recreational areas and open space which are urgently needed but relatively scarce in densely populated urban areas. The basic principle of all genunie new-town planning is the clustering of a variety of dwelling types—high-rise apartment buildings, garden apartments, town houses, and single-family detached homes—around common open space which results in relatively high residential densities without congestion. This is an extremely important consideration today when land near many metropolitan areas is not only scarce but expensive.

THE NEW-TOWN APPROACH TO COMMUNITY BUILDING

The new-town approach to community building differs from the conventional approach in three important respects: financing, design, and the legal controls over land use and ownership.

New-Town Versus Conventional Financing

Since new towns demand large-scale and long-term financing, their construction is mainly a field for limited-dividend corporations and for firms with large amounts of investment capital such as insurance companies and foundations, but increasingly it will be carried out by cooperatives, by unions, and especially by government, either as the principal agent or as the partner of a cooperative or other private endeavor. Because any new-town investor must count costs on a long-term basis, he tends to construct soundly; annual operating and maintenance expenses are more important to him than the original capital investment. Just the opposite is true for the conventional developer, who is principally concerned with the period between securing his mortgage and selling his product. Consequently, in spending money on a construction project, he tends to emphasize household gadgets and advertising more than home construction and site qualities which are conducive to durability and livability.

New-Town Versus Conventional Design Standards

A beautiful and livable urban environment requires a comprehensive design embracing the site and the form, the mass, and the details of every building, with attention to the relationship of each building to its neighboring structures and to the site as a whole—in short, the design must encompass all the visual surroundings. Thus, as he designs, the new-town planner envisages the future home life of individuals and families, as well as their lives as part of the community. He views these in terms of a grouping of residential buildings which enables every occupant to take utmost advantage of the sun and wind and that opens up pleasant, spacious, and varied views from every dwelling unit in every direction. He will also be guided by the landscape and by how its trees, streams, and rocks may best be preserved for the common enjoyment of the people who are going to form the community and whose lives from birth to old age will be molded by it. The speculative builder, on the contrary, takes the minimum risk and plays safe—he gives no more in size and quality than the scant requirements for an FHA-insured loan. As a result, his home interiors and exteriors and the relationship of his houses to each other and to their surroundings are characteristically pedestrian and dull.

New-Town Versus Conventional
Landownership and Land Use Controls

One of the principal lessons to be learned from European experience is that any attempt to significantly influence the location, magnitude, or physical form of urban growth requires public ownership or direct public control over a large part of the land in major metropolitan areas—especially on their growth peripheries. More specifically, private control over land use, especially where private ownership is fragmented into thousands of small parcels as in the United States, makes effective implementation of a national urban growth policy which promotes new-town development an impossible task. Once this lesson has been not only learned but accepted, our state governments will be the best instruments for gaining the necessary control of the land and planning its use, for they combine a metropolitan-wide perspective with decisive powers to override local governments and possess sufficient local political roots to make their exercising of such powers acceptable. The proper role of the federal government in shaping future urban growth, besides developing policy for this purpose, is to provide the states with the financial means to execute the policy, to subsidize private and public developers of socially and economically balanced communities, and to sponsor research into innovative approaches to the solution of key urban problems.

THE NEW-TOWN DEVELOPMENT PROCESS

The entire process of new-town development can be capsuled in the following five steps.

1. It is essential to purchase at a relatively low price a large amount of continuous land suitable for development and located near a strong real estate market.

2. There must be an overall plan for the community which offers a unique package of attractions for prospective residents, including such features as a variety of housing styles and densities; innovative architectural design; the thorough integration of well-landscaped open space with all buildings; the residential mixture

of people with varying ethnic, racial, and socio-economic backgrounds; residential proximity to jobs, schools, shopping centers, and recreational facilities within the new town; and complete separation of vehicular and pedestrian thoroughfares.

3. Recognition of the importance of transportation planning in new-town development is a fairly recent phenomenon. Research indicates that the first transportation study specifically prepared for a new town was not undertaken until 1958.[16] Many of the new communities which have been built in the recent past will eventually experience traffic problems because of lack of adequate early attention to this basic ingredient of community planning. This is not to suggest that all new towns will face problems identical with those of the old central cities. In some cases, not congestion but excessive dispersal will create serious problems; under-used roads built at a high cost and expensive to maintain represent a financial drain on the developer as well as the community. Consequently, the prospect of eliminating unnecessary roadway capacity by devoting careful attention to transportation systems early in the planning process should be an attractive one to both of these parties as well as to the agencies financing the project.

One major advantage in transportation planning for new communities is that the pattern of future land use, which is the basis for projecting travel demand, is relatively uncomplicated. By its very nature, a planned new community has distinctive land uses with specific characteristics and boundaries as determined in advance by the planner. Thus, internally generated traffic can be forecast with some precision. The problem facing the planner is to utilize intelligently the available data to arrive at values for trip generation which best suit the new town. In addition, however, transportation planning for a new community must take into consideration connections with surrounding urban development if the community is to become a viable part of the metropolitan regional fabric. Thus, planning of a new town built as a satellite to an existing central city is defective if it does not make adequate provision for population movement between the two urban areas as well as between the new town and other existing satellite communities. This would be especially important in a particular situation where the majority of the gainfully employed residents of a satellite new town work in the nearby central city or in one of the surrounding suburbs, and, in turn, some of the central city and suburban residents are employed in the new town.

4. The sale and rental of the initial residential units enhance the value of the nonresidential land in the new town, because the population on the site generates a market—a labor market for prospective industry and a selling market for prospective retail establishments. But it is also critical at this point for the local or state government to have complete control over land use for some distance around the new town in order to prevent the construction of competitive shopping centers and industrial estates.

5. The new town developer must retain control over all land within the new town designated for residential use, as well as that for commercial and industrial use, until the buildup of population and employment in the community sufficiently escalates land values so that he can sell or lease the land at prices which will result in revenues that more than counterbalance the long period at the beginning of the cycle when he was conducting a deficit operation. Indeed, the Federal Housing Administration (FHA) and the Veterans Administration (VA) which guarantee the developer's mortgages demand that the developer maintain control of his new town until it is substantially completed in order to reduce the risk of default and to assure that recreational and other amenities are equitably distributed throughout the community. For example, although Columbia, Maryland, was opened for occupancy in 1967, residents of the new town will not gain complete control of the Columbia Association which governs the new town until 1981.

Problems Inherent in the New Town Development Process

The new-town development process involves several critical problems, some of which will be difficult to resolve unless government provides private developers with more legal powers or the government itself becomes a more active participant in the process.

1. Unless a new-town developer is dealing with a large estate or a major land grant, assembling the necessary land parcels without letting everyone know what he is doing, which would inevitably raise land prices, is extremely difficult. Britain, Sweden, and other European countries grant their new-town developers eminent domain powers in procuring the land.

2. The new-town developer must choose a site close enough to

a large urban center so that there will be a market for his residential, commercial, and industrial properties, but if it is too close land becomes so expensive that there is not a sufficient differential between the initial buying price and the final selling price to enable him to realize a profit. Greater government control, not only over land use but over land prices, would certainly reduce this hazard.

3. A third problem, which is related to the first two, is that of getting sufficient start-up capital to acquire a site and improve it—that is, to install extensive utilities, streets, and other public facilities before any residents move in to help pay for them. It is difficult to convince most financiers that they should take such initial risks involved in new-town development and then wait for some time to realize a profit from their investment. Here is where the federal government's mortgage guarantees under the National Housing Acts of 1968 and 1970 have been extremely helpful, but these have now been cut off pending Office of Management and Budget (OMB) authorization to accept additional proposals. The last HUD commitment for this purpose was to the Newfields (Ohio) Development Corporation in October 1973; at present OMB is authorizing HUD to offer assistance only to already established new communities which are in financial difficulty.

4. One of the major arguments in favor of government assistance for new-town development under the Housing Acts of 1968 and 1970 was to provide decent housing in a suitable living environment for all Americans, including the economically disadvantaged segments of our society. Achievement of this goal was promoted to some extent by three HUD housing programs which were suspended on January 5, 1973: (1) the Rent Supplement Program, whereby the federal government paid the difference between 25 percent of a household's gross income and the FHA-approved rental for its dwelling unit, provided that household was eligible for public housing or was headed by an aged or physically handicapped person; (2) the Section 235 low- and moderate-income home-ownership assistance program under the Housing Act of 1968 whereby a mortgagee's interest rate could be reduced to as low as 1 percent; and (3) the Section 236 program, also under the Housing Act of 1968, whereby a mortgagee who built rental or cooperative units for occupancy by low- and moderate-income families could have his interest rate reduced to as low as 1 percent. How-

ever, in a 441-page HUD report entitled *Housing in the Seventies* produced by a one-hundred-member national policy review team between February and October 1973, all these federal housing subsidy programs were faulted on grounds of "equity"—that is, their alleged inability to assist more than a handful of the eligible American families. Of the 16-million households with annual incomes under $5,000, the study reported, 94 percent received no housing aid. Reaching all eligible families under the existing housing subsidy programs, it was estimated, would cost at least $35 billion a year in contrast to the $2.5 billion a year which was being spent at the time the study was conducted. Moreover, the study predicted a 20 percent foreclosure rate within ten years for the Section 236 rental program and contended that the Section 235 home ownership program was also actuarially unsound.[17]

With passage of the Housing and Community Development Act of 1974, however, a Rental Housing Assistance Payments Program was activated whereby payments are made to local public housing authorities to compensate them for those families living in public housing or in approved private housing who are paying 25 percent of their gross income for rent and yet a discrepancy exists between this amount and the FHA-approved rent for the dwelling unit. Then, in January 1976, a revised Section 235 home ownership program was implemented by HUD whereby families in the $9,000 to $11,000 income group can secure a 5 percent mortgage interest rate provided the purchase price of the home does not exceed $28,500 and the family can make a down payment equal to 3 percent of the first $25,000 and 10 percent of the remainder.[18]

5. Another problem of new-town development is that of securing a sufficient amount of commercial and industrial activity as a tax base to finance local government functions and to provide a reasonable degree of self-sufficiency with respect to the provision of goods and services and employment opportunities for the new town residents. Even with its extensive coercive controls over residential, commercial, and industrial land use, the British government has had to offer special financial incentives to induce companies to move out of London into new towns, a mechanism which our private new-town developers do not have at their disposal. However, it would be possible for state governments in the United States to provide financial incentives as well as to direct highway

construction in such a way as to make new towns more enticing to private business and industry. In addition, new towns might be specifically designated as sites for new government financed facilities such as hospitals, colleges, research laboratories, and utility companies in order to enhance their employment opportunities.

6. Once a core population has become established in a new town, they usually want to form their own government which can lead to ill-conceived demands for major alterations in the developer's plan for the community before construction has been substantially completed, destroying the very concept of the town which originally attracted them and jeopardizing the developer's investment. A variety of protective measures, such as those described below in greater detail, must be taken against such premature expressions of democratic rule. If the developer were a government body rather than a private agency, such interference might be less likely to occur, but if it did the turmoil would be no less disruptive. Probably every public official and businessman has occasionally thought how much easier his job would be if it weren't for voters or customers.

POTENTIAL SOLUTIONS FOR
LOCAL-GOVERNMENT PROBLEMS IN NEW-TOWN DEVELOPMENT

Another political problem inherent in new-town development, besides that of preserving the developer's interests while satisfying the desire of the new town residents to participate in the governance of their own affairs, is that of placating the concerns of long-established residents and local-government officials in the area. These concerns include the county government's fear of eventual control by the new-town population (for example, Columbia, Maryland, owns only 10 percent of the land in Howard County, but it already has one-third of the county's population); fear of the new town's becoming a financial drain on the county; resistance to demands from the new-town developer for changes in county zoning regulations; and resentment against the new-town developer for changing the "character" of the area from rural to urban. Among the techniques available to solve these problems are skip annexation, corporate control, state-agency control, contract control, and leasehold development, each of which has its advantages and disadvantages and requires some form of state legislation to make it feasible. Moreover, each of these structural responses requires intelligent and sensitive administration.[19]

Skip Annexation

By dispensation from state law, a major city could annex a noncontiguous tract of land for new-town development and serve either as the entrepreneur or the local government, or both, for the new community, thereby providing considerable political stability during its planning and development period. Moreover, the city's professionally staffed planning, public works, and social service departments could supervise the new town's development and extend needed services to its residents. One possible drawback to this measure is that some state governments might want to assume these responsibilities themselves. A second one is that many major cities today would be financially unable to assume the additional burden of new-town planning. A third possible disadvantage—the loss of a tax base by the small political jurisdictions within whose boundaries a new town is being developed—could be overcome if the city were to regard itself as the entrepreneur and receive leasehold income only, leaving tax returns for the smaller local governments in the area.

Corporate Control

The governing structure of Columbia, Maryland, is a nonprofit corporation created by the Maryland State Legislature to manage the town's properties and programs with the goal of providing the highest possible quality in amenities and services for the residents. Known as the Columbia Association, the corporation builds, operates, and maintains community facilities such as parks, swimming pools, tennis courts, golf courses, playgrounds, and meeting rooms and, with the residents, develops programs to enhance the quality of life in Columbia. Prior to 1976, the board of directors consisted of seven members, all of whom were representatives of the developer—Howard Research and Development Corporation, a joint venture of the Connecticut General Life Insurance Company and the Rouse Company. This board composition was required by the FHA and the VA which had insured the developer's mortgages and consequently insisted on protecting the developer's interests until the town was financially secure. Early in 1976, however, the board

of directors was enlarged to ten members, three of whom were
elected by the residents, one for each 4,000 dwelling units constructed and occupied at the time (a total of 12,000). By 1981,
when Columbia is expected to be "substantially complete," the
terms of all the seven original directors will have expired and the
residents will take over control of the corporation, electing all seven
members. Funding for the Columbia Association comes from assessment income; that is, each owner of residential, commercial, and
industrial property in Columbia must make an annual payment
equal to the assessed value of his property multiplied by a rate of
$.75 per $100 evaluation. While a property owner's first legal obli-
gation is his property tax to Howard County, payment of his annual assessment to the Columbia Association takes legal precedence
over the payment of the principal and interest on his mortgage.
The compulsory nature of the property owners' annual assessment,
in contrast to the voluntary character of homeowners' association
dues, assures that the community amenities for which the Columbia
Association is responsible will be equitably distributed and adequately maintained throughout the new town.[20]

Control by State Agency

A state could enact legislation to create a public benefit corporation with the power of eminent domain and the authority to
plan, develop, and manage new communities on a statewide basis.
Such an agency is the New York State Urban Development Corporation established in 1968 by the New York State legislature at
the insistence of former Governor Rockefeller. In addition to its
control over land use in new towns and its power to override local
zoning laws, a state development corporation can provide services
to new-town residents either directly or through contracts with
nearby local government units. While such a state agency might be
less likely than a private developer to be suspected of manipulating
new-town development plans in order to maximize profit, some opposition could arise to its creating the town without direct political
representation. This might be alleviated by the agency's creating
a local government with provision for a gradual assumption of
power by the new-town residents as planning objectives reached
completion.

Contract Control

The state government could create a private profit-making or nonprofit agency which would be under strict state or regional supervision to comply with the explicit terms of a contract in the development of a new town, with residents given the right to initiate court cases to ensure the protection of their interests.

Leasehold Development

Under this arrangement a development company retains title to the land in its new town, charging appropriate ground rents for various land uses under ninety-nine-year leases until a local government is created which may purchase the leasehold at a price ensuring the developer a profit. An appealing aspect of this arrangement is the potential for the new town to be taxless, using ground rent instead of property taxes to finance community improvements and government services.

The Benefits of New Towns

New towns are meant to develop in many directions, providing a variety of housing, jobs, and services for a wide range of socioeconomic classes in one place. Seven major benefits may be derived from such ideal communities.

1. In new towns we have a marvelous opportunity to create a new America by bringing together all races and classes of people on some neutral piece of land, which is much easier than trying to integrate neighborhoods where residents have a tendency to defend "their territory" when an "outsider" attempts to move in. Moreover, by providing a common tax base for a wide range of socioeconomic groups, new towns make it possible to provide optimum living conditions for everyone. In our national past, the "separate but equal" system proved to be unsuccessful in providing equal opportunities for good living and jobs for our minorities, and this was so judged by the Supreme Court in 1954. Practical fulfillment of the law is slow in coming, but as educational and income levels rise, larger segments of our population are demanding equal opportunities, and new towns are one means of assuring realization of their objectives.

2. The fact that new towns provide jobs for the majority of their employed residents means fewer traffic and transportation problems. If American new towns are as successful as their British counterparts, the tedious workday suburb-to-city and city-to-suburb journeys will be all but eliminated. As Wyndham Thomas, former director of Britain's Town and Country Planning Association, one-time mayor of the long-established new town, Hemel Hempstead, and general manager of the Crown Corporation (which recently undertook the development of the contemporary new town, Peter-borough), has stated: "As far as employment is concerned, the London new towns are almost self-sufficient. Of the 15 percent of the new-town residents who work outside, only about one in three travels to London. In all areas of activity there is a slowly increasing interchange with neighboring towns, while the commuting rate to London remains steady."[21]

Moreover, the street layout of new towns is designed for safety and efficiency, relieving pedestrians of the tensions which result from having to compete with automobiles, and separating local from through traffic without land-devouring multi-level inter-changes.

3. Because each new town has its own characteristic layout and attractions, it has a unique flavor. Indeed, each neighborhood within a new town is unique, allowing the citizen to feel some degree of identification and significance instead of the frustration and loneliness which often characterize big city social life. In fact, the very act of creating a new town can give people a new dimension of enthusiasm, provided they don't succumb to the temptation of simply building it.

4. New towns afford an excellent opportunity to implement a regional approach to the solution of urban problems. In Western Europe many countries are tying in urban renewal with the development of suburban new towns. If we had new towns developing as renewal was taking place in our central cities, displaced persons would have increased residential options. New towns also make mass transit more feasible because they concentrate population, reducing the need for an ever expanding highway system. Sweden's satellite towns, for example, which are linked to downtown Stockholm by a rapid rail system, feature very high population density

in residential areas clustered around the station stops so that thousands of people can live within walking distance of them. Moreover, for the convenience of satellite residents who commute by rail to jobs in Stockholm, as well as for nonworking residents, huge shopping centers have been built near each station. This situation is in striking contrast to our shopping centers which are built near expressway interchanges for the convenience of auto-driving residents who are scattered for miles across neighborhoods of low population density.

5. Since new-town populations are restricted in size, although they may vary from 50,000 to several hundred thousand, they are an important demonstration of how that fringe development which has plagued most of our large cities can be forestalled to provide more green space between urban developments. New towns not only offer a unique opportunity for improvements in environmental quality, but for the conservation of precious natural resources. By clustering development, new towns make possible the preservation of flood plains, open spaces, and lands that should not be used for construction purposes because they are geologically unstable. Moreover, the experimental orientation of new towns facilitates solutions to various pollution problems.

6. New towns can make a valuable contribution to national population policy, for there are some areas of the country which should be encouraged to grow and others which should be depopulated. In this context, new towns can serve as population reception and economic growth centers.

7. New towns could be one of the major forces propelling the American building industry into the twenty-first century because of their emphasis on innovative design and, in Europe, on mass production methods. In the United States, the highly successful Operation Breakthrough housing program launched by the Department of Housing and Urban Development under Secretary George Romney in 1969 proved conclusively that in our country too, mass produced housing can be as highly individualized and attractive in appearance as conventional custom-built housing. In this program twenty-two industrialized housing system producers demonstrated their innovative dwelling unit designs on nine planned unit developments (PUDs) in Jersey City, New Jersey; Kalamazoo, Michi-

gan; Indianapolis, Indiana; Memphis, Tennessee; St. Louis, Missouri; Macon, Georgia; Sacramento, California; Seattle, Washington; and King County, Washington.

RENEWING OUR CENTRAL CITIES
THROUGH NEW TOWNS IN-TOWN

Reasons for transforming our central cities are essentially the same as those for building new towns, for while the concept of "decentralization" generally has a beyond-the-city connotation it should be applied within the city as well. In other words, our central cities should be composed of many nuclei, with a complete set of city services in each district, making them more efficient administratively and more satisfying as places for people to live. Urban renewal must have the creation of socially significant districts in our central cities as its aim, with each district planned so that its corporate life has a validity of its own, rather than being simply a fragment or part of a total viscous mass. It is time to get away from the essentially negative approach involved in "removing the slums" or "doing something about rundown housing"; a great deal more can be gained from the new-town in-town approach which would undertake, stage by stage, to do *all* the things necessary to achieve a humane environment within our central cities.

CHOOSING AREAS FOR
NEW-TOWN IN-TOWN DEVELOPMENT

In every metropolis there are a few areas with a long and venerable historical tradition and/or a strategic location similar to Georgetown in Washington, D.C., Greenwich Village in New York City, and Old Town in Chicago which are highly conducive to new-town in-town development. Other more nondescript and amorphous sections of the city may be more difficult to transform into genuine communities, but with determination and imagination they, too, can be enhanced and revitalized by new town in-town projects. Hence, priorities must be established, for most cities cannot afford to undertake more than one or two such projects at a time. Ideally, a new-town in-town program should start in those areas where transformation of the environment is urgently needed and where improvements in physical environment and public services would make a valuable contribution to the success of various social programs, such as those directed at neighborhood stabilization, racial integration, and the reduction of poverty. It is important to realize that the total environment, not just housing, must be the focus of any new-town in-town program which hopes to be truly effective. A dramatic demonstration of the woe brought on by ignoring this fact is the infamous Pruitt-Igoe environmental housing experiment in St. Louis where $52 million in tax money went down the drain when, due to vandalism and crime, all but ten of the thirty-three eleven-story apartment buildings in the project stood vacant and sealed up for many months and were eventually demolished.[22]

A major feature of the original apartment building design in the Pruitt-Igoe project was a "skip stop" elevator system that would stop only at every third floor which would have an open gallery containing laundry facilities and storage bins. The galleries were to be "vertical neighborhoods" providing, in addition to the laundry and other facilities, a "close, safe playground." In order to increase neighborliness, no more than twenty families were to use each gallery. The floors between the galleries would consist exclusively of apartments. Finally, the entire complex was to be located on a 57-acre site with a "river of green running through it and no through streets." However, by the time the Pruitt-Igoe project was completed in 1955, several changes had been made in the original design. A plan to mix some townhouses with the apartment buildings had been rejected on the basis of a cost-benefit analysis conducted by the St. Louis Public Housing Authority. Other "economies" included eliminating the landscaping and public washrooms on the ground floor of the apartment buildings, leaving the steam pipes uninsulated, not painting the cinder-block galleries and other public areas, and not providing screens for the gallery windows. Although the project won an award for architectural design in 1958, by then the "economies" listed above had already produced some unexpected consequences: children urinated in hallways, burned themselves on exposed pipes, and fell out of gallery windows. Moreover, while the project had been designed for a racially mixed population—one-third white and two-thirds black—a heavy influx of hard-core poor families with numerous problems soon drove out most of the other residents. Demographically, this resulted in the project being inhabited almost exclusively by very large black households headed by women on welfare. For example, among the 10,736 people living at the Pruitt-Igoe project in 1965, there were only 900 men, many of them elderly, but there were over 7,000 children, 70 percent of whom were under twelve years of age. Subsequently, Pruitt-Igo became a symbol of all that is wrong with public housing projects in the United States. A 1969 survey of the residents disclosed that 41 percent of the adults had been robbed, 20 percent had been physically assaulted, and 39 percent had been insulted by teenagers.[23]

By 1972, total occupancy of the Pruitt-Igoe project had fallen to 2,788 persons as even the most down-and-out welfare recipients were unwilling to tolerate the constant threat of personal danger. It was estimated that rehabilitating the buildings to make them once again fit for human occupancy would cost more than $40 million and then there was no guarantee that addicts and vandals would not destroy and terrorize the buildings again. Then in the fall of 1972, the St. Louis Public Housing Authority decided to demolish the two worst buildings in the project and to remove the top seven stories of the others to convert them into more manageable four-story buildings. It was hoped that the resulting low-rises would be easier for the tenants to control against outsiders and would provide some sense of defensible space and physical security, but when this effort proved unsuccessful, the Public Housing Authority demolished the entire project in 1973. If there is one lesson to be learned from Pruitt-Igoe, it is that architecture can never solve the basic problem of an economic system that creates a lower class and effectively isolates it from the rest of society.[24]

THE IMPORTANCE OF STAGING
IN NEW-TOWN IN-TOWN DEVELOPMENT PROJECTS

Within each area chosen for new-town in-town development, staging—the planned step-by-step destruction and renewal of an area—is extremely important in order to minimize the dislocation of families and businesses. An equally important objective of staging, however, is to permit residents of the area to participate in the establishment of priorities with respect to the sequence of tasks involved in the project. Thus, the process would not necessarily start in the traditional manner with the demolition of decayed buildings, but with whatever tasks the residents felt demanded immediate attention—possibly the provision of additional employment opportunities in the area, the construction of new schools, the rehabilitation of commercial enterprises, or the provision of more and improved service facilities. In this way, new-town in-town projects can gradually create attractive and viable communities which serve the most salient needs of their inhabitants.

THE BENEFITS OF NEW-TOWN IN-TOWN DEVELOPMENTS

Finally, let us enumerate and discuss the major benefits to be derived by central cities from successful new-town in-town projects.

Vital Downtown Areas

Traditionally, one of the key features of big cities has been a glittering and exciting nightlife centered in the downtown area. Today, however, this area in most American cities is deserted at night, largely due to fear of criminal assault. If central cities are ever again to have vital downtown areas beyond the working hours, new-town in-town projects must redevelop them by installing very bright lights and providing heavy security measures; by offering merchants financial incentives to modernize their facilities in a creative manner; by cleaning important public buildings and floodlighting them; by replacing dilapidated buildings and parking lots with beautifully landscaped parks; by planting more trees, plants, and flowers along the streets and sidewalks; by placing benches, sculptures, and fountains in appropriate locations; by featuring a wide variety of indoor and outdoor eating and entertainment facilities for people of all ages, tastes, and financial circumstances; and by transforming the entire area into a pedestrian precinct, requiring people to park their cars in ramp garages (free or at nominal cost) on the periphery of the downtown area, from which shuttle buses could take them quickly to the center of activity.

A Wide Range of Housing Accommodations

One of the great "discoveries" of the past decade is that mixing various types of dwelling units—individual homes, townhouses, and high-rise apartments—can produce a very attractive residential complex as long as the buildings are aesthetically arranged in relation to one another. One example is Lafayette Park in downtown Detroit, an urban renewal project begun with private funds in 1947 and completed with federal funds between 1950 and 1964.

It is a racially integrated community (75 percent white and 25 percent black) whose middle- and upper-income households reside in a mixture of high-rise and low-rise dwelling units (a total of 2,773), 515 of which offer subsidized rents to the elderly.[25]

Self-contained developments, such as Chicago's Marina City, provide still another interesting central-city residential alternative. Opened for occupancy in 1960, Marina City has 896 apartment units—256 efficiencies renting for $185 to $230 per month; 576 one-bedroom apartments renting for $245 to $310 per month; and 64 two-bedroom apartments renting for $410 to $465 per month. Its 1,320 middle- and upper-income tenants enjoy within the same complex such amenities as convenience shops, a commissary, a liquor store, a restaurant with a coffee shop, cocktail lounge, and dining room, recreational facilities (a bowling alley, an ice-skating rink, and three cinemas), a beauty and barber shop, an art gallery, a flower shop, a valet, a bank, a travel agency, a sun deck, and a boat marina.[26] Since both Lafayette Park and Marina City were constructed in depressed areas, they constitute valuable precedents for new-town in-town projects, but, unfortunately, the former residents of these areas cannot afford to benefit from the "better way of life" provided.

In-Town Work Places

One of the traditional principles of city planning, the separation of homes and work places, was formulated at a time when almost all factories and other places of employment were regarded as nuisance facilities. But this situation has changed with the increasing use of electric power and with modern standards of plant construction and landscaping, as exemplified by the numerous industrial parks on the outskirts of central cities. Many disadvantaged persons have been effectively excluded from the labor market by this continuing movement of in-town plants and offices to the suburbs, causing unemployment and contributing to demoralization, poverty and such related inner-city problems as desertion, divorce, welfare dependency, crime, alcoholism, drug addiction, prostitution, and a high dropout rate from school among teenagers. Thus, even if a mixture of work places and homes in the central city were not ideal from the purely physical standpoint, it could be argued that this principle should be compromised in the interest of achieving more important social objectives. A new-town in-town project should strive to make this mixture as physically attractive as possible by developing compact (land is expensive in the central city) "industrial estates" suitable for a variety of nonnoxious industries, warehouses, and service agencies. High-rise plants renting space to many small industries might also be experimented with, substituting the efficiency of vertical transportation for the gains of one-floor operations. Moreover, through rehabilitation older buildings might be made suitable for various commercial and industrial operations.

Improved Community Facilities and Services

Contrary to current practice, the most modern schools, hospitals, libraries, cultural, and community centers should be built where they are needed most—in the low-income neighborhoods of central cities—to give these areas "new life" as well as a "new look" and to instill in their residents a feeling of pride and the conviction that somebody cares. Thus, a new-town in-town project might combine a junior college with a modern high school or work places with vocational schools in multi-unit arrangements to not only stimulate the educational advancement of the residents, but to enhance the appearance of the development area. There is also a drastic need in low-income central city neighborhoods for places where little theater groups, jazz combos, and other performing groups can display their talents and entertain sizable audiences. Such facilities might encourage the formation of more such groups and, hence, the development of latent talents among the residents of depressed central city areas.

Here, then, in the new-town in-town concept, we have the guidelines for the creation of truly great and beautiful American cities where humanistic values dominate and where full use is made of the evolving partnership in urban affairs between government and private enterprise. Almost every metropolis in the United States should be able to complete at least five or six new-town in-town projects each decade, and even our older cities should be able to create a completely renewed environment for their citizens within a generation or so. In fact, the achievement of this objective by the year 2000 should be of top priority among our national urban goals. Together with the new-towns program, it constitutes a fitting challenge for a great nation.

The American people and their leaders should become as strongly committed, both in theory and practice, to the "domestic Marshall Plan" which has been outlined herein as they were to the original Marshall Plan for the reconstruction of Western Europe following World War II, to the Alliance for Progress in Latin America, to the Peace Corps program for the social and economic enrichment of underdeveloped nations throughout the world, and to the space program. If this commitment were made, the United States would not only regain much of the prestige it has lost abroad in recent years and instill renewed hope in America's youth and minorities, but, confident in the fact that it had conquered the Great Depression of the 1930s with the New Deal and the urban crisis of the 1970s with a "domestic Marshall Plan," this country would be better prepared to cope effectively with the equally difficult if not more difficult challenges of the twenty-first century.

Chapter Notes

INTRODUCTION

1. Philip M. Hauser, "Urbanization: An Overview," in *The Study of Urbanization*, ed. Philip M. Hauser and Leo F. Schnore (New York: John Wiley and Sons, 1965), pp. 6–7; *Urban Man and Society*, ed. Albert N. Cousins and Hans Nagpaul (New York: Knopf, 1970), p. 8.
2. Oswald Spengler, *The Decline of the West*, vol. II (New York: Knopf, 1928), p. 107.

CHAPTER 1

1. J. Fletcher Wellemeyer and Frank Lorimer, Appendix, *Population Bulletin* 18 (Feb. 1962): 19.
2. Philip M. Hauser, "Urbanization: An Overview," p. 6.
3. Ibid.
4. Ibid.
5. Ibid.
6. Ibid.
7. Ibid., p. 7.
8. United Nations, Department of Economic and Social Affairs, *Growth of the World's Urban and Rural Population, 1920–2000*, Population Studies No. 44 (New York, 1969), pp. 56, 67.
9. Ibid.
10. Eric E. Lampard, "Historical Aspects of Urbanization," in *The Study of Urbanization*, ed. Philip M. Hauser and Leo F. Schnore (New York: John Wiley and Sons, 1965), p. 523.

11. Robert J. Braidwood and Gordon R. Willey, eds., *Courses Toward Urban Life: Archeological Considerations of Some Cultural Alternates* (Chicago: Aldine Publishers, 1962), p. vi.

12. Eric E. Lampard, "Historical Aspects of Urbanization," p. 525.

13. Robert M. Adams, "The Origins of Cities," *Scientific American* 203 (September, 1960): 48.

14. V. Gordon Childe, "The Urban Revolution," *Town Planning Review* 21 (April, 1950): 3–17.

15. John A. Wilson, "Egypt Through the New Kingdom," in *City Invincible: Symposium on Urbanization and Cultural Development in the Ancient Near East* [Oriental Institute, 1958], ed. Carl H. Kraeling and R. M. Adams (University of Chicago Press, 1960), p. 126.

16. Eric E. Lampard, "Historical Aspects of Urbanization," p. 523.

17. Ibid., p. 546.

18. Gideon Sjoberg, *The Preindustrial City: Past and Present* (New York: The Free Press of Glencoe, 1960), p. 6.

19. Ronald P. Dore, *City Life in Japan* (Berkeley: Univ. of California Press, 1958), p. 170.

20. Ernestine Friedl, "Lagging Emulation in Post-Peasant Society: A Greek Case," *American Anthropologist* 66 (June, 1964): 569–586.

21. Daniel Lerner, *The Passing of Traditional Society* (New York: The Free Press of Glencoe, 1958), pp. 52–54; Oscar Lewis, *The Children of Sanchez* (New York: Random House, 1961), pp. xxviii–xxix.

22. Gideon Sjoberg, "Cities in Developing and Industrial Societies: A Cross-Cultural Analysis," in *The Study of Urbanization*, ed. Philip M. Hauser and Leo F. Schnore (New York: John Wiley and Sons, 1965), pp. 226–227.

23. Peter Suzuki, "Village Solidarity Among Turkish Peasants Undergoing Urbanization," *Science* 132 (September 30, 1960): 891–892.

24. John Kenneth Galbraith, "The Poverty of Nations," *Atlantic Monthly*, (Oct. 1962), pp. 47–53; Bert Hoselitz, "Cities of India and Their Problems," *Annals of the Association of American Geographers* 49 (1959): 223–231; M. N. Svrinas, *Caste in Modern India* (London: Asia Publishing House, 1962), Chs. 1 and 6; Arthur Niehoff, *Factory Workers in India, Publications in Anthropology, No. 5* (Milwaukee, Wis.: Milwaukee Public Museum, 1959).

25. Mark G. Field, "Alcoholism, Crime, and Delinquency in Soviet Society," *Social Problems* 3 (October, 1955): 100–109; William R. Vizzard, "Taiyo-zoku: A Youth Problem in Japan," *Sociologus* 9 (1959): 162–178.

26. Daniel Bell, "Russia's Eroding Ideology," *New Leader* 46 (15 Apr. 1963): 18–23.

27. George Ginsburgs, "Objective Truth and the Judicial Process in Post-Stalinist Soviet Jurisprudence," *American Journal of Comparative Law* 10 (Winter-Spring, 1961): 53–75.

28. Walter Laqueur and Leopold Labedz, eds., *The Future of Communist Society* (New York: Praeger, 1962), p. 161.

29. R. D. McKenzie, *The Metropolitan Community* (New York: McGraw-Hill, 1933), p. 70.
30. Sylvia F. Fava, ed., *Urbanism in World Perspective* (New York: Thomas Y. Crowell, 1968), p. 43.
31. Ibid.

CHAPTER 2

1. William H. Form, "The Place of Social Structure in the Determination of Land Use: Implications for a Theory of Urban Ecology," *Social Forces* 32 (May, 1954): 317–323.
2. Martin Meyerson and Edward C. Banfield, *Politics, Planning, and the Public Interest* (New York: The Free Press of Glencoe, 1955), pp. 300–302.
3. Gideon Sjoberg, "The Rise and Fall of Cities: A Theoretical Perspective," *International Journal of Comparative Sociology* 4 (September, 1963): 107–120.
4. Gideon Sjoberg, "Theory and Research in Urban Sociology," in *The Study of Urbanization*, ed. Philip M. Hauser and Leo F. Schnore (New York: John Wiley and Sons, 1965), p. 177.
5. *Urban Man and Society* (Introduction: n. 1), p. 89.
6. Stuart Dodd, "A System of Operationally Defined Concepts for Sociology," *American Sociological Review* 4 (Oct. 1939): 619–634.
7. *Urban Man and Society*, p. 85.
8. Robert Park, *Human Communities: The City and Human Ecology* (New York: The Free Press of Glencoe, 1952), p. 16.
9. Sidney M. Willhelm and Gideon Sjoberg, "Economic vs. Protective Values in Urban Land Use Change," *American Journal of Economics and Sociology* 19 (Jan. 1960): 151–160.
10. Robert Redfield, *The Folk Culture of Yucatán* (University of Chicago Press, 1941), p. 154; Louis Wirth, "Urbanism as a Way of Life," *American Journal of Sociology* 44 (July 1938): 12.
11. Lewis Mumford, *The City in History* (New York: Harcourt, Brace, and World, 1961), p. 571.
12. Milla Aissa Alihan, *Social Ecology* (New York: Columbia University Press, 1938); Warner E. Gettys, "Human Ecology and Social Theory," *Social Forces* 18 (May 1940): 469–476.
13. Walter Firey, *Land Use in Central Boston* (Cambridge: Harvard University Press, 1947); A. B. Hollingshead, "A Re-Examination of Ecological Theory," *Sociology and Social Research* 31 (January–February, 1947): 194–204.
14. Daniel R. Miller and Guy E. Swanson, *The Changing American Parent* (New York: John Wiley and Sons, 1958).
15. Oscar Lewis, "Urbanization Without Breakdown: A Case Study," *Scientific Monthly* 75 (July, 1952): 31–41.
16. A. L. Epstein, *Politics in an Urban African Community* (Manchester Uni-

versity Press, 1958); Aidan Southall, ed., *Social Change in Modern Africa* (London: Oxford University Press, 1961); Peter Marris, *Family and Social Change in an African City* (Northwestern University Press, 1962).

17. Roger Le Tourneau, *Fès: Avant le Protectorat* (Casablanca: Société Marocaine de Librairie et d'Edition, 1949); Horace Miner, *The Primitive City of Timbuctoo* (Princeton University Press, 1953).

18. Robert J. Smith, "Pre-Industrial Urbanism in Japan: A Consideration of Multiple Traditions in a Feudal Society," in *City and Village in Japan*, ed. Thomas C. Smith (University of Chicago Research Center in Economic Development and Cultural Change, 1960), pp. 241–257; Marshall B. Clinard, "A Cross-Cultural Replication of the Relation of Urbanism to Criminal Behavior," *American Sociological Review* 25 (Apr. 1960): 253–257.

19. Radhakamal Mukerjee, *Social Ecology* (London: Longmans Green, 1945); Theodore Caplow, "Urban Structure in France," *American Sociological Review* 17 (Oct. 1952): 544–549.

20. Christen T. Jonassen, "Cultural Variables in the Ecology of an Ethnic Group," *American Sociological Review* 14 (Feb. 1949): 32–41; Jerome K. Myers, "Assimilation to the Ecological and Social Systems of a Community," *American Sociological Review* 15 (June 1950): 367–372; Albert Seeman, "Communities in the Salt Lake Basin," *Economic Geography* 14 (July 1938): 300–308.

21. Robert E. Dickinson, *The West European City* (London: Routledge and Kegan Paul, 1951); Emrys Jones, *A Social Geography of Belfast* (London: Oxford University Press, 1960); G. E. von Grunebaum, *Islam*, American Anthropological Association, Memoir No. 81, Chapter 8 (1955).

22. Jane Jacobs, "Downtown Is For People," in *The Exploding Metropolis*, edited by editors of *Fortune* (Garden City, N.Y.: Doubleday, 1958), pp. 157–184; Paul Meadows, "The Urbanists: Profiles of Professional Ideologies," in *1963 Yearbook, School of Architecture* (Syracuse, N.Y.: Syracuse University, 1963).

23. Harold Orlans, *Stevenage* (London: Routledge and Kegan Paul, 1952); Peter Marris (n. 2:16).

24. Otis Dudley Duncan "From Social System to Ecosystem," *Sociological Inquiry* 31 (Spring, 1961): 140–149.

25. Jack P. Gibbs and Walter T. Martin, "Urbanization, Technology, and the Division of Labor: International Patterns," *American Sociological Review* 27 (October, 1962): 667–677.

26. Ibid., p. 677.

27. William F. Ogburn, "Inventions of Local Transportation and the Pattern of Cities," in *Cities and Society: The Revised Reader in Urban Sociology*, ed. Paul K. Hatt and Albert J. Reiss, Jr. (New York: The Free Press of Glencoe, 1957), p. 281; Amos Hawley, *Human Ecology* (New York: Ronald Press, 1950), p. 421.

28. Floyd Dotson and Lillian Ota Dotson, "Urban Centralization and Decentralization in Mexico," *Rural Sociology* 21 (March 1956): 41–49; Noel P.

Gist, "The Ecology of Bangalore, India: An East-West Comparison," *Social Forces* 35 (May 1957): 356–365.

29. Scott Greer, *The Emerging City: Myth and Reality* (New York: The Free Press of Glencoe, 1962).

30. Ibid., pp. 54, 56.

31. Robert N. Bellah, "Durkheim and History," *American Sociological Review* 24 (Aug. 1959): 461.

CHAPTER 3

1. Thomas A. Reiner, *The Place of the Ideal Community in Urban Planning* (Philadelphia: University of Pennsylvania Press, 1963), pp. 22–24.

2. John W. Reps, *The Making of Urban America* (Princeton University Press, 1965), p. 439.

3. Alice Felt Tyler, *Freedom's Ferment* (University of Minnesota Press, 1944), pp. 121–122, 124–125.

4. John W. Reps, pp. 455–456; Alice Felt Tyler, pp. 200–201, 203–204.

5. Ralph Thomlinson, *Urban Structure: The Social and Spatial Character of Cities* (New York: Random House, 1969), p. 284.

6. Ibid., p. 285.

7. Thomas A. Reiner, p. 39.

8. Ebenezer Howard, "A Path to Real Reform," in *A Place to Live: The Crisis of the Cities*, ed. Wolf von Eckhardt (New York: Dell Publishing Co., 1967), p. 363.

9. Gurney Breckenfeld, *Columbia and the New Towns* (New York: Ives Washburn, 1971), p. 38.

10. Frederic J. Osborn and Arnold Whittick, *The New Towns: The Answer to Megalopolis* (London: Leonard Hill, 1969), p. 59.

11. Gurney Breckenfeld, p. 40.

12. Osborn and Whittick, p. 85.

13. Gurney Breckenfeld, p. 41.

14. Ibid., pp. 41–42.

15. Thomas A. Reiner, p. 157.

16. Voltaire, "Le Mondain," *Oeuvres Complètes*, vol. X (Paris, 1877), pp. 83–86.

17. Adam Smith, *The Wealth of Nations* (1776; rpt. Baltimore: Penguin Books, 1937), pp. 390–391.

18. Ibid., p. 358.

19. Ibid., pp. 392–393.

20. William Wordsworth, "The World," *Oxford Book of English Verse* (New York: Oxford University Press, 1931), p. 609; William Blake, "London," *The Portable Blake*, ed. Alfred Kazin (New York: Viking Press, 1946), p. 112.

21. Karl Marx and Friedrich Engels, "The Housing Question," in *Selected Works of Karl Marx and Friedrich Engels*, ed. V. Adoratsky and D. Rjazanov (Moscow: Marx-Engels-Lenin Institute, 1927–35), pp. 627–628.

22. Ibid.

23. Jane Jacobs, *The Death and Life of Great American Cities* (New York: Random House, 1961), p. 20.

24. Roy Lubove, *Community Planning in the 1920s: The Contribution of the Regional Planning Association of America* (Pittsburgh: University of Pittsburgh Press, 1963), pp. 83–84.

25. Lewis Mumford, *The Culture of Cities* (New York: Harcourt, Brace and Co., 1938), p. 374.

26. Alvin Boskoff, *The Sociology of Urban Regions* (New York: Appleton-Century-Crofts, 1970), p. 368.

27. Lewis Mumford, *The Culture of Cities*, p. 188.

28. Ibid., p. 251.

29. Ibid., p. 560.

30. Marvin D. Koenigsberg, "Urban Development: An Introduction to the Theories of Lewis Mumford," in *Urbanism in World Perspective*, ed. Sylvia Fava (n. 1:30), p. 580.

31. Louis K. Loewenstein, ed., *Urban Studies: An Introductory Reader* (New York: The Free Press of Glencoe, 1971), p. 516.

CHAPTER 4

1. Statement by J. Vink of the Netherlands, in United Nations, *The Future Patterns and Forms of Urban Settlement: Proceedings of the Seminar*, vol. I (New York: The United Nations, 1968), p. 16.

2. Myles Wright, "Regional Development: Problems and Lines of Advance in Europe," *Town Planning Review* 36 (Oct. 1965): 147.

3. H. Wentworth Eldredge, ed., *Taming Metropolis*, vol. II (New York: Doubleday and Company, 1967), pp. 1146–1147.

4. Ibid., p. 1156.

5. *Town Planning and Ground Exploitation in Amsterdam* (City of Amsterdam Press, Publicity, and Information Bureau, 1967), pp. 5, 31.

6. Interview with Dr. C. Wegener Sleeswijk, Town Planning Section, Public Works Department, Amsterdam, May 2, 1972.

7. "In Bijlmermeer the Amsterdam Citizen of Today Finds the Environment of Tomorrow" (City of Amsterdam Press, Publicity, and Information Bureau, 1969), p. 3.

8. Sleeswijk interview.

9. "In Bijlmermeer the Amsterdam Citizen of Today Finds the Environment of Tomorrow," pp. 2–3.

10. Ibid., pp. 2, 4.

11. Sleeswijk interview.

12. Kell Aström, *City Planning in Sweden* (Stockholm: The Swedish Institute, 1967), pp. 23, 27, 59.

13. Office of International Affairs, *HUD International Brief* (Washington, D.C.: U.S. Department of Housing and Urban Development, June 1972), p. 2.

14. Kell Aström, pp. 60–61.

15. Ibid.

16. David Pass, *Vallingby and Farsta: From Idea to Reality* (Stockholm: National Swedish Building Research, 1969), pp. 364–365.
17. Interview with Ola Källström, Information Officer, City of Stockholm, May 24, 1972.
18. Ibid.
19. Ibid.
20. David Pass, pp. 125–126, 129, 133.
21. Källström interview.
22. Ibid.
23. David Pass, pp. 288, 304.
24. *HUD International Brief*, June 1972, pp. 10–12.
25. Interview with Arne T. Bergqvist (AB Farsta Centrum), developer of Farsta Center, June 30, 1970.
26. Ibid.
27. Kell Aström, p. 157.
28. Bergqvist interview.
29. Uolevi Itkonen, "Welfare Activities in Tapiola" (Tapiola, Finland: The Finnish Housing Foundation, 1970), p. 1.
30. Heikki von Hertzen, "Practical Problems in New Town Development," New Towns Seminar, Tapiola, Finland, August 13, 1965 (The Finnish Housing Foundation), p. 1.
31. "Tapiola General Information" (The Finnish Housing Foundation, 1970), p. 2.
32. Ibid.
33. Ibid.
34. Uolevi Itkonen, p. 4.
35. Interview with Aarne Ervi, architect of Tapiola's town center, July 3, 1970.
36. Antoni R. Kuklinski, "The Role of Growth Poles and Growth Centers in Regional Development" (Geneva, Switzerland: United Nations Research Institute for Social Development, 1968), p. 1.
37. Lloyd Rodwin, "British and French Urban Growth Strategies," in *Toward a National Urban Policy*, ed. Daniel P. Moynihan (Basic Books, Inc., 1970), pp. 273–274.
38. Gurney Breckenfeld (n. 3:9), p. 65.
39. Ibid., p. 68.
40. Lloyd Rodwin, p. 278.
41. Gurney Breckenfeld, p. 69.
42. Lloyd Rodwin, p. 279.
43. Gurney Breckenfeld, p. 48.
44. Ibid., p. 49.
45. Ibid., p. 51.
46. Interview with Miss Helen Moeller, Department of the Environment, June 11, 1970.
47. Ibid.
48. Ibid.

49. Osborn and Whittick (n. 3:10), p. 376.
50. Interview with G. K. Davie, Cumbernauld Development Corporation, June 10, 1970.
51. Ministry of Housing and Local Government, *The New Towns* (London: Her Majesty's Stationery Office, 1970), p. 37.
52. G. K. Davie interview.
53. Ibid.
54. Osborn and Whittick, p. 386.
55. Ibid., pp. 380–381.
56. Ray Thomas, *Aycliffe to Cumbernauld* (London: PEP Publishers, 1969), p. 930.
57. G. K. Davie interview.
58. Frank Schaffer, *The New Town Story* (London: MacGibbon and Kee, Ltd., 1970), pp. 203–204.
59. Book Review Section, *Town and Country Planning* 37 (Jan.-Feb. 1969): 86.
60. G. K. Davie interview.
61. *Cumbernauld New Town* (Cumbernauld, Scotland: Cumbernauld Development Corporation, 1970), pp. 3–5.
62. Ray Thomas, pp. 923–924.
63. Book Review Section, *Town and Country Planning* 37: 86.
64. *Cumbernauld New Town*, p. 5.
65. Ray Thomas, pp. 915, 917, 925.
66. G. K. Davie interview.
67. Interview with J. Goepel, New Towns Commission for Crawley information officer, Crawley, England, June 17, 1970.
68. New Towns Commission for Crawley, "Quarterly Report on Development Progress," April 1, 1973.
69. Osborn and Whittick, pp. 186–187.
70. Ibid., pp. 189–190.
71. New Towns Commission for Crawley, "Quarterly Report," April 1, 1973.
72. J. Goepel interview.
73. Ibid.
74. Ibid.
75. Ibid.
76. Central Office of Information for British Information Services, *The New Towns of Britain* (London: Her Majesty's Stationery Office, 1972), p. 13.
77. J. Goepel interview.
78. Commission for New Towns, *Crawley* (London: Ministry of Housing and Local Government, 1970), pp. 11–12.
79. Osborn and Whittick, pp. 197–199.
80. Ibid., p. 200.
81. Helen Moeller interview.
82. Ibid.
83. Gurney Breckenfeld, p. 26.
84. Ibid., pp. 81–82.

85. J. B. Cullingworth, *Town and Country Planning in England and Wales* (University of Toronto Press, 1964), pp. 223, 266.

86. Kell Aström (n. 4:12), p. 113.

87. Frederic Gutheim, "Continental Europe Offers New Town Building Experience," in *Taming Metropolis* (n. 4:3), p. 837.

CHAPTER 5

1. Donald Canty, ed., *The New City* (New York: Frederick A. Praeger, 1969), pp. 85–86.

2. Ibid., p. 87.

3. Ibid., p. 86.

4. Arthur B. Gallion and Simon Eisner, *The Urban Pattern: City Planning and Design* (Princeton, New Jersey: D. Van Nostrand, 1963), p. 55.

5. John W. Reps (n. 3:2), pp. 272, 314, 351, 402.

6. Ibid., p. 415.

7. Charles L. Sellers, "Early Mormon Community Planning," *Journal of the American Institute of Planners* 28 (Feb. 1962): 25.

8. Donald Canty, pp. 89, 93.

9. John W. Reps, p. 421.

10. Advisory Commission on Intergovernmental Relations, *Urban and Rural America: Policies for Future Growth* (Washington, D.C.: Superintendent of Documents, U.S. Government Printing Office, 1968), p. 68.

11. Stanley Buder, "The Model Town of Pullman: Town Planning and Control in the Gilded Age," *Journal of the American Institute of Planners* 33 (Jan. 1967): 8.

12. John W. Reps, p. 427.

13. Ibid., p. 428.

14. Ibid., p. 427.

15. Letter from Fred K. Hefferly, secretary-treasurer, United Mine Workers of America, Denver, Colorado, April 18, 1962, quoted in James B. Allen, *The Company Town in the American West* (University of Oklahoma Press, 1966), pp. 64–65.

16. Ibid., p. 36.

17. John W. Reps, pp. 429–430.

18. Ibid., p. 430.

19. Donald Canty, p. 98.

20. Clarence S. Stein, *Toward New Towns for America* (Liverpool, England: Liverpool University Press, 1958), pp. 14–15.

21. Ibid., p. 21.

22. Ibid., p. 27.

23. Ibid., p. 39.

24. Advisory Commission, *Urban and Rural America: Policies for Future Growth*, p. 70.

25. Clarence S. Stein, p. 37.

26. Ibid., p. 65.

27. Ibid., pp. 69, 72.

28. Advisory Commission, *Urban and Rural America: Policies for Future Growth,* p. 75.
29. Ibid.
30. Ibid., p. 71.
31. Miles L. Colean, *Housing for Defense* (New York: The Twentieth Century Fund, 1940), pp. 17–18.
32. Ibid., p. 26.
33. Clarence S. Stein, p. 120.
34. Ibid., pp. 119–121.
35. Ibid., pp. 127–128, 181, 187.
36. Gurney Breckenfeld (n. 3:9), p. 119.
37. Ibid., pp. 119–120.
38. Charles N. Glaab and Theodore Brown, *A History of Urban America* (New York: The Macmillan Company, 1967), p. 303.
39. Information provided by Aelred J. Gray, Graduate School of Planning, University of Tennessee, and former chief of the TVA regional planning staff.
40. Information provided by the United States Energy Research and Redevelopment Administration, Richland Operations Office, P. O. Box 550, Richland, Washington 99352.
41. Gurney Breckenfeld, p. 128.
42. Ibid., pp. 127–128.
43. Ibid., p. 125.
44. "Cities: Pairing the Old and New," *Time* 97 (March 1, 1971): 15.
45. Ibid., pp. 15–16.
46. Ibid., p. 16.
47. Steven V. Roberts, "Adolescent 'New Town' Grows in Arizona," *New York Times,* April 6, 1971, p. 36.
48. "New Town Takes Form," *American City* 82 (October 1967): 109.
49. Eleanore Carruth, "The Big Move to New Towns," *Fortune* 84 (Sept. 1971): 149.
50. Ibid., p. 150.
51. James Bailey, ed., *New Towns in America: The Design and Development Process* (New York: John Wiley and Sons, 1973), p. 97.
52. Ibid., p. 127.
53. Patricia Degener, "Reston, City in the Country," *St. Louis Post-Dispatch,* January 19, 1971, p. 5A.
54. Gurney Breckenfeld, pp. 132–133.
55. Ibid., pp. 133–134.
56. Ibid., pp. 135–137.
57. Ibid., p. 139.
58. Ibid., pp. 138–139.
59. Ibid., p. 137.
60. Ibid., pp. 140–141.
61. Ibid., p. 142.

62. "A Brief History of Reston, Virginia" (Reston, Va.: Gulf Reston, Inc., 1972), pp. 31–32, 34.
63. Information provided the author by the Marketing Department, Gulf Reston, Inc., during telephone call, February 6, 1976.
64. "Inside Reston, Virginia," an unpaged booklet prepared by Gulf Reston, Inc., 1972.
65. Ibid.
66. James W. Rouse, "Cities That Work for Man—Victory Ahead," address presented at the University of Puerto Rico, San Juan, Puerto Rico, October 18, 1967, p. 5.
67. Ibid., pp. 5–7.
68. Information provided the author by the Columbia Information Center during telephone call, February 6, 1976.
69. Robert Gladstone and Harold F. Wise, "New Towns Solve Problems of Urban Growth," in *Regional New Towns: Alternatives in Urban Growth* (Detroit, Michigan: Metropolitan Fund, Inc., 1970), p. 21.
70. Ibid.
71. Ibid.
72. "Visitor's Guide to Columbia" (Howard Research and Development Corporation, 1975), p. 30.
73. Ibid., pp. 40, 42.
74. Quoted in Gurney Breckenfeld, p. 16.
75. Chester Rapkin, "New Towns for America," *Journal of Finance* 22 (May 1967): 213.
76. Donald Canty, p. 172.
77. Eleanore Carruth, p. 96.
78. Ibid.
79. Ibid., p. 97.
80. Ibid., pp. 97, 147.
81. *Congressional Record*, February 4, 1971, p. E491, and December 8, 1971, pp. E13151–E13152.
82. Ibid., December 8, 1971, p. E13152.
83. Ibid., February 4, 1971, p. E491.
84. Ibid., December 8, 1971, p. E13152.
85. Ibid.
86. Eleanore Carruth, pp. 97, 147.
87. "HUD-Guaranteed New Communities," *HUD Challenge*, August 1972 (Washington, D.C.: U.S. Department of Housing and Urban Development), p. 17.
88. Ibid., pp. 14–15.
89. Ibid., pp. 13–14.
90. *HUD News*, June 30, 1972, pp. 1–2.
91. Ibid., pp. 3–5.
92. Ibid., October 4, 1972, pp. 1–4.
93. Ibid., February 16, 1973, pp. 1–3, 5.

94. Ibid., November 15, 1973, pp. 1, 3–4.
95. Eleanore Carruth, pp. 148–149.
96. Ibid., p. 148.
97. Ibid.
98. Triton Foundation, *Triton City: A Study of a Prototype Floating Community* (Washington, D.C.: U.S. Government Printing Office, 1968); Athelstan Spilhaus, "Experimental City," *Daedalus*, Fall 1967, pp. 1129–1141; Athelstan Spilhaus, "The Experimental City," *Science* 159 (Feb. 16, 1968): 710–715.
99. Hoyt Gimlin, "New Towns," *Editorial Research Reports* 2 (Nov. 6, 1968): 822 (International City Management Association, Washington, D.C. 20036).
100. Donald Canty, p. 172.

CHAPTER 6

1. Advisory Commission, *Urban and Rural America: Policies for Future Growth*, pp. 13–14.
2. Gurney Breckenfeld (n. 3:9), p. 22.
3. Daniel P. Moynihan (n. 4:37), pp. 6–7.
4. Gurney Breckenfeld, p. 10.
5. Marion Clawson, "Urban Sprawl and Speculation in Suburban Land," *Land Economics* 38 (May 1962): 99, 111.
6. Daniel P. Moynihan, p. 7.
7. Gurney Breckenfeld, p. 7.
8. Daniel P. Moynihan, pp. 6, 8–9.
9. Leo Molinaro, "Truths and Consequences for Older Cities," *Saturday Review* 54 (May 15, 1971): 29.
10. Wolf von Eckhardt, "A Fresh Scene in the Clean Dream," *Saturday Review* 54 (May 15, 1971): 22–23.
11. Louis K. Loewenstein (n. 3:31), pp. 90–91.
12. Daniel P. Moynihan, pp. 15–16.
13. Quoted by Wolf von Eckhardt, "Urban Design," in Daniel P. Moynihan, p. 113.
14. Ibid., p. 114.
15. Ibid., p. 117.
16. Wilson L. Hugh, *Cumbernauld New Town Traffic Analysis Report* (Cumbernauld, Scotland: Cumbernauld Development Corporation, 1958).
17. Kenneth R. Harney, "Massive HUD Report Hits Hard at Subsidies," *The Washington Post*, October 27, 1973, F-16, Column 1.
18. Information provided the author by the Public Information Office, U.S. Department of Housing and Urban Development, Washington, D.C. during a telephone call, February 13, 1976.
19. Roger Marz, "Local Government and New-Town Development," in *Regional New Towns: Alternatives in Urban Growth* (Detroit, Michigan: Metropolitan Fund, Inc., 1970), pp. 42–43.

20. Information provided the author by the Columbia Association Office during a telephone call, February 13, 1976.
21. Wyndham Thomas, Director of the British Town and Country Planning Association, in a letter to the author, January 25, 1966.
22. *Congressional Record*, March 6, 1972, p. E2030.
23. Lee Rainwater, *Behind Ghetto Walls* (Chicago: Aldine Publishing Company, 1970), p. 309.
24. J. John Palen, *The Urban World* (New York: McGraw-Hill Book Company, 1975), pp. 259–261.
25. Information provided the author by the Detroit Housing Commission during a telephone call, February 13, 1976.
26. Information provided the author by the Marina City Sales and Rental Office during a telephone call, February 13, 1976.

Bibliography

BOOKS AND BOOKLETS

Abrams, Charles. *The City Is the Frontier*. New York: Harper and Row, 1965.

Adrian, Charles, and Press, Charles. *Governing Urban America*. New York: McGraw-Hill, 1972.

Alihan, Milla A. *Social Ecology*. New York: Columbia University Press, 1938.

Allen, James B. *The Company Town in the American West*. Norman, Okla.: University of Oklahoma Press, 1966.

Allen, Muriel I., ed. *New Communities: Challenge for Today*. Washington, D.C.: The American Institute of Planners Task Force on New Communities, 1968.

Altshuler, Alan A. *The City Planning Process*. Ithaca, N.Y.: Cornell University Press, 1965.

American Institute of Architects. *New Towns in America: The Design and Development Process*. New York: John Wiley and Sons, 1973.

Anderson, Nels, ed. *Urbanism and Urbanization*. Leiden, The Netherlands: E. J. Brill, 1964.

Anderson, Nels, and Ishwaran, K. *Urban Sociology*. New York: Asia Publishing House, 1965.

271

Andrews, Richard B. *Urban Growth and Development: A Problem Approach.* New York: Simmons-Boardman Publishing Corp., 1962.

The Application of the New Towns Concept. The Hague: International Union of Local Authorities, 1964.

Ashworth, William. *The Genesis of Modern British Town Planning.* London: Routledge and Kegan Paul, 1954.

Aström, Kell. *City Planning in Sweden.* Stockholm: The Swedish Institute, 1967.

Babcock, Richard F. *The Zoning Game.* Madison, Wis.: University of Wisconsin Press, 1966.

Bacon, Edmund N. *Design of Cities.* New York: Viking Press, 1967.

Bellush, Jewel, and Hausknecht, Murray. *Urban Renewal: People, Politics, and Planning.* Garden City, N.Y.: Anchor Books, 1967.

Benevolo, Leonardo. *The Origins of Modern Town Planning.* Cambridge, Mass.: M.I.T. Press, 1967.

Berry, Brian J. L., and Meltzer, Jack. *Goals for Urban America.* Englewood Cliffs, N.J.: Prentice-Hall, 1967.

Beshars, James M. *Urban Social Structure.* New York: The Free Press of Glencoe, 1962.

Beveridge, William Henry. *New Towns and the Case for Them.* London: University of London Press, 1952.

Beyer, Glenn. *Housing and Society.* New York: The Macmillan Company, 1965.

Biddle, William W. *Community Development Process.* New York: Holt, Rinehart and Winston, 1965.

Blijstra, J. *Town Planning in the Netherlands Since 1900.* Amsterdam: P. N. Van Kampen and Zoon, 1965.

Blumenfeld, Hans, and Spreiregen, Paul D., eds. *Modern Metropolis: Its Origins, Growth Characteristics, and Planning.* Cambridge, Mass.: M.I.T. Press, 1967.

Bollens, John C. *The Metropolis: Its People, Politics, and Economic Life.* New York: Harper and Row, 1965.

Bor, Walter. *The Making of Cities.* New York: Barnes and Noble, 1972.

Boskoff, Alvin. *The Sociology of Urban Regions.* New York: Appleton-Century-Crofts, 1970.

Braidwood, Robert J., and Willey, Gordon, R., eds. *Courses Toward Urban Life: Archeological Considerations of Some Cultural Alternates.* Chicago: Aldine Publishers, 1962.

Branch, Melville C. *Planning: Aspects and Application.* New York: John Wiley and Sons, 1966.

Breckenfeld, Gurney. *Columbia and the New Towns.* New York: Ives Washburn, 1971.

Breese, Gerald, ed. *The City in Newly Developing Countries: Readings on Urbanism and Urbanization.* Englewood Cliffs, N.J.: Prentice-Hall, 1969.

British Information Services. *The New Towns of Britain.* London: Her Majesty's Stationery Office, 1969.

Broadey, Maurice. *Planning for People.* London: The Bedford Square Press of the National Council of Social Service, 1968.

Burgess, Ernest W., and Bogue, Donald J. *Contributions to Urban Sociology.* Chicago: University of Chicago Press, 1964.

Callow, Alexander B. *American Urban History.* New York: Oxford University Press, 1969.

Canty, Donald, ed. *The New City.* New York: Frederick A. Praeger, 1969.

Cary, L. J., ed. *Community Development as a Process.* Columbia, Mo.: University of Missouri Press, 1970.

Central Office of Information. *The New Towns.* London: Her Majesty's Stationery Office, 1970.

Chapin, Francis Stuart, Jr. *Urban Land Use Planning.* Urbana, Ill.: University of Illinois Press, 1965.

————, and Weiss, Shirley F., eds. *Urban Growth Dynamics in a Regional Cluster of Cities.* New York: John Wiley and Sons, 1962.

Chermayeff, S., and Tzonis, A. *Shape of Community.* Baltimore: Penguin Books, 1971.

Clinard, Marshall B. *Slums and Community Development.* New York: The Macmillan Company, 1966.

Commission for the New Towns. *Crawley.* London: Ministry of Housing and Local Government (now Department of the Environment), 1970.

Cousins, Albert N., and Nagpaul, Hans, eds. *Urban Man and Society: A Reader in Urban Sociology.* New York: Alfred A. Knopf, 1970.

Crecine, J. *Financing the Metropolis.* Vol. 4. Beverly Hills, Calif.: Sage Publications, 1970.

Crosby, Theo. *Architecture: City Sense.* New York: Reinhold Publishing Company, 1965.

Cullingworth, J. B. *Town and Country Planning in England and Wales.* Toronto: University of Toronto Press, 1964.

Cumbernauld Development Corporation. *Cumbernauld New Town.* Cumbernauld, Scotland, 1970.

Davis, Kingsley. *Modern Urban Revolution.* New York: Random House, 1967.

Department of Public Works. *Town Planning and Ground Exploitation in Amsterdam.* Amsterdam, 1967.

Dickinson, Robert E. *The West European City.* London: Routledge and Kegan Paul, 1951.

Dore, Ronald P. *City Life in Japan.* Berkeley: University of California Press, 1958.

Doxiades, Constantinos A. *Between Dystopia and Utopia.* Hartford, Conn.: Trinity College Press, 1968.

_____. *Urban Renewal and the Future of the American City.* Chicago: Public Administration Service, 1966.

Duff, A. C. *Britain's New Towns: An Experiment in Living.* London: Pall Mall Press, 1961.

Duhl, Leonard J. *The Urban Condition: People and Policy in the Metropolis.* New York: Basic Books, 1963.

Duncan, Otis D., et al. *Metropolis and Region.* Baltimore: The Johns Hopkins Press, 1960.

Editors of *Fortune. The Exploding Metropolis.* Garden City, N.Y.: Doubleday, 1958.

Eichler, Edward P., and Kaplan, Marshall. *The Community Builders.* Berkeley: University of California Press, 1967.

Eldredge, H. Wentworth. *Taming Metropolis.* Vols. 1 and 2. Garden City, N.Y.: Anchor Books, 1967.

Elias, E. C.; Gillies, James; and Riemer, Svend. *Metropolis: Values in Conflict.* Belmont, Calif.: Wadsworth Publishing Company, 1964.

Epstein, A. L. *Politics in an Urban African Community*. Manchester, England: Manchester University Press, 1958.

Everett, Robinson O., and Leach, Richard H., eds. *Urban Problems and Prospects*. Dobbs Ferry, N.Y.: Oceana Publications, 1965.

Ewald, William R., Jr., ed. *Environment and Policy: The Next Fifty Years*. Bloomington, Ind.: Indiana University Press, 1968.

Faltermayer, Edmund K. *Redoing America*. New York: Harper and Row, 1968.

Farsta Centrum, AB. *Farsta*. Stockholm, 1959.

————. *Farsta Centre*. Stockholm, 1961.

Fava, Sylvia F., ed. *Urbanism in World Perspective*. New York: Thomas Y. Crowell, 1968.

Firey, Walter. *Land Use in Central Boston*. Cambridge, Mass.: Harvard University Press, 1947.

Fiser, Webb S. *Mastery of the Metropolis*. Englewood Cliffs, N.J.: Prentice-Hall, 1962.

Frieden, Bernard J. *The Future of Old Neighborhoods: Rebuilding for a Changing Population*. Cambridge, Mass.: M.I.T. Press, 1964.

————, and Morris, Robert, eds. *Urban Planning and Social Policy*. New York: Basic Books, 1968.

Gallion, Arthur B., and Eisner, Simon. *The Urban Pattern: City Planning and Design*. Princeton, N.J.: D. Van Nostrand, 1963.

Gans, Herbert J. *People and Plans: Essays on Urban Problems and Solutions*. New York: Basic Books, 1968.

Geen, Elizabeth; Lowe, Jeanne R.; and Walker, Kenneth. *Man and the Modern City*. Pittsburgh: University of Pittsburgh Press, 1963.

Gentili, Giorgio. *The Satellite Towns of Stockholm*. Stockholm: Department of Planning and Building Control, 1960.

Gibbs, Jack P. *Urban Research Methods*. Princeton, N.J.: D. Van Nostrand, 1961.

Gittings, James A. *Life Without Living: People of the Inner City*. Philadelphia: Westminster Press, 1966.

Glaab, Charles N. *The American City: A Documentary History*. Homewood, Ill.: The Dorsey Press, 1963.

————, and Brown, A. Theodore. *A History of Urban America.* New York: The Macmillan Company, 1967.

Goodman, R. *After the Planners.* New York: Simon and Schuster, 1971.

Goodman, William I., ed. *Principles and Practice of Urban Planning.* Washington, D.C.: International City Managers' Association, 1968.

Gordon, Mitchell, *Sick Cities.* New York: The Macmillan Company, 1963.

Gottmann, Jean. *Megalopolis.* New York: The Twentieth Century Fund, 1961.

————, and Harper, Robert A., eds. *Metropolis on the Move.* New York: John Wiley and Sons, 1967.

Grebler, Leo. *Urban Renewal in European Countries.* Philadelphia: University of Pennsylvania Press, 1964.

Green, Constance M. *The Rise of Urban America.* New York: Harper and Row, 1965.

Greer, Scott. *The Emerging City.* New York: The Free Press of Glencoe, 1962a.

————. *Governing the Metropolis.* New York: John Wiley and Sons, 1962b.

————. *Urban Renewal and American Cities.* Indianapolis: Bobbs-Merrill, 1965.

————; McElrath, Dennis L.; Minar, David W.; and Orleans, Peter. *The New Urbanization.* New York: St. Martin's Press, 1968.

Gruen, Victor. *The Heart of Our Cities.* New York: Simon and Schuster, 1964.

Gutkind, Erwin A. *The Twilight of Cities.* New York: The Free Press of Glencoe, 1962.

Hadden, Jeffrey K., and Borgatta, Edgar F. *American Cities: Their Social Characteristics.* Chicago: Rand McNally and Co., 1965.

Hadden, Jeffrey K.; Musotti, Louis H.; and Larson, Calvin J. *Metropolis in Crisis.* Itasca, Ill.: F. E. Peacock Publishers, 1967.

Hall, Peter G. *World Cities.* New York: McGraw-Hill, 1966.

Harlow Development Corporation. *History of Harlow.* Harlow, England, 1968.

Hatt, Paul K., and Reiss, Albert J., Jr., eds. *Cities and Society*. New York: The Free Press of Glencoe, 1957.

Hauser, Philip M., ed. *Handbook for Social Research in Urban Areas*. Paris: UNESCO, 1964.

————, and Schnore, Leo F., eds. *The Study of Urbanization*. New York: John Wiley and Sons, 1965.

Hawley, Amos. *Human Ecology*. New York: Ronald Press, 1950.

————, and Zimmer, B. *The Metropolitan Community: Its People and Government*. Beverly Hills, Calif.: Sage Publications, 1970.

Hellman, Hal. *The City in the World of the Future*. New York: M. Evans and Company, 1970.

Herber, Lewis. *Crisis in Our Cities*. Englewood Cliffs, N.J.: Prentice-Hall, 1965.

Hirsch, Werner Z. *Urban Life and Form*. New York: Holt, Rinehart and Winston, 1963.

Howard, Ebenezer. *Garden Cities of Tomorrow*. Cambridge, Mass.: M.I.T. Press, 1965.

Hunter, David R. *The Slums: Challenge and Response*. New York: The Free Press of Glencoe, 1964.

International City Managers' Association (now International City Management Association, Washington, D.C.). *New Towns: A New Dimension of Urbanism*. Chicago, 1968.

Isenberg, Irwin, ed. *The City in Crisis*. New York: The H. W. Wilson Company, 1968.

Jackson, John N. *Surveys for Town and Country Planning*. London: Hutchinson University Library, 1963.

Jacobs, Jane. *The Death and Life of Great American Cities*. New York: Random House, 1961.

————. *The Economy of Cities*. New York: Random House, 1969.

Johnson-Marshall, Percy. *Rebuilding Cities*. Chicago: Aldine Publishing Company, 1966.

Jones, Emrys. *A Social Geography of Belfast*. London: Oxford University Press, 1960.

Kanter, R. M. *Commitment and Community*. Cambridge, Mass.: Harvard University Press, 1972.

Kent, T. J. *The Urban General Plan.* San Francisco: Chandler Publishing Company, 1964.

Keyes, Scott. *Urban and Regional Studies at U.S. Universities.* Baltimore: The Johns Hopkins Press, 1964.

Klotsche, J. Martin. *The Urban University and the Future of Our Cities.* New York: Harper and Row, 1966.

Kraeling, Carl H., and Adams, R. M., eds. *Symposium on Urbanization and Cultural Development in the Ancient Near East.* Chicago: University of Chicago Press, 1960.

Kulski, Julia E. *Land of Urban Promise.* South Bend, Ind.: University of Notre Dame Press, 1967.

Lampard, Eric E. "Urbanization and Social Change: On Broadening the Scope and Relevance of Urban History." In *The Historian and the City,* edited by Oscar Handlin and John Buchard. Cambridge, Mass.: M.I.T. Press, 1963.

Laqueur, Walter, and Labedz, Leopold, eds. *The Future of Communist Society.* New York: Frederick A. Praeger, 1962.

Leinwand, G. *The City as a Community.* New York: Simon and Schuster, 1970.

————, ed. *Governing the City.* New York: Simon and Schuster, 1971.

Lerner, Daniel. *The Passing of Traditional Society.* New York: The Free Press of Glencoe, 1958.

Le Tourneau, Roger. *Fès: Avant le Protectorat.* Casablanca: Société Marocaine de Librairie et d'Edition, 1949.

Lewis, David. *Pedestrian in the City.* Princeton, N.J.: D. Van Nostrand, 1966.

————. *Urban Structure.* New York: John Wiley and Sons, 1968.

————. *The Growth of Cities.* New York: John Wiley and Sons, 1971.

Lewis, Oscar. *The Children of Sanchez.* New York: Random House, 1961.

Loewenstein, Louis K., ed. *Urban Studies: An Introductory Reader.* New York: The Free Press of Glencoe, 1971.

Lowe, Jeanne. *Cities in a Race with Time.* New York: Random House, 1967.

Lubove, Roy. *Community Planning in the 1920's: The Contri-*

bution of the Regional Planning Association of America.
Pittsburgh: University of Pittsburgh Press, 1963.

_____. *The Urban Community: Housing and Planning in the Progressive Era.* Englewood Cliffs, N.J.: Prentice-Hall, 1967.

Lynch, Kevin. *The Image of the City.* Cambridge, Mass.: The Technology Press, 1960.

McKelvey, Blake. *The Urbanization of America, 1860–1915.* New Brunswick, N.J.: Rutgers University Press, 1963.

_____. *The Emergence of Metropolitan America: 1915–1966.* New Brunswick, N.J.: Rutgers University Press, 1968.

Mackenzie, R. D. *The Metropolitan Community.* New York: McGraw-Hill, 1933.

Mackesey, Thomas W. *History of City Planning.* Oakland, Calif.: Council of Planning Librarians, 1961.

McQuade, Walter, ed. *Cities Fit to Live In.* New York: The Macmillan Company, 1971.

Mahood, H. R. *Urban Politics and Problems.* New York: Charles Scribner and Sons, 1969.

Maier, Henry W. *Challenge to the Cities: An Approach to a Theory of Urban Leadership.* New York: Random House, 1966.

Malt, Harold. *Furnishing the City.* New York: McGraw-Hill, 1970.

Mandelker, Daniel R. *Green Belts and Urban Growth.* Madison, Wis.: University of Wisconsin Press, 1962.

Marris, Peter. *Family and Social Change in an African City.* Evanston, Ill.: Northwestern University Press, 1962.

Marx, Karl, and Engels, Friedrich. *Selected Works.* 2 vols. Moscow, 1958.

Maxwell, James A. *Financing State and Local Governments.* Washington, D.C.: The Brookings Institution, 1969.

Mayer, Albert. *The Urgent Future.* New York: McGraw-Hill, 1967.

Merlin, P. *New Towns: Regional Planning and Development.* London: Methuen and Co., 1971.

Metropolitan Fund, Inc. *Regional New Towns: Alternatives in Urban Growth.* Detroit, Mich. 211 West Fort Street, 1970.

Meyer, John. *The Urban Transportation Problem*. Cambridge, Mass.: Harvard University Press, 1965.

Meyerson, Martin, and Banfield, Edward C. *Politics, Planning, and the Public Interest*. New York: The Free Press of Glencoe, 1955.

Meyerson, Martin; Tyrwhitt, Jacqueline; Falk, Brian; and Seklar, Patricia. *Face of the Metropolis*. New York: Random House, 1963.

Miller, Daniel R., and Swanson, Guy E. *The Changing American Parent*. New York: John Wiley and Sons, 1958.

Miner, Horace. *The Primitive City of Timbuctoo*. Princeton, N.J.: Princeton University Press, 1953.

Ministry of Housing and Local Government. *Old People's Flatlets at Stevenage*. London: Her Majesty's Stationery Office, 1966.

————. *The Needs of New Communities: A Report on Social Provisions in New and Expanding Communities*. London: Her Majesty's Stationery Office, 1967.

————. *Grouped Flatlets for Old People: A Sociological Study*. London: Her Majesty's Stationery Office, 1968.

————. *The New Towns*. London: Her Majesty's Stationery Office, 1970*a*.

————. *People and Planning*. London: Her Majesty's Stationery Office, 1970*b*.

Mowry, George E. *The Urban Nation, 1920–1960*. New York: Hill and Wang, 1965.

Moynihan, Daniel P. *Toward a National Urban Policy*. New York: Basic Books, Inc., 1970.

Mukerjee, Radhakamal. *Social Ecology*. London: Longmans Green, 1945.

Mumford, Lewis. *The Culture of Cities*. New York: Harcourt, Brace and Company, 1938.

————. *The City in History*. New York: Harcourt, Brace and World, 1961.

————. *The Urban Prospect*. New York: Harcourt, Brace and World, 1968.

Murphy, Raymond E. *The American City: An Urban Geography*. New York: McGraw-Hill, 1966.

National Commission on Urban Problems. *Building the American City*. Washington, D.C.: U.S. Government Printing Office, 1968.

National Committee on Urban Growth Policy. *The New City*. New York: Frederick A. Praeger, 1969.

Nicholson, J. H. *New Communities in Britain: Achievements and Problems*. London: National Council of Social Service, 1961.

Niehoff, Arthur. *Factory Workers in India, Publications in Anthropology, No. 5*. Milwaukee: Milwaukee Public Museum, 1959.

Orlans, Harold. *Stevenage: A Sociological Study of a New Town*. London: Routledge and Kegan Paul, 1952.

Osborn, Frederic J. *Greenbelt Cities*. London: Faber and Faber, 1946.

––––––, and Whittick, Arnold. *The New Towns: The Answer to Megalopolis*. London: Leonard Hill, 1969.

Park, Robert. *Human Communities: The City and Human Ecology*. New York: The Free Press of Glencoe, 1952.

Pass, David. *Vallingby and Farsta: From Idea to Reality*. Stockholm: National Swedish Building Research, 1969.

Pell, Claiborne. *Megalopolis Unbound: The Supercity and the Transportation of Tomorrow*. New York: Frederick A. Praeger, 1966.

Perin, Constance. *With Man in Mind*. Cambridge, Mass.: M.I.T. Press, 1970.

Perloff, Harvey S., ed. *Planning and the Urban Community*. Pittsburgh: University of Pittsburgh Press, 1961.

––––––. *The Quality of the Urban Environment*. Baltimore: The Johns Hopkins Press, 1969.

Planning Advisory Group. *The Future of Development Plans*. London: Her Majesty's Stationery Office, 1965.

Price, Douglas. *The Metropolis and Its Problems*. Syracuse, N.Y.: Syracuse University Press, 1960.

Purdom, Charles B. *The Building of Satellite Towns*. London: J. M. Dent and Sons, 1949.

Redfield, Robert. *The Folk Culture of Yucatán*. Chicago: University of Chicago Press, 1941.

Reiner, Thomas A. *The Place of the Ideal Community in Urban Planning*. Philadelphia: University of Pennsylvania Press, 1963.

Reissman, Leonard. *The Urban Process*. New York: The Free Press of Glencoe, 1964.

Report of the Commission for the New Towns for the Period Ending March 31, 1969. London: Her Majesty's Stationery Office, 1969.

Reps, John W. *The Making of Urban America: A History of City Planning in the United States*. Princeton, N.J.: Princeton University Press, 1965.

Richardson, H. W. *Urban Economics*. Baltimore: Penguin Books, 1971.

Robson, W., and Regan, D. *Great Cities of the World: The Government, Politics and Planning*. 2 vols. Beverly Hills, Calif.: Sage Publications, 1972.

Rockefeller Brothers Fund. *The Use of Land*. New York: Thomas Y. Crowell Co., 1973.

Rodwin, Lloyd. *The British New Towns Policy*. Cambridge, Mass.: Harvard University Press, 1956.

————, ed. *The Future Metropolis*. New York: Braziller, 1961.

————. *Nations and Cities: A Comparison of Strategies for Urban Growth*. Boston: Houghton Mifflin Company, 1970.

Rogers, David. *The Management of Big Cities*. Beverly Hills, Calif.: Sage Publications, 1971.

Royal Commission on Historical Monuments. *Peterborough New Town*. London: Her Majesty's Stationery Office, 1969.

Saarinen, Eliel. *The City: Its Growth, Its Decay, Its Future*. Cambridge, Mass.: M.I.T. Press, 1965.

Schaffer, Frank. *The New Town Story*. London: MacGibbon and Kee, 1970.

Schlivek, Louis B. *Man in the Metropolis*. Garden City, N.Y.: Doubleday, 1965.

Schmandt, Henry J., and Bloomberg, Warner, Jr., eds. *The Quality of Urban Life*. Vol. 3. Beverly Hills, Calif.: Sage Publications, 1969.

Schnore, Leo F. *The Urban Scene: Human Ecology and De-mography*. New York: The Free Press of Glencoe, 1965.
———, and Fagin, Henry. *Urban Research and Policy Plan-ning*. Vol. 1. Beverly Hills, Calif.: Sage Publications, 1967.
Schuchter, Arnold. *White Power/Black Freedom*. Boston: Bea-con Press, 1968.
Scott, Mellier G. *American City Planning Since 1890*. Berkeley: University of California Press, 1971.
Second Report on Physical Planning in the Netherlands. The Hague: Government Printing Office of The Netherlands, 1966.
Senior, Derek. *The Regional City*. Chicago: Aldine Publishing Co., 1966.
Simmel, Georg. "The Metropolis and Mental Life." In *Cities and Society: The Revised Reader in Urban Sociology*, edited by Paul K. Hatt and Albert J. Reiss, Jr. New York: The Free Press of Glencoe, 1957.
Sirjamaki, John. *The Sociology of Cities*. New York: Random House, 1964.
Sjoberg, Gideon. *The Preindustrial City: Past and Present*. New York: The Free Press of Glencoe, 1960.
Smerk, George M., ed. *Readings in Urban Transportation*. Bloomington, Ind.: Indiana University Press, 1968.
Smith, Adam. *The Wealth of Nations*. Reprint. Baltimore: Pen-guin Books, 1937.
Smith, W. F. *Housing: The Social and Economic Elements*. Berkeley: University of California Press, 1971.
Southall, Aidan, ed. *Social Change in Modern Africa*. London: Oxford University Press, 1961.
Spengler, Oswald. *The Decline of the West*. Vol. 2. New York: Alfred A. Knopf, 1928.
Spiegel, Erika. *New Towns in Israel*. New York: Frederick A. Praeger Publishers, 1967.
Spiegel, Hans B. C. *Citizen Participation in Urban Develop-ment*. 2 vols. Washington, D.C.: Center for Community Affairs, NTL Institute for Applied Behavioral Science, 1968–1969.
Spreiregen, Paul D. *Urban Design: The Architecture of Towns and Cities*. New York: McGraw-Hill, 1965.

Starr, Roger. *The Living End: The City and Its Critics.* New York: Coward-McCann, 1966.

Stein, Clarence S. *Toward New Towns for America.* Liverpool, England: Liverpool University Press, 1958.

Steiner, Oscar H. *Downtown USA.* Dobbs Ferry, N.Y.: Oceana, 1964.

Stipe, Robert E., ed. *Perception and Environment: Foundations of Urban Design.* Chapel Hill, N.C.: The Institute of Government, The University of North Carolina, 1966.

Strauss, Anselm L. *Images of the American City.* New York: The Free Press of Glencoe, 1961.

Strong, Ann Louise. *Open Space for Urban America.* Washington, D.C.: U.S. Urban Renewal Administration, 1965.

―――. *Planned Urban Environments.* Baltimore: The Johns Hopkins Press, 1971.

Svrinas, M. N. *Caste in Modern India.* London: Asia Publishing House, 1962.

Sykes, A. J.; Livingstone, J. M.; and Green, M. *Cumbernauld '67: A Household Survey and Report.* Stirling, Scotland: Jamieson and Munro, 1967.

Taylor, Lord, and Chave, Sidney. *Mental Health and Environment in a New Town.* London: Longmans, 1964.

Theodorson, George A., ed. *Studies in Human Ecology.* Evanston, Ill.: Row, Peterson, 1961.

Thomas, Ray. *Aycliffe to Cumbernauld: A Study of Seven New Towns in Their Regions.* London: PEP Publishers, 1969.

Thomlinson, Ralph. *Urban Structure: The Social and Spatial Character of Cities.* New York: Random House, 1969.

Triton Foundation. *Triton City: A Study of a Prototype Floating Community.* Washington, D.C.: U.S. Government Printing Office, 1968.

Tyler, Alice Felt. *Freedom's Ferment.* Minneapolis: University of Minnesota Press, 1944.

United Nations. *Report of the United Nations Symposium on the Planning and Development of New Towns.* New York, 1966.

―――. *Planning of Metropolitan Areas and New Towns.* New York, 1967.

_____. *Proceedings of the Seminar: Future Patterns and Forms of Urban Settlement.* Vol. 1. New York, 1968.

_____. Department of Economic and Social Affairs, Population Studies, No. 44, *Growth of the World's Urban and Rural Population, 1920–2000.* New York, 1969.

_____. *Urbanization in the Second United Nations Development Decade.* New York, 1970.

United States Advisory Commission on Intergovernmental Relations. *Metropolitan Social and Economic Disparities: Implications for Intergovernmental Relations in Central Cities and Suburbs.* Washington, D.C.: U.S. Government Printing Office, 1965.

_____. *Urban and Rural America: Policies for Future Growth.* Washington, D.C.: U.S. Government Printing Office, 1968.

United States Conference of Mayors, Special Committee on Historic Preservation. *With Heritage So Rich.* New York: Random House, 1966.

United States Congress, Joint Economic Committee. *Urban America: Goals and Problems.* Washington, D.C.: U.S. Government Printing Office, 1967.

United States Department of Housing and Urban Development. *Urban Land Policy—Selected Aspects of European Experience.* Washington, D.C.: U.S. Government Printing Office, 1969.

United States President's Science Advisory Committee. *Restoring the Quality of Our Environment.* Washington, D.C.: U.S. Government Printing Office, 1965.

United States Urban Renewal Administration. *Open Space for Urban America.* Washington, D.C.: U.S. Government Printing Office, 1965.

Urban Land Institute. *Federally Assisted New Communities: New Dimensions in Urban Development.* Washington, D.C.: The Urban Land Institute, 1973.

Von Eckhardt, Wolf, ed. *A Place to Live: The Crisis of the Cities.* New York: Dell Publishing Company, 1967.

Von Hertzen, Heikki, and Spreiregen, Paul D. *Building a New Town: Finland's New Garden City, Tapiola.* Cambridge, Mass.: M.I.T. Press, 1970.

Warner, Sam Bass, ed. *Planning for a Nation of Cities.* Cambridge, Mass.: M.I.T. Press, 1966.

Warren, Robert O. *Government in Metropolitan Regions.* Davis, Calif.: Institute of Governmental Affairs, University of California, 1966.

Weaver, Robert C. *Dilemmas of Urban America.* New York: Atheneum, 1969.

Webber, Melvin M., et al. *Explorations into Urban Structure.* Philadelphia: University of Pennsylvania Press, 1964.

Weissbourd, Bernard, and Channick, Herbert. *An Urban Strategy.* Santa Barbara, Calif.: Center for the Study of Democratic Institutions, 1968.

White, L. E. *New Towns: Their Challenge and Opportunity.* London: The National Council of Social Service, 1951.

White, Morton G. *The Intellectual Versus the City from Thomas Jefferson to Frank Lloyd Wright.* Cambridge, Mass.: Harvard University Press, 1962.

Whyte, William H., Jr. *Man and the Modern City.* Pittsburgh: University of Pittsburgh Press, 1963.

————. *The Last Landscape.* Garden City, N.Y.: Doubleday, 1968.

Willbern, York. *The Withering Away of the City.* Bloomington, Ind.: Indiana University Press, 1966.

Willhelm, Sidney M. *Urban Zoning and Land Use Theory.* New York: The Free Press of Glencoe, 1962.

Willmann, John B. *The Department of Housing and Urban Development.* New York: Frederick A. Praeger, 1967.

Wilson, James Q., ed. *Urban Renewal: The Record and Controversy.* Cambridge, Mass.: M.I.T. Press, 1967.

————. *The Metropolitan Enigma.* Cambridge, Mass.: Harvard University Press, 1968.

Wingo, Lowden, ed. *Cities and Space: The Future Use of Urban Land.* Baltimore: The Johns Hopkins Press, 1966.

Wirth, Louis, *On Cities and Social Life.* University of Chicago Press, 1964.

Wright, Frank Lloyd. *Living City.* New York: Horizon Press, 1963.

Zimmerman, Joseph F., ed. *Government of the Metropolis.* New York: Holt, Rinehart and Winston, 1968.

JOURNAL ARTICLES, INFORMATION SHEETS,
RESEARCH MONOGRAPHS, SEMINAR
AND SYMPOSIUM REPORTS

Adams, Robert M. "The Origin of Cities." *Scientific American* 203 (Sept. 1960) : 48.

Bell, Daniel. "Russia's Eroding Ideology." *New Leader* 46 (15 April 1963) : 18–23.

Bellah, Robert N. "Durkheim and History." *American Sociological Review* 24 (Aug. 1959) : 461.

Buder, Stanley. "The Model Town of Pullman: Town Planning and Control in the Gilded Age." *Journal of the American Institute of Planners* 33 (Jan. 1967) : 8.

Bull, D. A. "New Town and Town Expansion Schemes." *Town Planning Review* 38 (July 1967) : 103–114, and 38 (Oct. 1967) : 165–186.

Caplow, Theodore. "Urban Structure in France." *American Sociological Review* 17 (Oct. 1952) : 544–549.

Carruth, Eleanore. "The Big Move to New Towns." *Fortune* 84 (Sept. 1971) : 149.

Champion, Anthony. "Recent Trends in New Town Densities." *Town and Country Planning* 38 (May 1970) : 252–254.

Childe, V. Gordon. "The Urban Revolution." *Town Planning Review* 21 (April 1950) : 13–17.

"Cities: Pairing the Old and New." *Time,* 97 (March 1, 1971) : 15–16.

City of Amsterdam Press, Publicity, and Information Bureau. "In Bijlmermeer the Amsterdam Citizen of Today Finds the Environment of Tomorrow." Amsterdam, The Netherlands, 1969. 4 pages.

Clark, Colin. "Employment in New Towns." *Journal of the Town Planning Institute* 52 (Jan. 1966) : 11–14.

Clinard, Marshall B. "A Cross-Cultural Replication of the Relation of Urbanism to Criminal Behavior." *American Sociological Review* 25 (April 1960) : 253–257.

Commission on Population Growth and the American Future. *Population Growth and the American Future.* Washington, D.C.: U.S. Government Printing Office, 1972.

Cumbernauld Information Center. "Cumbernauld New Town." Cumbernauld, Scotland, 1970. 7 pages.

Degener, Patricia. "Reston, City in the Country." *St. Louis Post-Dispatch*, Jan. 19, 1971, p. 5A.

Dodd, Stuart. "A System of Operationally-Defined Concepts for Sociology." *American Sociological Review* 4 (Oct. 1939) : 619–634.

Domestic Council Committee on National Growth. *Report on National Growth, 1972*. Washington, D.C.: U.S. Government Printing Office, 1972.

Dotson, Floyd, and Dotson, Lillian. "Urban Centralization and Decentralization in Mexico." *Rural Sociology* 21 (March 1956) : 41–49.

Duncan, Otis Dudley. "From Social System to Ecosystem." *Sociological Inquiry* 31 (Spring 1961) : 140–149.

Ellis, Alan E. "Leasehold Reform in the New Towns." *Town and Country Planning* 37 (Jan.-Feb. 1969) : 39–42.

Field, Mark G. "Alcoholism, Crime, and Delinquency in Soviet Society." *Social Problems* 3 (Oct. 1955) : 100–109.

Form, William. "The Place of Social Structures in the Determination of Land Use: Implications for a Theory of Urban Ecology." *Social Forces* 32 (May 1954) : 317–323.

Freeman, Orville L. "Towards a National Policy on Balanced Communities." *Minnesota Law Review* 53 (June 1969) : 1163–1178.

Friedl, Ernestine. "Lagging Emulation in Post-Peasant Society: A Greek Case." *American Anthropologist* 66 (June 1964) : 569–586.

"The Future of Britain's New Towns: Views of the Three Political Parties." *Town and Country Planning* 38 (Jan. 1970) : 64–67.

Galantry, Ervin. "Black New Towns." *Progressive Architecture* 49 (Aug. 1968) : 126–131.

Galbraith, John Kenneth. "The Poverty of Nations." *Atlantic Monthly*, 210 (Oct. 1962) : 47–53.

Gans, Herbert J. "The Balanced Community." *Journal of the American Institute of Planners* 27 (Aug. 1961) : 176–184.

Garvey, John, Jr. "What Can Europe Teach Us About Urban Growth?" *Nation's Cities* 7 (April 1969) : 13–18.

Gettys, Warner E. "Human Ecology and Social Theory." *Social Forces* Vol. 18 (May 1940) : 469–476.

Gibbs, Jack P., and Martin, Walter T. "Urbanization, Technology, and the Division of Labor: International Patterns." *American Sociological Review* 27 (Oct. 1962): 667–677.

————, and Schnore, Leo F. "Metropolitan Growth: An International Study." *American Journal of Sociology* 66 (Sept. 1960) : 160–170.

Gimlin, Hoyt. "New Towns." *Editorial Research Reports*, Vol. 2, November 6, 1968. Congressional Quarterly, Inc., 1735 "K" Street, Washington, D.C.

Ginsburgs, George. "Objective Truth and the Judicial Process in Post-Stalinist Soviet Jurisprudence." *American Journal of Comparative Law* 10 (Winter-Spring 1961) : 53–75.

Gist, Noel P. "The Ecology of Bangalore, India: An East-West Comparison." *Social Forces* 35 (May 1957) : 356–365.

Gladstone, Robert. "New Towns' Role in Urban Growth Explored." *Journal of Housing* 23 (Jan. 1966) : 29–36.

————, and Wise, Harold F. "New Towns Solve Problems of Urban Growth." *Public Management* 48 (May 1966) : 128–139.

Gutheim, Frederick. "Europe Offers New Town Builders Experience." *Public Management* 48 (April 1966) : 99–107.

Gutman, Robert, and Rabinovitz, Francine F. "The Relevance of Domestic Urban Studies to International Urban Research." *Urban Affairs Quarterly* 1 (June 1966) : 45–64.

Hancock, Macklin L. "New Towns: Are They the Answer to Current Urban Sprawl?" *Journal of Housing* 22 (Oct. 1965) : 469–471.

Harris, Britton. "Urban Development Models: New Tools for Planning." *Journal of the American Institute of Planners* 31 (May 1965) : 90–182.

Hawkes, John, and McKie, Robert. "Greater Peterborough: Amenities and Social Change." *Town and Country Planning* 37 (Jan.-Feb. 1969) : 10–16.

Hodge, Patricia L., and Hauser, Philip M. "The Challenge of America's Metropolitan Population—1960 to 1985." Research Report No. 3. Washington, D.C.: National Commission on Urban Problems, 1968.

Holford, William G. "British New Town Planning." *Journal of the American Institute of Architects* 15 (Jan. 1951): 46–50.

Hollingshead, A. B. "A Re-Examination of Ecological Theory." *Sociology and Social Research* 31 (Jan.-Feb. 1947): 194–204.

Hoselitz, Bert. "Cities of India and Their Problems." *Annals of the Association of American Geographers* 49 (June 1959): 223–231.

Itkonen, Uolevi. "Welfare Activities in Tapiola." Tapiola, Finland: The Finnish Housing Foundation, 1970.

Jonassen, Christen T. "Cultural Variables in the Ecology of an Ethnic Group." *American Sociological Review* 14 (Feb. 1949): 32–41.

Korpivaara, Eero. "Tapiola: An Experiment in Urban Planning." *American-Scandinavian Review* 56 (March 1968): 32–41.

Lean, W. "Economics of New Town Size and Form." *Journal of the Town Planning Institute* 52 (July-Aug. 1966): 262–264.

Lewis, Oscar. "Urbanization Without Breakdown: A Case Study." *Scientific Monthly* 75 (July 1952): 31–41.

MacMurray, Trevor. "British Town Planning in Transition." *Technology Review* 72 (June 1970): 47–55.

"Making American Cities More Livable." *Saturday Review,* January 8, 1966, entire issue.

Mangiamele, J. F. "Controlling the Growth of New Towns." *Town and Country Planning* 32 (April 1964): 178–180.

Mannheim, Ernest. "Theoretical Prospects of Urban Sociology in an Urbanized Society." *American Journal of Sociology* 6 (Nov. 1960): 226–230.

Mayer, Albert. "A New-Town Program." *Journal of the American Institute of Architects* 15 (Jan. 1951): 5–10.

————. "Trends in New Town Development." In *Planning 1952.* Chicago: American Society of Planning Officials, 1952, pp. 64–71.

————. "Green-Belt Towns in the USA." *Town and Country Planning* 37 (Jan.-Feb. 1969) : 35–38.

Meadows, Paul. "The Urbanists: Profiles of Professional Ideologies." *1963 Yearbook—School of Architecture.* Syracuse, N.Y.: Syracuse University, 1963.

Morris, Robert L. "The Impact of New Towns." *Nation's Cities* 7 (April 1969) : 8–11.

————. "What Can the Cities Learn from New Town Experience?" *Nation's Cities* 7 (May 1969) : 19–22.

————. "Prospects for Coexistence: New Towns and Old Cities." *Nation's Cities* 7 (June 1969) : 39–41.

Moynihan, Daniel P. "Urban Conditions." *Annals of the American Academy of Political and Social Science* 371 (May 1967) : 159–177.

Myers, Jerome K. "Assimilation to the Ecological and Social Systems of a Community." *American Sociological Review* 15 (June 1950) : 367–372.

"A New Approach to New-Town Planning." *Architectural Forum* 121 (Aug.-Sept. 1964) : 194–199.

"New Towns: Philosophy and Reality." *Building Research* 3 (Jan.-Feb. 1966).

"New Town Takes Form." *American City* 82 (Oct. 1967) : 109.

Ogilvy, A. A. "The Self-Contained New Town." *Town Planning Review* 39 (April 1968) : 38–54.

Perkins, G. Holmes. "New Towns for America's Peacetime Needs." *Journal of the American Institute of Architects* 15 (Jan. 1951) : 11–15.

Perloff, Harvey. "New Towns In-Town." *Journal of the American Institute of Planners* 32 (May 1966) : 155–161.

————. "Modernizing Urban Development." *Daedalus* 96 (Summer 1967) : 789–800.

Peterson, William. "The Ideological Origins of Britain's New Towns." *Journal of the American Institute of Planners* 34 (May 1968) : 160–170.

Pickard, Jerome P. "Dimensions of Metropolitanism." Urban Land Institute Research Monograph 14. Washington, D.C., 1967.

Rapkin, Chester. "New Towns for America." *Journal of Finance* 22 (May 1967) : 208–219.

Riboud, Jacques. "New Towns for a New Civilization." *Town and Country Planning* 38 (June 1970) : 281–284.

Roberts, Steven. "Adolescent 'New Town' Grows in Arizona." *New York Times*, April 6, 1971, p. 36.

Rodgers, H. B. "Women and Work in New and Expanding Towns." *Town and Country Planning* 37 (Jan.-Feb. 1969) : 23–27.

Rosow, Irving. "The Social Effects of the Physical Environment." *Journal of the American Institute of Planners* 27 (May 1961) : 127–133.

Ross, J. B.; The Runcorn Development Corporation; Bland, K. W.; and Bilsby, Leslie. "The Role of Private Enterprise in New Towns." *Town and Country Planning* 36 (Jan.-Feb. 1968) : 99–107.

Schmertz, M. F. "Shaping the Community in an Era of Dynamic Social Change." *Architectural Record* 140 (July 1966) : 189–206.

Seeman, Albert. "Communities in the Salt Lake Basin." *Economic Geography* 14 (July 1938) : 300–308.

Sellers, Charles L. "Early Mormon Community Planning." *Journal of the American Institute of Planners* 28 (Feb. 1962) : 25.

Sjoberg, Gideon. "The Rise and Fall of Cities: A Theoretical Perspective." *International Journal of Comparative Sociology* 4 (Sept. 1963) : 107–120.

Smith, Robert J. "Pre-Industrial Urbanism in Japan: A Consideration of Multiple Traditions in a Feudal Society." *Economic Development and Cultural Change* 9 (Oct. 1960) : 241–257.

Spilhaus, Athelstan. "Experimental City." *Daedalus* 96 (Fall 1967) : 1129–1141.

————. "The Experimental City." *Science* 159 (16 Feb. 1968) : 710–715.

Spreiregen, Paul D. "The Practice of Urban Design: Some Basic Principles." *Journal of the American Institute of Planners* 39 (June 1963) : 59–74.

Suzuki, Peter. "Village Solidarity Among Turkish Peasants Undergoing Urbanization." *Science* 132 (30 Sept. 1960) : 891–892.

"Symposium: New Towns." *Washington University Law Quarterly* (Feb. 1965), pp. 1–104.

"Symposium: Private Participation in New Towns." *Town and Country Planning* 38 (Jan. 1970): 72–76.

Tapiola Information Center. "Tapiola General Information." Tapiola, Finland, 1970. 3 pages.

Thompson, Wayne E. "Prototype City—Design for Tomorrow." *Public Management* 48 (Aug. 1966): 212–217.

Tisdale, Hope. "The Process of Urbanization." *Social Forces* 20 (March 1942): 311–316.

Vizzard, William R. "Taiyozoku: A Youth Problem in Japan." *Sociologus* 9 (1959): 162–178.

Von Eckhardt, Wolf, "The Case for Building 350 New Towns." *Harper's Magazine* 231 (Dec. 1965): 85–94.

Von Grunebaum, G. E. *Islam.* American Anthropological Association, Memoir No. 81, 1955.

Von Hertzen, Heikki. "Practical Problems of New Town Development." New Towns Seminar, Tapiola, Finland, August 13, 1965. 4 pages.

Weaver, Robert C. "New Towns: Federal Proposals May Solve City Problems." *Public Management* 48 (June 1966): 154–159.

Wellemeyer, J. Fletcher, and Lorimer, Frank. "Appendix." *Population Bulletin* 18 (Feb. 1962): 19.

Whittick, Arnold. "Towards New Towns in Scandinavia." *Town and Country Planning* 32 (Feb. 1964): 83–87.

————. "The Architecture of New Towns." *Town and Country Planning* 37 (Jan.-Feb. 1969): 28–33.

————. "Cumbernauld—Outstanding Success or Failure?" *Town and Country Planning* 38 (May 1970): 236–240.

————; Buck, Hadley; and Pitt, Gillian. "Central Areas of New Towns." *Town and Country Planning* 38 (Jan. 1970): 15–24.

Willhelm, Sidney M., and Sjoberg, Gideon. "Economics vs. Protective Values in Urban Land-Use Change." *American Journal of Economics and Sociology* 19 (Jan. 1960): 151–160.

Willmott, Peter. "East Kilbridge and Stevenage: Some Characteristics of a Scottish and an English New Town." *Town Planning Review* 34 (Jan. 1964) : 307–316.

Wirth, Louis. "Urbanism as a Way of Life." *American Journal of Sociology* 44 (July 1938) : 1–24.

Wright, Myles. "Regional Development: Problems and Lines of Advance in Europe." *Town Planning Review* 36 (Oct. 1965) : 147.

Index

Mary Jo Huth is professor of sociology at the University of Dayton.

After receiving her M.A. from Indiana University and a Ph.D. from St. Louis University, she taught at St. Mary's College, Notre Dame, Indiana. She has served as a public administration fellow with the Department of Housing and Urban Development and as a research sociologist with the National Bureau of Standards, Center for Building Technology.

Dr. Huth is past chairman, Indiana State Committee on the Status of Women and is a member of the Education Advisory Committee of the Ohio Civil Rights Commission.

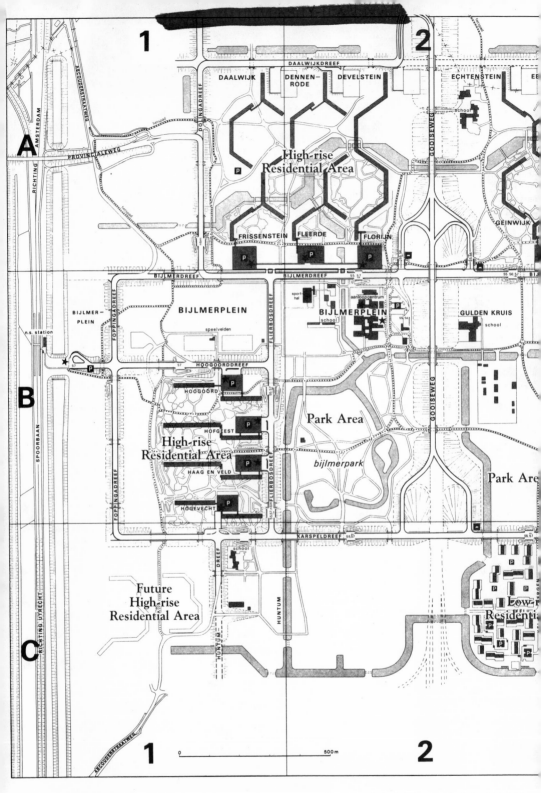